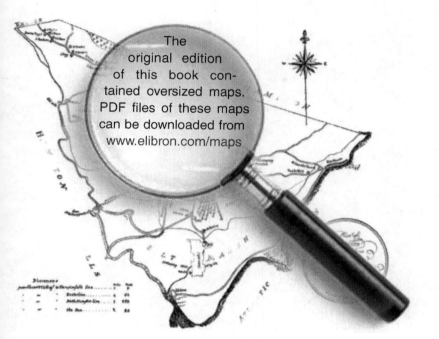

WALTER WESTON

MOUNTAINEERING

AND

EXPLORATION

IN THE

JAPANESE ALPS

Elibron Classics
www.elibron.com

MOUNTAINEERING AND EXPLORATION IN THE JAPANESE ALPS.

MOUNTAINEERING AND EXPLORATION

IN

THE JAPANESE ALPS.

BY THE REV. WALTER WESTON,

M.A., F.R.G.S.; MEMBER OF THE ALPINE CLUB;
MEMBER OF THE ASIATIC SOCIETY OF JAPAN; MEMBER OF THE GEOGRAPHICAL SOCIETY
OF TOKYO, JAPAN.

LATE BRITISH CHAPLAIN, KOBE, JAPAN.

WITH MAPS AND 35 ILLUSTRATIONS.

LONDON:

JOHN MURRAY, ALBEMARLE STREET.

1896.

BRADBURY, AGNEW, & CO. LD., PRINTERS,
LONDON AND TONBRIDGE.

TO THE

COMPANIONS OF MY TRAVELS.

Ὅταν τύχῃ τις εὐνοοῦντος οἰκέτου,
Οὐκ ἔστιν οὐδὲν κτῆμα κάλλιον βίῳ.

PREFACE.

In the Japan of to-day the world has before it a unique example of an Eastern people displaying the power to assimilate and to adapt the civilization of the West whilst still preserving its own national dignity unimpaired. It is, moreover, more than probable that there awaits this remarkable race a future rich in developments, such as it is at present impossible to forecast, so capable are they of almost any degree of self-sacrifice for the advancement of the national prestige.

Upon these considerations, however, fascinating as they are, it is beside my purpose to dwell in this book. I have, on the contrary, confined myself to an attempt to give a record of four years' holiday wanderings in the high mountain regions of Central Japan, and the main grounds on which I have ventured to describe my travels in detail are that they have taken me off the beaten tracks into districts practically unknown to the outside world. There

I have found a grandeur and a wildness in the scenery
such as is seldom associated with the typical Japanese
landscape, whilst the primitive customs and superstitions
of the hospitable peasants with whom I had the privilege
of much pleasant intercourse, are in their way scarcely
less remarkable. The substance of several of these
chapters has already appeared, in another form, in the
columns of the "Japan Mail," to the Editor of which
I am glad to acknowledge my obligations.

It is now my privilege also to offer my grateful
thanks to the various friends who have helped me in the
preparation of my book : to Mr. William Gowland,
F.C.S., &c., late of the Imperial Japanese Mint, the
first European explorer of the Hida-Shinshū range, for
valuable notes on its Botany and Geology ; to Mr. B. H.
Chamberlain, Emeritus Professor of Japanese in the
Imperial University of Tōkyō, for varied information,
especially on some superstitions and local customs ; to
my travelling companions, Messrs. H. W. Belcher and
H. J. Hamilton, for most of the photographs—the first
taken of their kind—from which the illustrations are
reproduced ; and also to H.E. Sir Ernest Satow, K.C.M.G.,
H.B.M.'s Minister at Tōkyō ; and to Mr. Noel E. Buxton,
for kind assistance in different ways. Useful hints have
been furnished on various points by the writings of

Dr. J. J. Rein on Japan. Finally, my best thanks are due to Mr. John Murray for the kindness and courtesy which have made it a genuine pleasure to produce this work under his auspices.

WALTER WESTON.

EGGISHORN,
  SWITZERLAND,
    August, 1896.

NOTE.—The design on the binding of this book is copied from the device of the Tomoe-kō, one of the principal societies of Japanese Pilgrim-Mountaineers (see p. 269). These societies are the nearest equivalent in the far-East to our European Alpine Clubs. The Tomoe-kō numbers some thousands of members, and recognises as its Patron Spirit the canonized climber known as Tōkō-Shutoku Reijin.

CONTENTS.

CHAPTER I.

PAGE

CHAPTER II.

CHAPTER III.

CHAPTER IV.

CHAPTER V.

CHAPTER VI.

CHAPTER VII.

CHAPTER VIII.

LIST OF ILLUSTRATIONS.

MOUNTAINEERING AND EXPLORATION
IN THE JAPANESE ALPS.

CHAPTER I.

Books and bookmakers—Pleasant surprises—A parable in bronze—A
terra incognita—A curious tramway—Karuisawa—A terrible eruption
—Ascent of a famous volcano—Noisy neighbours—George and Louisa
—Companions in misfortune.

In his delightful little encyclopædia of "Things
Japanese," my friend Professor Chamberlain has shown
that "Of making many books there is no end" is a dictum
pre-eminently true of works of travel in Japan. And a
curious fact is that the space of time dealt with by each
succeeding visitor to the "Land of the Rising Sun"
has been growing gradually less, from "Nine Years in
Nipon" to "Three Weeks in Japan:" so that we may
not, after all, despair of reaching the Ultima Thule in
this respect before the publication of that great work
with which I have heard the public threatened—"Five
Minutes in Japan," in two vols.

So frequently do these books appear that writers almost

stumble on each other's heels in the literary race ; certainly
they usually succeed, metaphorically speaking, in treading
on each other's toes. A Japanese writer has, not without
justice, somewhat bitterly complained of the numbers of
foreign tourists who come to his country, and after rushing
through it " at the rate of forty miles an hour " (though
the average speed of the express trains is only about half
that pace), then hurry home to record their impressions
and pose as authorities on what they have only glanced at
by the way.

The present writer wishes to steer clear of these
reproaches. The notes of travel and observation detailed
in the following pages are only offered after some six
seasons of exploration and research in what are almost the
least known, though in many respects the most interesting
regions in Japan. For there, where the mainland attains
its greatest width, the mountain ranges reach their
grandest proportions, and the inhabitants are often the
most delightful to deal with. He has found that, in spite
of the epigrammatic *dicta* of certain tourists, there are in
Japan birds that *do* sing, flowers that give forth the most
delicious scent, and babies that can cry to a degree that
should satisfy the most exacting.

In the precincts of an ancient temple * near my former

* Nōfukuji, in Hyōgo.

THE DAIBUTSU AT THE TEMPLE OF NOFUKUJI, HYŌGŌ

P. 8.

Japanese home there sits the most remarkable, though the youngest, member of that numerous family of *Daibutsu* ("Great Buddha") so familiar to the traveller in this country. The features, it is true, wear the conventional expression typical of that absolute calm and passionless condition, that Nirvana to which the devout Buddhist aspires. But on the forehead, in place of the little boss of metal that stands for the sacred "jewel of the law," the artist has fixed an electric light! In some respects it is certainly a speaking likeness, a parable in bronze, of the Japan of to-day, with all the novelties of modern civilisation engrafted on the old-world ways and thoughts that have for so many centuries characterized this most remarkable race.

The traveller is nowhere so struck with this extraordinary contrast, or combination, of ancient and modern, as when he leaves behind the great capital and busy treaty-ports, with their reproductions of our own British navy, or of the military system of our Teutonic neighbours, and penetrates into the interior of Central Japan. For it is there, amongst the great mountains, in close intercourse with the simple, kindly country-folk who dwell beneath their shadows, that we seem to feel ourselves transported into almost another world. Our intellectual surroundings, at any rate, are rather those of the ninth century than of the nineteenth.

The present writer was first induced to turn his attention to the great range so well called the "Japanese
Alps," by an enthusiastic account of their appearance given
by Professor Chamberlain some years ago. The result of
repeated visits has been continued revelations of a grandeur
and scenic beauty unequalled elsewhere in this country,
of whose area no less than seven-eighths is composed of
mountains. Owing, however, to the fact that travel is
here often of the roughest description, these wild fast-
nesses have hitherto been "a charmed circle within a
charmed circle," isolated by Nature almost as much as
the whole country was formerly isolated by man. And
yet nowhere within the whole bounds of the Empire can
we find so great a variety of Nature's beauties, for though
the peaks bear no glaciers on their sides, nothing else is
wanting, from the richness of sub-tropical vegetation to
almost Alpine snows. When the dark cone of Fuji has
laid aside its white mantle, many of these great granite
giants of the "Hida range" still retain the glittering
slopes of snow upon their sides.

A piping hot day towards the end of July, four years
ago, saw my friend H. W. Belcher (then Consulting
Engineer to the Sanyo Railway Company) and myself *en
route* from Yokohama on the first stage of our journey to
make the acquaintance of the great mountains which as yet
we only knew by name. An eight hours' shaking up by

train on the narrow track that winds across the sun-scorched plain of Musashi at length deposited us, dusty and perspiring, at Yokokawa, then the terminus of the Tōkyō-Takasaki line at the southern foot of the Usui-tōge. Close at hand rose the broken ridges of Myogi-San, that strange skeleton of a volcano, whose fantastic towers offer such great attractions for the rock-climbing athlete. Our own time was limited, however, and we were obliged to forego the pleasure. In the hope of reaching our destination - Karuisawa—before nightfall, we decided to take the horse-tramway which in those days crawled up the sinuous windings of the Usui Pass, reaching its highest point at nearly 4,000 feet, and then making a sudden plunge down into the hill-encircled plain. The journey, though only a dozen miles in length, on this occasion occupied nearly three hours. The cars were small, light, and very uncomfortable, and as the rails were not very firmly laid on the somewhat narrow path, the ride proved fairly exciting. So frequently used the cars to slip off the rails that the coolie-conductor was provided with a small crow-bar to hoist the wheels into position. The driver of the scraggy ill-fed pair of horses took it all as a matter of course, and seized at every slip an opportunity for a smoke. It is in some respects a pity that the tram has now been super-seded by the train, as the former was far more exciting, and could be especially recommended to persons of a sluggish

liver, inasmuch as the ride in the car afforded almost as
much up and down exercise as if one were astride one's
steed.   A continued drizzle shut out the view of the
romantic scenery of the pass, and night fell as we descended
to Karuisawa and made our way along the muddy village
streets to the Banshokwan inn, where we found comfortable quarters, and food cooked in "foreign" style.

On the following morning, by way of getting into
training, and in hopes of gaining a distant view of our
Alpine range, we started for the ascent of Asama-yama
(8,282 feet), the mountain which shares with Aso-san (in
Kyūshū) the reputation of being the finest example of an
active volcano in Japan.   As seen from the level plain of
Karuisawa (3,000 feet), its dull red-streaked form presents
the appearance of a single cone.   As a matter of fact it
is really only the tall outpost of a long range.   During
the last few years several eruptions have seemed imminent,
but since 1783 no actual damage has been done.   In that
year, however, a dreadful catastrophe took place.   A
mighty stream of lava devastated a famous forest, and
destroyed various villages on the north slope of the
mountain.   A dense cloud of ashes transformed day into
night, and the cornfields, which stretched for miles
towards the Usui-tōge, were turned into a desert, whilst
nearly fifty of the adjoining villages, together with
hundreds of their inhabitants, were destroyed.   In addition

to the numerous deer, dogs, monkeys, and other animals that were killed by the red-hot stones and ashes, many died of hunger through the vegetation being buried several feet deep under the matter thrown out from the volcano.

Our innkeeper having provided us with a guide (said, by those who got a premium for recommending him, to be good), we started at 9 A.M. for our peak, the rain having hindered us from getting off earlier. A walk of two hours over gently rising meadow land brought us into a narrow valley leading up to a sort of *col* between the main peak and Ko Asama ("the baby Asama"), an excrescence on its N.E. shoulder. Near this our "guide," who had previously twice lost his way in the forest of larches and pines, again went hopelessly wrong, and was consequently dismissed to the rear of the caravan, as in that ignominious position we found he was capable of less harm. At an altitude of about 6,000 feet we emerged from the now thinning forest on to the cinders and loose ashes of the bare cone, whose inclination now steepens to about 35°. Over this a faint track, marked out by little cairns, leads us to the edge of the outermost and oldest crater lip. The busy hum proceeding from a swarm of hornets that had made their nest in a hole amongst the cinders here induced us to quicken our pace. As we overtopped the ridge a keen wind from the N.E. drove us to take shelter in a deep ditch rent in the lava on the other side.

From here an easy walk of fifteen minutes landed us at one o'clock on the edge of the mighty crater, from whose honeycombed sides vast volumes of sulphurous steam roll up with a roar that rises and falls with awful weirdness. In the distance it resembles a great waterfall, or the thundering of the breakers on the Pacific shore, heard in the stillness of night. The circumference of the crater is about 1,300 yards, but its yet unfathomed depth is probably greater still. Those who have made the ascent of the volcano, as I have since done, by night, and looked down into the cavernous abyss at the fires below, will never forget the unearthly scene.

The dense curtain of clouds that rolled around the summit of our peak shut off all but an occasional glimpse of distant scenes. Far off to the south the dark cone of Fuji San appeared for a second as if suspended between heaven and earth, and again through a sudden rift in the mist westwards, the dark wall of the Japanese Alps loomed up imposingly.

On turning to descend, we saw the clouds had now gathered so dense as to entirely shut out all traces of our downward way. Having paid no particular attention to landmarks in our excitement at the strange scene as we were nearing the crater edge, we found ourselves simply standing on the circumference of a circle of puzzling sameness, and all appeals to our " guide " only drew forth the admission that he was lost, as he only knew the way in fine weather! "That," however, "*might* be the right direction," he ventured, pointing to a great precipice of lava that formed one side of a great chasm, now visible for a moment through the mist. A few minutes more spent in wandering about in the vain search for signs of a track showed that our coolie was really worse than useless, and at length an appeal was made to the compass, with the result that we were soon, though off all traces of a path, at any rate getting down somehow. Following the edge of a deep-cut chasm on the east slope of the cone, a rough descent over the bare lava and cinders led us at last out of the chilly clouds into the warm brightness of the summer sun, and soon we saw stretching below us the fresh green expanse of the meadows that deck the volcano's lower slopes. All inconveniences then were forgotten in the delightful tramp through the long grass, gay with flowers of every hue. At a height of some 1,100 feet above Oiwake, the village to which we were now descending, on the side of Asama-yama, we passed a curious waterfall hidden among the trees, the reddish tint of the water and of the underlying rock giving it among the natives the name of " the blood cascade."

At Oiwake, half a dozen miles west of Karuisawa, we struck the famous Nakasendō, the " middle of the mountains road." Oiwake was once a place of some importance,

but it is now, like many other villages in this neighbourhood, nearly ruined by the railway between Karuisawa and
Naoetsu, which has diverted traffic almost entirely from the
well-known highway.

After our first day's training tramp, with the prospect of
a long journey on the morrow, we were naturally anxious
to get a good night's rest at our inn, and so went early to
futon.   But no sooner had we lain down upon the piles of
soft cotton-stuffed quilts that in Japanese inns do duty for
beds, than a hideous uproar began in the adjoining room.
We knew quite well what it meant, and our hearts sank
within us.   A native dinner party was on, and with only a
thin paper partition between ourselves and the half-dozen
revellers and their attendant musicians, the chorus of
hand-clapping to the rhythm of the songs, mingled with
the tuneless strumming of the *samisen* (the Japanese
banjo), our sufferings were complete.   For the native inn
ensures but little of privacy or quiet to travellers sharing
adjacent rooms.   If your next-door neighbour happens to
be curious about you and your belongings, he has only to
rub a little hole in the thin paper panes of the *shōji* that
separate you from him, and apply his eye to the hole, to be
able to see as much as if he were sharing the apartment
with you.   Or if he merely cares to listen to your
conversation, he can hear with perfect ease, so long as he
only keeps quiet himself.   Happily, however, when he is

not alone, the chances of his acting as eavesdropper are usually very remote, for unless a man's companion be either deaf or dumb, the conversation never flags.

One can never think of the extraordinary loquacity of this vivacious people without recalling the ungallant but cutting sarcasm of a certain French writer : " la langue des femmes est leur épée, et elles *ne la laissent pas rouiller.*" Happily for our Japanese friends, however, they are able to sleep, apparently under all circumstances. Moreover their childlike lack of self-consciousness spares them much of the annoyance from which we English so often suffer, and consequently the broadest hints from the other side of a paper partition too often pass unheeded.

In the case of my companion and myself, unhappily, remonstrances with our fellow guests proved fruitless. The landlord, on being appealed to, comforted us with the assurance that if we could only hold out until twelve o'clock, we should have peace, as at that hour a police regulation would compel the carousals to come to an end. And so at last the howling and handclapping began to grow less distracting, and shortly after midnight quiet was restored. But only to be once more broken. This time the disturbance proceeded from without, and was due to the unexpected arrival of two American tourists travelling *en grand seigneur* with an interpreter. They had made the ascent of Asama-yama, we were afterwards told, from

the opposite side to ourselves, but had met with a similar
and even worse fate, having, with the assistance of their
local guide, completely lost their way, and wandered down
the mountain to Komoro on the Nakasendō.   Here, late
in the evening they took the train for Karuisawa, $13\frac{1}{2}$
miles distant, but that too broke down, and it was not
until towards 1 A.M. that they reached their destination.

CHAPTER II.

THE growing popularity of Karuisawa as a summer
resort for foreign residents, with its cool climate and varied
walks in the hills that encircle the pleasant plain, has
induced enterprising native shop-keepers to establish
stores for the sale of foreign provisions. At one of these
we were able to stock our small canteen by way of sup-
plementing the flimsy diet we knew we should get at the
native country inns. A railway journey of five-and-
twenty miles on the Naoetsu line took us to the old
castle town of Ueda, where, as we saw our train slowly
steaming out of the station on its way to the western
coast, we knew we had said good-bye to such traces of
civilisation for the rest of our wanderings.

It is odd, now that one is again at home, to hear the
question, " And are there any railways in Japan? " For

only the other day, after replying to it for the tenth
time, an interesting handbook to railway and steamboat
travelling in Japan, kindly presented to me by Hayashi
Gonsuke, Esq., H.I.J.M.'s Consul-General in London, stated
that at the end of 1895, no less than 2,248 miles of railway were open, shared by twenty-nine companies. And I
may add, moreover, that besides being able to cross the
main island at its widest part by rail, one can get a much
longer railway journey in one continuous direction in
Japan, than is possible between John o' Groats and Land's
End. Under the patient tuition of able English engineers,
a knowledge of the science of railway construction has
been rapidly acquired, and most creditable results have
been achieved, for Japan is a country where many difficulties have to be overcome, owing partly to the hilly
nature of the ground, and also to the liability to inun-
dation in many of the plains through which the main
lines pass. Generally speaking, the travelling accommodation is inferior to that on English railways, but much
less so than the difference in fares would imply. The
charges per mile are only about one, two, and three
farthings for third, second, and first classes respectively.

Shortly after 1 P.M. found us trundling in *jinrikisha*
across the mountain-guarded vale in which Uyeda lies,
along the path which passes westwards over the Hōfukuji-
tōge towards Matsumoto. The broad stream of the Chiku-

magawa is crossed by an ugly iron bridge with staring
white painted girders where once a picturesque bridge of
boats joined the banks. After the cool air of Karuisawa's
elevated plateau, the fierce heat in the gradually narrowing valley was almost stifling. But a capitally made road,
in the freshness of its youth, enabled our sturdy pairs of
runners to spin along with ease as far as Urano, where the
seven miles they had traversed justified a halt for the
everlasting *ippuku* (" one whiff ") in which the soul of the
coolie so delights.

As we looked backwards from the shady verandah of
the neat wayside *chaya* ("tea-house") down the sunlit
vale, the far-off walls of the old castle keep of Uyeda
gleamed white against the dark trees of the hills beyond
the river, the astonishing clearness of the air almost
annihilating the distance between us and them. From
Urano the face of the road, here wrinkled with age and
worn by the small torrents that are formed by every
downpour of rain, grew uncomfortably rough, and the
jinrikisha jolted with such difficulty over the big stones
washed bare of soil, that we determined to lighten the
work of our coolies and to lessen our own sufferings by
walking to the top of the pass. For fourteen miles the
steep pathway climbed over almost treeless hills, winding
in and out of bald grassy slopes formed of volcanic scoriæ
and exposed to the full blaze of the afternoon sun. At

6 o'clock the summit, 4,500 feet, was reached, and then
from a little knoll on the left of a gap in the ridge, we
suddenly found ourselves for the first time in full view
of the great mountain range on which our hearts were
set.

Coming unexpectedly as the prospect did, we were
almost startled by its magnificence. The whole of the
central and southern part of the chain rose up before us
westwards like a great barrier between the broad plain of
Matsumoto that lay at our feet, and the lonely province of
Hida beyond.   Snow-seamed ridges and noble peaks of
10,000 feet and more in height stand up in dark sharp
outline against the opalescent sky of the dying day.
Yarigatake, the "Spear Peak," the Matterhorn of Japan;
Jōnendake, with its graceful triangular form, that recalls
in miniature the Weisshorn, queen of the Pennine Alps;
and further southward the massive double-topped Norikura,
the "Saddle mountain," each arrests the eye with a
characteristic profile.

Afternoon soon faded away into night as we feasted our
gaze on the splendid panorama, for there is little twilight
in these low latitudes, even at high altitudes, and day dies
suddenly and young. A rough descent down the steep
stony track by the side of a mountain torrent that rose
near the summit of the pass on its western side, brought
us under cover of darkness through the quaint hamlet of

Hōfukuji, which owes its name to an old Buddhist temple now falling into decay. Another ascent beyond this, and then the path pierced its way through a damp dark tunnel in an intervening spur of the hills before gradually dropping down into the Matsumoto plain. Jumping into our *jinrikisha* when more level ground was reached we sped merrily on, our coolies gaining in pace and good spirits as we drew near our destination.

The outskirts of the town of Matsumoto were reached at 10 P.M., the distance of thirty miles having taken 9 hours to traverse. The townsfolk still passing to and fro in the busy main street turned startled aside as we rattled up to the door of the Shinanoya inn, where we were received with the politest of welcomes from Sasai Motoji, the young landlord whose acquaintance has, since that first meeting, been one of the most interesting features of my repeated visits to this neighbourhood. He is a curious character altogether. His large hooked Jewish nose, so unusual for a Japanese, would have furnished a grand argument for that eccentric individual who laboured so hard to prove that in the Japanese he had discovered the "lost Ten Tribes." His business practices would have given even still more countenance to the theory, although in fairness I can only add that he always took great interest in our plans. And though his charges sometimes a little startled us, his knowledge of the neighbourhood makes him an

c

invaluable ally when mountain expeditions are con-
templated. For such expeditions no better starting point
than Matsumoto can be chosen. A busy town of 20,000
inhabitants, it lies in the middle of a fertile plain on one
of the main roads that connect the Nakasendō with the
western coast of Japan, and various by-paths lead to
the passes that cross the main mountain mass near its
southern end. The repeated attempts my companions
and I have made to obtain bread, aided by personal
instruction in the art of baking in "foreign style,"
have at last induced the local *panya* (baker) to try his
hand, and with fair success. Beef, of a muscular sort,
beer, milk, and ice are to be had ; whilst at a native
provision-store one can not only get a substance that is
alleged to be butter, but I have also seen certain tins
labelled with the inviting legend, "This apricots is very
sweetest !"

Near the northern entrance to the town the pagoda-like
tower of the ancient fortress rises from the wide expanse
of rice-fields and mulberry orchards, like a castle on a
mammoth chess-board. The white plaster of its walls is
rapidly peeling off, but even in its decay the old keep is
stately, and its topmost storey affords a grand near view of
the tall peaks that rise abruptly beyond the western outskirts of the plain.

Monday, August 3rd, at 9 A.M., saw us at last fairly

launched on our expedition, viz., the third ascent of Yarigatake, the tip of whose "spear" is now seen peeping over the shoulder of Jōnendake like the steeple of some distant church. In his polite anxiety on our behalf, our landlord insisted on accompanying us on the first stage of our journey, which took us a dozen miles south-west of Matsumoto to Hashiba, a hamlet that guards the approach to one of the most picturesque valleys in the Japanese Alps.

Having sent on our baggage in advance by pack horse, we followed in *jinrikisha*, as the road is fairly passable for such vehicles for the first half-dozen miles. Near the hamlet of Murasaki, however, the track grows extremely rough, so we dismissed our coolies and proceeded on foot. Leaving behind us the mulberry orchards, for this plain is one of the great centres of silkworm culture, we plunged into the grateful shade of a dark forest of sweet-scented pines, which stretches for a distance of several miles until at length the pathway leaves it and passes along a hillside above the right bank of the Adzusagawa. The valley into which we have now entered gradually narrows, but on the opposite side the tall steep hills are cultivated almost to their summits with millet, *daikon* (the Japanese radish), &c. Soon the dark cottages of Hashiba appear ahead, and then we round a little rocky promontory that pushes itself out into the stream, and mount up the stony path that

constitutes the only street of which the village boasts.
Our Matsumoto landlord lost no time in commending us
and our plans to the interest of the host of the modest inn,
the " Shimidzuya," and he, in his turn, at once set about
the task of securing the services of local bear-hunters
as guides upon our expedition. Whilst these were being
searched for, we were able to take stock of our surroundings. Hashiba, a hamlet of some sixty or seventy
houses, is perched on the right bank of the swift Adzusagawa, at the entrance to whose picturesque valley it stands,
on the road that goes westwards over the main mountain
chain, by the Nomugi Pass, to Takayama, the capital town
of the secluded province of Hida. A fine ingeniously
constructed wooden bridge, called Zōsui-bashi, connects
Hashiba with Shimajima, a twin village on the opposite
side of the stream. These two places are chiefly inhabited
by thrifty peasants, whose main occupations are silkworm
culture and charcoal burning, or by hardy hunters, who fish
the neighbouring streams and chase the big game (bears,
boars, deer, and chamois) that abound in the more inaccessible mountain regions.

After a little search, our new acquaintance, the landlord
of the " Shimidzuya," succeeded in producing a couple of
sturdy *ryōshi* (hunters), who, in their turn, on hearing our
plans, enlisted the services of a third, and so our party was
completed. The eldest of the trio was a lithe, active fellow,

who had already twice climbed Yarigatake, but for a
Japanese he was unusually reticent. The other two were
short, thick-set young fellows, who looked capable of
carrying-work to any extent. Many were the good wishes
that sped us on our way as we moved off from the
village inn—"Please honourably condescend to come back
quickly ; " " Deign to proceed at your august leisure ; "
and so on, for even the country folk can make the politest
of speeches, and intercourse with them soon teaches us
that genuine refinement is the exclusive possession of no
one class. The conventional phrases may often, it is true,
mean a good deal less than at first sound their literal
meaning implies, but all the same this universal courtesy
helps to make the wheels of social intercourse run the more
smoothly. It reminds one sometimes of the politeness of a
certain politician of bygone days, of whom it was asserted
that even the very tones in which he asked you for a pinch
of snuff were more potent than the clearest logic. As we
passed over the bridge, the hunters drew our attention to
the water of the stream, which they said had the remarkable property of rendering unusually white the complexions
of those who wash in it. I am inclined to think, however,
from the faces of the men, that it can only be the gentler
sex by whom it is used. During a delay on the part of
our men to rearrange the baggage, which included a small
tent, camera, and canteen, Belcher and I were invited to

step into a wayside silk filature, such as we constantly meet with in these regions, to see the winders at their work. The simple machinery for winding off the silk from the cocoons is driven by water-power, and gives employment to a score of bright-faced girls, varying from twelve to twenty years of age. Their neat appearance helped us to credit the story about the river water, and the startled glances of shy curiosity as we suddenly entered the long narrow room told prettily how unusual was the sight of the face of a foreigner. To most, if not to all, it would be the first such experience, and would furnish a topic of conversation for days to come.

But I feel I am lingering by the way too long. Leaving behind us the filature and the quaint cottages of Shima-jima, we passed due west through a wide, well-cultivated vale, until this suddenly narrowed, and, turning more to the north, contracted into a wild and picturesque valley. All signs of human habitations had vanished. On the left tall precipices rise from the river brink, bearing here and there in the crevices in their sides bushes of azaleas, or creepers hanging in graceful festoons of vivid green over the face of the rocks. On the right tower lofty hills to a height of 3,000 feet and more above the valley, clad from base to summit with forests of pines, interspersed with birch and other trees. Sometimes the track is cut in the face of the cliff, or, again, it has to be carried along narrow platforms of small fir logs lifted by struts of timber high above the stream. Occasionally it passes over the débris of a landslip, for here and there the hillside, denuded by wood-cutters of its timber, slides down, and every trace of a path is swept away. At a distance of some seven miles from Shimajima our coolies suddenly halted. Pointing to a little log cabin half hidden in the foliage on the left bank of the river, "There," they said, "is the *Dashi-no-sawa koya* (*koya* = hut), and the smoke you see coming out of the window shows the caretaker is inside." The hut in question turned out to be the property of the Nōshōmushō, the Imperial Board of Agriculture, which controls the construction of certain mountain roads, and also regulates timber-felling in districts where the forests are Government property. Here we were to put up for the night, so we crossed the stream by a curious bridge, formed of long pine poles inclined sideways at an angle of 30°, and, on entering the hut, were received with a civil welcome by the guardian, who apologised for the "meanness of the accommodation," as his phrase put it, but hoped that under the circumstances it would be excused. A wood fire was burning in an open space in the middle of the raised floor, and glad we were of its warmth, for though the altitude of the spot is but 3,700 feet, the valley is so shut in by the high mountains on either hand that little sunshine can find an entrance. But though the fire was grateful and com-

forting, the smoke was the reverse, for the volumes emitted
from the freshly cut logs almost filled the small room, and,
as no chimney gave it outlet, a good deal found its way
into our eyes and nostrils, and the only way of getting
relief was to lie on the floor face downwards, an exceedingly inconvenient posture for hungry men with dinner
waiting.   However, the attractions of curried fowl (the
inimitable Halford's), and Japanese rice, supplemented
with cocoa, marmalade, and the bread bought at Karuisawa,
were too strong to be resisted, and the feast proceeded.
Dinner over, we turned in, or, more strictly speaking,
turned over, for the floor of the hut formed bedstead as
well as chair.

The caretaker kindly provided my friend and myself
with a *futon* apiece to serve as mattress, whilst the
knapsacks and tent rolled up formed our pillows.   With
heads close to the cracks in the walls of the hut, and feet
to the fire, the company bade each other " Good-night ! "—
" *O yasumi nasai* " (" honourably deign to rest "), and soon
a chorus of snores burst forth.   Unlike myself, my companions slept soundly, regardless of the presence of the
small tormentors inseparable from every Japanese dwelling-
place.   For this hut, unhappily for me, not only gives
shelter to at least eight persons, but also finds accommodation for fleas innumerable.   As I invariably found that
these creatures, when on the nightly war-path, skipped my

friend to feed on me, he endeavoured to console me with
the flattering remark that though their manners might
be bad their taste was decidedly good, and he felt it an
honour, not to say pleasure, to travel with a companion so
universal an object of attention. An old Japanese priest
once tried to prove to me the longevity of the species by
stating that representatives of it, which had been left in a
woodcutter's hut near the Nakasendō when the owner
deserted it, were found 64 years afterwards still alive
and active.

Our start on Tuesday morning was delayed by a steady
downpour until 9·30, and then again, after a distance of a
mile or so had been covered, fresh torrents drove us to take
shelter in a woodcutter's shanty by the side of the torrent.
At 2·30 P.M. we left the occupants of this queer structure
of branches and bark still smoking their diminutive pipes,
and moved on up the ravine. At length we found ourselves at the foot of the pass, which now climbs the great
forest-covered hillside that shuts in the head of the valley.
Dense dwarf-bamboo and tall stinging nettles make the
pull up the sinuous windings of the now fading track
unusually stiff, and each step brings down fresh showers
of moisture from the heavily laden leaves. By 5 o'clock
we were on the top of the Tokugō-tōge (*tōge* = pass), 7,100
feet above the sea, which crosses between the summits of
Nabekamuriyama on the north, and Kasumigadake on the

south. The view from near the highest point of the pass is
one of the grandest in Japan, so entirely does it differ in
character from the ordinary mountain landscapes with their
rounded outlines and verdure-clad slopes.

With the broad white pebbly bed of the Azusagawa
sweeping round its southern foot, the tall form of Hodakayama (known also as Hodakadake) rises before us face to
face. The highest granite peak in Japan, 10,150 feet
above the sea, its towers and pinnacles, that spring from
ridges seamed with snow, give it its picturesque name,
"the mountain of the standing ears of corn." Northwards a great *arête* connects it with Yarigatake, whose
monolithic peak is yet hidden by intervening wooded
heights, but as we descend a little to the left a fine view
greets us of the pyramid of Jōnendake standing due north
of our pass and separated from it by Chōgadake and
Nabekamuriyama ("the mountain of the cauldron upside-
down ").

. From the summit of the pass a rough scramble down the
loose broken rocks of a torrent bed took us in an hour and
a half to a meadow bordering on the left bank of the
Adzusagawa, where amidst the trees we found another of
the huts belonging to the Nōshōmushō. The only human
being in the lonely valley was an old hunter whom we
found by the river-side fishing for the trout in which these
mountain streams abound. From him we purchased a

H. J. Hamilton, phot.

HODAKA-YAMA (MYOJIN-DAKE).

[P. 26.

dozen fish, varying in weight from half a pound upwards,
and when dinner was done, we spread our tent upon the
floor, laid down our native straw rain-coats as mattresses,
and so passed the night as before.

A glorious sky greeted us as we left the hut at 6·15 A.M.,
and made our way through the long grass of the meadow
to the river's brink. A little careful search revealed a
practicable ford, though the feat of stepping from boulder
to boulder with the waist-deep current sweeping sideways
with considerable force was none of the easiest. And yet
without the least misgiving our sturdy companions invited
us to "mount up" and go across the swirling waters
pick-a-back. For four or five miles beyond the ford we
traversed the right bank, passing sometimes through the
dense undergrowth in the forest that clothed the lower
slopes of Hodakayama, or again amongst the smooth
boulders in the bed of the river.

At length the valley divided, and a counsel of war was
called to settle our route. "The ravine on the right,"
said the oldest of the hunters, "is long, but the way is
known, as the former parties who climbed Yarigatake both
took that route. If, however, you want 'sport,' you will
find the left, though probably shorter, more interesting, and
the way we shall have to find for ourselves." "The left
let it be," we said, and without further delay we turned
our faces to the north-west and applied ourselves gaily to

our task. That the new route, up the Yoko-ō-dani ("*tani*"
or *dani* = valley), was interesting we soon discovered.
A struggle for half a mile or so through the thick brushwood, and over the interlacing roots of trees near the bank
of the wild torrent, landed us at a cave in the side of the
ravine. Here we deposited the bulk of our baggage, as our
hunters assured us we should easily get back before nightfall. After a good meal we set out in light marching
order, taking with us food for "tiffin," a Cardigan jacket
each, and Belcher's camera. Up the rough torrent bed we
scrambled, leaping from boulder to boulder, over water
that seethed and boiled as it dashed madly down its rocky
channel. Occasionally we were compelled to wade through
the icy-cold current from side to side, or to take to the
rough banks and fight our way with axe and knife through
the tangled mass of creepers and bushes that barred the
way.

At a height of 6,930 feet the first snow was reached,
and then, as the vegetation grew more sparse, the way
grew easier, for it was possible to stick to dry land.
Above us, on the left, rose the precipitous eastern ridge of
Hodakayama, whose sides here hold slopes of glistening
snow scored by the volleys of stones that shoot down from
the crags above. A grand bit of climbing was afforded
as we reached the foot of a cliff over which a fine cascade
tumbled with thunderous roar into its rocky basin. On

T. Hori, *phot.*

RIDGE S. OF YARIGATAKE.

surmounting this we found ourselves on the edge of a wide
snow-field, with white slopes hanging on the sides of the
amphitheatre of wild and rugged peaks. Rain, however,
now came down once more, and almost completely shut out
what must in many respects be the most striking view in
the whole of Japan, and soon we were completely soaked.
Up the slippery snow we went, and then, bearing to the
right, scrambled up broken rocks to a gap in the ridge
beyond which we now knew our " Spear Peak " lay
hidden. With our upward progress our spirits rose, and
soon we overtopped the *arête* and looked beyond to the
left where the sharp top of Yarigatake loomed up dimly
through the rain. How terribly distant, though, he
seemed ! It was now 2 P.M., and evidently we had still
plenty of work to do. Racing down the slopes of snow on
the north side of the *col*, we pushed our way through or
over the flat-topped masses of *goyo-no-matsu* (" five-needle-
pine ") that fringed them, and then came out into a wilderness of rocks scattered about in the wildest confusion as
they had been torn off by disintegration and hurled down
from the cliffs above. In the middle of this desolation we
found a curious sort of natural cave formed by huge stones
leaning against each other, but admitting of entrance at
either end. Here, our leader informed us, we had rejoined
the original route up the mountain, and to celebrate that
fact the trio sat down to smoke their pipes, and then

began to make a fire of pine branches to cook their rice, evidently having no intention of moving on for some time. It was now 4 o'clock; the wind whistled through the cavern in such a way that, wet and cold as we were, we felt it unwise to linger. .

On requesting the men to proceed, we met with a flat refusal. It was too late in the afternoon, they said; "we shall be benighted; and besides, if we attempt the final peak, the wet condition of the steep rocks will make it impossible for us to scale them." They then suggested that we should stay where we were, and finish the ascent on the following morning. This motion, however, was negatived without a division, and as they declined to make any further proposal, Belcher and I left them smoking their pipes and blowing their fire, and applied ourselves to the remainder of the climb alone. Hungry as we were, however, this was no easy matter. The little food we had we knew we must keep to last us until the morrow, for it was quite plain we should not get within reach of the Yokoō-dani cave, where we had left our provisions, for many hours. However, we struggled on, clambering over the sharp hard rocks, whose smooth slippery surface under our hobnailed boots recalled unpleasantly the tiresome moraines of glaciers in the Alps. A more agreeable reminder, however, was the Alpine bell, the *Schizocodon soldanelloides,* the Japanese kinsman of the *Soldanella alpina,* encircling with its beautiful flowers the slopes of snow across which, from time to time, our line of ascent was directed. The Japanese species is both larger and lovelier than its western congener, and as it is also found in the early spring at low altitudes it covers a more extensive zone. By 5 o'clock we had nearly reached the southern base of the final peak. On the west, steep cliffs fall abruptly to the valley of the Gamada-gawa, but the distant prospect was hidden in clouds. All we could see was the stony wilderness we had just traversed, with its dreary slopes of snow, the narrow jagged *arête* on which we stood, and, through the swathing mists, the lower portion of the great rock pinnacle that gives Yarigatake its expressive title. The smooth slabs of porphyry breccia of which the peak is chiefly built, showed that in their wet and slippery state they would need the greatest care, for a slip might readily prove fatal here, and going would be consequently slow. At length we reached an ugly gap in the *arête*, which had to be passed before the "spear" could be attacked, and just as we were stopping to discuss its crossing we were surprised to hear shrill shouts proceeding from below. Presently through the mists peered the excited face of our "leading guide." In almost agonizing tones he begged us not to persist in our attempt. "You have no idea," he protested, "of the inaccessible nature of those upper rocks," pointing vaguely into the clouds, "and in their

present condition you are running a risk that is absolutely
unjustifiable."

Though not disposed to take the hunter's declaration
without liberal discount, a few feet further scrambling
induced us to reconsider our position and to climb down
to where he stood gesticulating below, and then to return
to the cave where the two younger men were expectantly
waiting. Their rice they had cooked and eaten, but the
ever-recurring *ippuku* ("one whiff") was still proceeding.
Our main object was now to get down as quickly as
possible to the spot at which the men told us we should
find a "grand shelter" for the night, situated in a ravine
parallel to and westward of the one up which we had
ascended, and lying on the route taken by the parties who
had made the previous ascents.

Leaving the cave shortly before 6 P.M., we hurried
down the rocks and snow slopes with all speed, for we had
far to go, and it was a case of racing against nightfall.
In spite of the rain, the glissades were delightful,
though the hunters, shod with straw sandals, gear quite
unsuited for such a mode of progression, preferred to
descend by the rocks. The tame ptarmigan, that have
their home in the low "creeping pine" (as the *goyo-
no-matsu* is sometimes called), peered curiously out of
their hiding places as we passed by, and then scurried
back to wonder what the unwonted sight could mean.

For 3,000 feet or so our descent was quick, but when the torrent was reached progress slackened, and it was not until after 7 o'clock that, soaking wet, we reached our wished-for goal. After the glowing accounts given of the attractions of the spot by our coolies, a rapid survey of the actual surroundings came upon us as somewhat of a surprise. We had not actually expected an hotel, nor yet a tea-house; indeed, our wildest hopes did not aspire even to *futon*, or food. As a matter of fact, the *Akasaka no iwagoya* ("the Red Cliff cave") consisted simply of a huge wedge of rock some 25 feet long by 20 wide, and about 15 in height, lying on the left bank of the Adzusa-gawa, a mile or two below its source. On the opposite side of the stream a wide bare channel in the dark pine forest marked the track of a spring avalanche of snow, the white slope of which still lay gleaming through the tall trees below. One end of our wedge was tilted up at a sufficient angle to enable us to get a fair amount of shelter underneath, but the ground was wet, and the rain dripping from above made matters worse. However, darkness quickly came down, so we set to work to make the best of our situation. With brushwood and pine-branches we soon succeeded in raising a cheerful blaze, but Belcher and I both agreed we had never before realized how long wet garments took to dry, as one by one each separate article had its turn before

D

the fire. At length we were outwardly comfortable enough to think of the claims of the inner man which by this time was sorely in need, for we had made no meal for over ten hours, and the day's work had been unusually trying.

An inspection of the contents of the larder revealed a small tin of sausages, a morsel of bread, a bit of kola chocolate (with the earthiest of flavours), and a little brandy which we had brought in case of emergencies. Our coolies we were glad to find were well supplied with rice, and the clayey character of our chocolate they by no means despised. Dinner over, our surroundings took on a more cheerful aspect, and the mildest of jokes were received with uproarious merriment. Then we went to bed; that is to say, each of us possessed himself of a flat piece of pine bark by way of mattress, and whilst Belcher once more made a pillow of his camera case, I laid my head peacefully on the softest piece of rock handy. The hunters themselves occupied three sides of the fire, whilst we had to be content with one side between us. No sooner had we "gone to bark," than my friend and I fell fast asleep, but after three hours of blissful slumber our cramped positions began to tell, and stiffened limbs asked to be stretched for relief. So oddly were we fixed though, that this involved the thrusting of one's feet either into the fire or into the face of the neighbouring sleeper, so a compromise had to be effected by the two of us changing places and huddling up from time to time in varying postures—and so the night passed away.

As soon as daylight had penetrated into our secluded valley we were ready to move, but the pouring rain delayed us several hours. The usual time spent in cooking break- fast and packing up was now not needed, for there was nothing to cook, and no baggage to pack. Our coolies, however, spared us a little of their rice, and as the narrow strip of clouds above the ravine began to part, the blue sky appeared, and with the ceasing rain we began the descent of the torrent. The work was similar to that of the previous day, but rather less arduous, though the recent rains had swollen the stream, and in many places it had to be forded waist deep. By 10·45 we had rejoined our tracks of yesterday at the junction of the two valleys, and whilst two of the men went up to fetch the baggage we had left at the Yokoōdani cave, Belcher and I stretched ourselves on the smooth warm stones on the edge of the river bed, basking in the bright sunshine, and watching with admi- ration the skill of our remaining hunter, as with a hastily improvised rod and line, he landed silvery trout from the clear stream close by. By the time we were again on the march after lunch our porters had a distinctly lighter load. On our way down to the Azusagawa ford we startled an eagle in the act of devouring its quarry in the shape of a *ten* (*anglicè* marten), which it dropped as we approached ; as the smoke from the gun of one of our hunters cleared away after an ineffective shot, we saw the magnificent creature circling high above the cliffs on the opposite side of the valley.   Crossing the river once more, we passed through the meadow near the Nōshōmushō hut, but before we could reach the top of the Tokugō Pass, 2,000 feet above, we were again overtaken by the rain, which came down in sheets, and soaked us through and through.   Our men were now getting tired, for they had worked well all through the day, and it was only by dint of a special spurt that we could hope to escape being benighted.   As we breasted the summit of the *col* and descended the steep slippery slopes of wet bamboo grass, we found the modest mountain streamlet had grown, through the heavy rain, into a roaring yellow torrent, and considerable steadiness was called for as in the deepening twilight we crossed the narrow pine poles that here and there did duty for a bridge.   Shortly after dark we were under the welcome shelter of the hut at Dashi-no-sawa, discussing over our trout the events of the past three days.   The caretaker was delighted to receive the gift of the marten, which he promptly skinned, spitted on a stick, and roasted in the red-hot embers for his dinner.   On the following day we were once more in Hashiba, where we parted from our hunters, who were made happy by being paid off at the rate of a dollar (then worth 3*s.* 3*d.*) a day apiece. We then retraced our steps to Matsumoto, finding the pathway by the river near Hashiba badly damaged by the recent rains. At Murasaki we were lucky enough to get *jinrikisha*, in which we drove to the town. Just as we were entering one of the main streets I suddenly heard behind me a loud shout, followed by a crash, and, on glancing round, was greeted by the sight of Belcher standing on his head in the road, and flourishing his heels to the astonishment of the startled bystanders, whilst the coolie lay sprawling under the skyward-pointing shafts of the *jinrikisha.* It transpired that the man had abruptly, without due warning, stopped to speak to a friend by the roadside, and as he unexpectedly lost control over the vehicle, this general toss-up backwards was the consequence.

A cheery welcome greeted us as we pulled up, this time with more deliberation, at the front of the Shinanoya inn, where we learned from Sasai Motoji that he, too, had not been without his adventures since we parted. On his way back from Hashiba earlier in the week, he was riding a pack-horse on a path above the river, when the earth gave way, and hurled himself and his horse into the swollen stream some twenty feet beneath. As we remembered the spot, it seemed a marvel that either man or beast should have escaped, and that unharmed.

CHAPTER III.

SOME forty miles south-west of Matsumoto, on the east and west sides respectively of the valley of the famous Kisogawa, stand two commanding peaks—Komagatake ("the foal mountain"), in the province of Shinshū, the tallest member of the large family all known by that name —and Ontake ("the august mountain"), whose reputation as a sacred summit is second only to that of Fujisan herself.

As both of these can be ascended from Fukushima, a picturesque village on the Nakasendō, Saturday morning, at 7·15, saw us starting in unusual style for that place. "Style," on this occasion, was represented by a *basha*, a native carriage of peculiar construction, drawn by a weedy undersized horse, whose driver was clad in blue cotton drawers, with a dilapidated hat and jacket of European pattern. Although the clatter made by the *basha* was far more than enough to startle any pedestrians we might meet on the road long before reaching them, a small boy was added as " conductor," his duty being to blow a tin horn to warn persons from the way of our Juggernaut car. We soon found out that the thing is intimately connected with suffering, as, though its speed rarely exceeds four miles an hour, and is seldom dangerous to travellers on foot, the discomforts it inflicts on the passengers it carries are often considerable. To those who have never ridden in one it is difficult to give a fair idea of its peculiarities, but the nearest approach to it yet seen in England would seem to be the deer-cart which Hood describes in "The Epping Hunt :"

> " In shape like half a hearse, but not
> For corpses in the least."

Its appearance has been compared to a cross between an ambulance waggon and a prison van, and certainly the feelings to which it conduces are often appropriate to either of those conveyances.

Our obliging landlord again insisted on starting us off in true Japanese fashion, by bearing us company, as a sort of courier, on the first part of our journey. As we left the town, with wheels rattling, horn blowing, and driver whistling at his beast, and passed across the "moor of the Kikyō" (so called from the quantities of the beautiful bluebell for which the locality is famed), a fine prospect greeted our view. On the east rise the hills, over which the Nakasendō comes from the celebrated Lake of Suwa, and far beyond which rise the blue outlines of the mountain-mass of Kōshū. On the west tower the great peaks whose company we have left, with the sharp top of Yarigatake shooting up above the shoulder of Jōnendake, and calling forth from one of us, at any rate, the resolution to return another year to plant an iron heel upon the giant's head. Straight before us stands the less lofty range that forms the watershed between the Saigawa, which flows northwards into the Sea of Japan, and the Kisogawa, which empties itself into the Pacific Ocean. Four miles out from Matsumoto, at the village of Murai, a stately grove of dark cryptomeria and *Pinus Thunbergi* overshadows a small shrine dedicated to the two great goddesses of far-off Ise. At Seba our road loses itself in the Nakasendō, famous above all highways in Japan for the beauty of its valleys and the wildness of its deep-cut ravines. Romantic bridges lead us from side to side of the Saigawa, whose emerald waters now flash far below through some narrow defile, or, again, flow placidly at hand along some gradually opening vale.

At Sakurazawa a wayside cottage displays for sale an assortment of bear- and chamois-skins, trophies of the chase from the neighbouring mountains. Beyond this a grandly-situated bridge marks the northern limit of the district of Kiso, which stretches for a distance of 50 miles down the

Nakasendō, as far as Ochiai. The timber grown on the forest-clad hill-sides throughout its entire length is amongst the finest in the country, and is known as "the five trees of Kiso"—viz., the beech, horse-chestnut, Spanish chestnut, maple, and walnut, often of enormous size.

On reaching Narai, we parted regretfully with our Matsumoto friend, but bade a glad good-bye to the *basha*, which we now dismissed after a six hours' jolting, during which we had made but 22 miles. At the village we engaged a pack-horse, and forthwith began to climb the steep winding road that goes over the Tōrii-tōge, crossing the watershed already spoken of at a height of 4,200 feet. The pass gains its title from one of the large *tōrii** (sacred gateway), so familiar to travellers in Japan, that crowns its summit. As the *tōrii* is always connected with the idea of approach to some sacred spot, such as temple or shrine, this one has its *raison d'être* in the fact that it leads, though a score of miles away, to the foot of the holy mountain Ontake, whose dark serrated ridge, streaked with snow, we now saw standing out boldly against the clear blue sky. As we reached the *tōrii*, we found ourselves

---

* The derivation of this word is a vexed question. Authorities are divided between *tōru*, "to pass through," and *tori*, "a bird" (referring to the sacred poultry which used to be kept in temple precincts). It has been pointed out to me by Sir William Conway as a curious coincidence, that the word *turan* is used for the same kind of gateway in North India.

on the ridge that forms the water-parting between the
basins of two rivers, which share with the Tonegawa the
honour of the name *San-dai-kai*, or " Three Great Rivers "
of Japan.   As the Saigawa flows N.E. from here into
the Sea of Japan near Niigata, under the name of the
Shinano-gawa, it carries with it the drainage of most of
the east side of the Japanese Alps.   On the west of the
pass, almost at our feet, spreads the broad valley containing the head waters of the noble Kisogawa, which
emerges from the mountainous region to which it gives
its name, to embrace, with its many-mouthed delta, the
wide and fertile plain of Owari, the district so awfully
devastated by earthquake and flood in the autumn
of 1891.

A well-engineered road drops down in serpentine
windings from the top of the ridge to Yabuhara, a
village 1,000 feet below.   Here, in every cottage, one
sees for sale scores of the wooden combs worn by women,
the original of which is said to have been invented by
the wife of Izanagi-no-mikoto.   The latter person is
spoken of in Japanese mythology as the creator of all
things, father of the sun and moon, and ancestor of the
human (*i.e.*, the Japanese) race.   It is a curious fact that
this pair are represented on the artistic diploma of
membership of the Imperial Geographical Society of
Tōkyō as watching over the fair land they are alleged

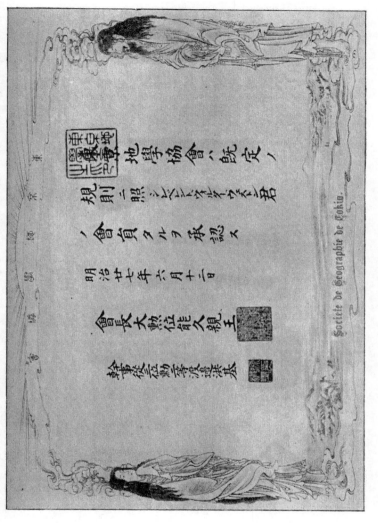

Société de Géographie de Tokio.

DIPLOMA OF THE TŌKYŌ GEOGRAPHICAL SOCIETY.

to have created out of the foam of the waves of the ocean.

A sudden turn in the road some six miles beyond Yabuhara brings into view the rugged form of Komagatake, and before the afternoon has closed we are resting near its western base at Fukushima. The Matsutaya inn here affords a lovely view of the Kisogawa flowing under its picturesque bridge, by brown cottages, whose overhanging eaves, weighted with blocks of stone, recall the châlets of Switzerland. The busy little town is a place of some importance, owing partly to its position as a centre of the silkworm culture, evidence of which meets us in the shape of several tall buildings with whitewashed walls, the filatures where the silk-winding is carried on.

A more curious sight, however, is the hundreds of little coloured streamers that flutter from the eaves of the numerous inns that line the village street on either hand. They are the flags presented by the various bands of pilgrims who have come year by year from all parts of Central Japan to make the ascent of Ontake. Each flag denotes the fact that the journey hither has been accomplished, and marks out, for the subsequent patronage of other members of the same club, the inn with which the donors have been so well pleased. They remind one of the *Führer-buch* of Alpine guides,

or of the stars that mark approval of favourite hotels in
" Murray " or " Baedeker."

A quiet week-end at Fukushima was succeeded by an
ascent of the sacred peak of Ontake, when for the first
time we were introduced to the strange hypnotic practices
of certain of the pilgrim bands who visit the mountain
during the summer months.   For Ontake is a sort of
Delphi of Japan, and pale-faced ascetics climb it annually
to seek communion with the spirits of deified or canonized
heroes who are believed to be more accessible within the
precincts of the " august peak " than elsewhere.   As I
subsequently repeated the ascent in additionally interesting
circumstances, I must refer the reader to a later chapter*
for a recital of these strange experiences.   In the
meantime I want to take him on to Agematsu, a pictur-
esquely-situated village on the Nakasendō, six miles south
of Fukushima, and our starting point for the crossing of
Komagatake.   Below the village the Buddhist temple of
Rinzenji opens its grounds to admit us to one of the most
curious and charming prospects of river scenery in Japan,
known far and wide as *Nezame-no-toko,* " the bed of
awakening."   The origin of the name is a matter of
dispute.   Some hold it to refer to the story of the Rip
van Winkle of Japan, who is said to have waked up here

* Chap. XIII.

after his long slumber of a hundred years. Others maintain that the name comes from the startling effect produced upon the spectator by the unusual beauty of the surrounding scenery. Below the bank on which the temple stands at the foot of a grandly-wooded hill, a cluster of curious water-worn rocks cramp the Kisogawa into a narrow channel. The most remarkable of these is the huge platform, some 80 yards by 20, which forms the "bellevue" that gives the place its name. Others are known as the "mat-rock," the "screen-rock," or the "rock of the black cap," from their suggestive shapes. A similar collection may be seen near Ochiai, thirty-five miles further south, but in Japanese estimation *Nezame-no-toko* is the most wonderful, and the native guide-book quoted in "Murray," affirms that "Its noble character can scarcely be fully appreciated by the mind, nor adequately described in language."

The evening of our arrival at Agematsu was spent in preparations for the crossing of Komagatake in a single day. The mountain, over 10,000 feet in height, stands like a mighty screen, the culminating point in the Kiso range, separating the Kiso district from the neighbouring valley of the Tenryūgawa, for which we were bound. By " making a *col* of the peak," as Alpine parlance has it, we could save the extra time that would otherwise have been taken by crossing the range at a lower point; and, in

addition, the certainty of an enjoyable climb, with the
possibility of good views, was too good to be lost.

Although our landlord prophesied the failure of our
expedition, he certainly did his best to help us to succeed.
After pointing out that the climb involved not only an
ascent and descent of 7,500 feet each, but also a walk of
over thirty miles, he set to work to get us the best trio of
coolies he could find to act as porters for our baggage.
This we reduced to the smallest possible amount, as we
wished to travel as lightly as possible.   After packing up
the rest we gave it to our host for conveyance to Kobe by
Tsu-un-kwaisha.   This concern, whose name is usually
rendered " Express Company," has offices scattered about
the principal highways of traffic in Japan, each flying a
white flag adorned with the letter E repeated eight times.
Its name, unfortunately, is all that is "express" about it,
for as time is *not* regarded as money in Japan, such
companies are by no means to be "relied upon for punc-
tuality and despatch."   On this occasion our things were
delivered at their destination in a mouldy and disreputable
condition, having travelled at the " express " speed of
seventy miles in a fortnight.

A brilliant morning on August 12th gladdened our
eyes as we strode away from our inn amidst the usual
shower of kindly farewells from the assembled household
kneeling on the front verandah.   The orthodox *torii* that

spans the track leading to the mountain, turned our footsteps due east from the southern end of the village, and an
hour's walk over cultivated slopes brought us to a Shintō
shrine, where a grand view of Ontake burst upon us.
Crossing the white granite boulders of the bed of the
Namekawa, we plunged into a dense forest of horse-
chestnut, firs, and beech, a faint track leading us to the
foot of a cascade, above which we scrambled up the bed of
a watercourse and over the interlacing roots of trees at a
steep angle. Then the slope eased off a little, and the
cool scented shade of the pine forest above made the climb
delightful to a degree. As we got on to the southern
ridge of the mountain at a height of 8,000 feet and
emerged into an open space known as *En-kem-ba*—" the
place of the distant prospect,"—a fine panorama lay before
us of the southern giants of the Hida range, whilst the
Nezame-no-toko near Agematsu was clearly distinguish-
able in the bed of the Kisogawa over 5,000 feet below.
The forest trees now became smaller and more sparse,
and at length gave way to creeping pine and rhododendron. The flowers of the latter shrub, which is also found
on other high peaks in Central Japan, about the end of
July impart a charming colouring to the surroundings.

Higher up the ridge, a bronze image, pedestalled upon a
jutting rock against the sky line, does honour to Shimmei
Reijin, the first pilgrim-mountaineer to make the ascent of

Komagatake.   The track then led us to the edge of a precipitous face of rock which we traversed to the foot of the final peak, where we discovered an erection that reminded us of the familiar club huts on Swiss mountains. This we found tenanted by a caretaker and his son, the sight of whom suggested to one of our coolies that they should be invited to change places with the remaining pair, whose shortness of wind and slowness of foot had already begun to make the success of our expedition somewhat doubtful.   The want of breath was less owing to the exertions of climbing than to the monkey-like chattering that scarcely ceased for five minutes during the whole of the ascent.   I regretted I had not at the start induced them to adopt the plan of putting pebbles in the mouth for the purpose of keeping it moist and so alleviating thirst. It would have compelled them to keep their mouths shut, and the pebbles would not only have promoted the flow of saliva but also prevented the torrent of aimless babbling and consequent loss of breath.

Whilst the arrangements for the change of porters were being carried out, Belcher and I walked on alone to the summit, some 500 feet above the hut.   It consists of a narrow broken ridge of disintegrated granite rocks, in the crevices of which are hidden a few Alpine flowers, including one much like edelweiss in colour and shape. The highest point is known as Shakujō-ga-take, "the

Crozier peak," from its supposed resemblance, at a distance, to the staff adorned with metal rings used by Buddhist priests, an article which reminds one of a gigantic baby's coral and bells. The little shrine of plain pine wood on the top dedicated to the "Spirit of the mountain," commands a magnificent panorama, for Komagatake is the highest summit (10,100 feet) in the centre of the mainland, and the view it affords is of almost unrivalled extent. The native "Murray" describes it in hyperbole, as one that embraces three dozen mountains and 8,000 valleys. Due west the outline of Hakusan, the "white mountain" of Kaga, is faintly visible beyond the southern shoulder of Ontake, whilst a little closer the jagged outline of the Japanese Alps stretches northwards to the Sea of Japan. To the north-east, a mingled column of smoke and steam curling white against a deep blue sky reminds us that the fires of Asamayama are still burning. Eastwards the eye ranges from peak to peak of the beautiful Koshū mountains, on whose southern flank the graceful pyramid of Akaiishi-san rises above a snow-streaked ridge. But the grandest feature of this vast panorama, 150 miles almost in diameter, is the great truncated cone of Fuji, seen in vignette between two of the triple tops of Shirane San (in Kōshu). Its height is curiously foreshortened from the fact that nothing is seen of the intervening country that separates it from the range of which it seems

E

to form a part. Immediately below us, on the east—so near that it almost appears possible to throw a stone into its winding current—the Tenryūgawa rolls down the valley from its source in Lake Suwa, to cleave its way southwards into the mass of wooded heights that finally lose themselves in the blue haze towards the Pacific. A few hundred feet down the east side of the main ridge lay a lovely little lake known as Shima-ike, "the lake with the island." Its appearance suggests, what is known to be a fact, that Komagatake has been closely connected with volcanic up-heavals in ancient times. After leaving the top, our descent lay over broken rocks, whose lower portions were covered with *haimatsu* and various flowering shrubs, but further down steep stretches of dwarf bamboo made "going" slippery, and we were glad to reach the forest of beeches, firs, &c., where footing was more secure. Then, in a fine grove of tall red pines, a pilgrim's hut suggested rest and refreshment. As we left the forest, at a height of about 5,000 feet, we came out on rounded spurs covered with tall rank grass, which finally merged in the cultivated fields that formed the floor of the valley.

At 7 P.M., just twelve hours after leaving Agematsu, we were stumbling in the deepening twilight up a stony path to the door of the Ton-ya, an old-fashioned hostelry at Inabe, the village from which this district of the Inakaidō gets its title. Immediately on our arrival, as we sat down on the edge of the polished verandah floor to take off our boots before stepping up on to the smooth mats of our room, we were informed that the "honourable hot bath" was ready, and invited to "honourably deign to get in." A kindly consideration often breaks through the usual rule of letting guests occupy the bath in order of arrival at the inn, and the "foreigner" is generally given the first dip.

Odd as it may seem to English ideas, one bath does duty for the whole establishment, without change of water. All the guests having taken their turn at par-boiling in the oval wooden tub (which is heated by a charcoal fire at the bottom of an iron pipe that passes through the water), the male members of the household follow; for in this land of frequent topsy-turvydom it is *place aux messieurs*, not *aux dames*. The ladies of the family generally follow later on, then the domestics, and it is seldom before midnight that the splashing and chattering ceases and peace is restored. No one uses soap in the water, and the towels are simply pieces of soft cotton about 20 inches by 10, stamped with some pretty pattern. Sometimes a pair of wooden clappers are provided, by rapping which together each departing bather announces to the next that his turn has now arrived. In the above circumstances it is needless to add that the appearance of

the overnight's water before the bath is emptied in the
morning leaves much to be desired.

Never was a bath more welcome than on that evening
after our long tramp. It was with a sense of well-earned
repose that we threw ourselves down on the soft *futon* in
our *yukata* (native dressing-gowns of soft thin cotton), and
fell-to on the little bowls of soup, fish, and rice, that
seemed more appetising than ever we had found them
before. As Inabe stands on a fairly busy country road we
were able next day to call *jinrikisha* to our aid for the
journey of 30 miles down the valley to Tokimata, where
the rapids of the Tenryūgawa are best approached.
Much time was lost in wrangling over fares, as the *shafu*
(runners) were few, their spirit independent, and their
charges exorbitant. At 8.30 A.M., however, we were off,
and as we trundled along the rough dusty road we looked
up with satisfaction at the grey summit of the shattered
ridge of our peak, little dreaming of the sad tragedy of
which it was to be, three weeks later, a silent witness.
Mountain accidents are so rare in Japan, partly because
only the easiest peaks are usually ascended, that this
is perhaps worth recording. The account is abridged
from the *Asahi Shimbun*, one of the leading vernacular
journals.

On September 8th three native Christian students
started from the east side of Komagatake to make the

ascent without guides. Their progress was, however, so slow that before they could reach the summit night overtook them, and they were compelled to lie down wrapped in their blankets, and to wait for dawn. About midnight a violent storm came on, and from the exposed ridge on which they lay, their blankets, and the knapsack containing their food, were blown away into space, and it was only by clinging desperately to the rocks that they escaped being carried away themselves. When day broke the wind abated, but the unfortunate travellers, unused to such rough experiences, began at once to descend. By the time they had reached the Shimagaike, one of the three, Ando by name, completely exhausted, gave in, and was left by his companions, who promised to return with assistance. They had only struggled on a little further when Utsumi also collapsed, and Iriye, the last, went on alone. In the meantime another party of climbers, on their way down the mountain, were attracted by groans to the spot where Ando was lying by the lake, but after giving him a couple of cakes of *mochi* (pounded rice) they strangely enough abandoned him and passed on, only to discover Utsumi lower down. Him they treated in the same way, but when they reached the foot of the mountain the alarm was given to the pastor of a little Christian church in the neighbourhood, who immediately started off with a relief party to the rescue. At midnight they reached the spot where Utsumi had been seen, but no traces of him were to be found. A detachment of coolies was left behind to search for him while the rest went up to the help of Ando. The poor fellow, however, was found lying dead beside the lake just where he had been deserted. It was eventually discovered that Utsumi had recovered sufficient strength to make his way down safely, though terribly exhausted.

Curiously enough, just before the above disaster, another accident, though fortunately without serious results, occurred on the opposite side of the mountain. This time the victim was a foreigner, who also had attempted the climb without a guide. Losing his way during the ascent of the main ridge he suddenly found himself on the top of a precipitous landslide, which immediately gave way under his feet, hurling him down a considerable distance amidst an avalanche of rocks and earth. He succeeded, happily, in descending back to Agematsu in safety, *minus* his helmet—which in breaking the force of a blow on the head from a stone, was knocked off and disappeared—but *plus* a large collection of bruises and wounds.

From Inabe to Tokimata our ride took us down the broad valley of the Tenryūgawa on its right bank under the shadow, first of Komagatake, and then of its lower but still imposing neighbour Ena-San, in Mino. At one point we passed through a magnificent belt of pine trees, which stretches from the base of the hills to the river's brink. Between Akao and Iijima, the conformation of the plateau over which the road runs exhibits interesting traces of terraces, and shows that what is now a wide plain was once the bed of a mighty river, of which the Tenryūgawa is but the diminutive modern representative. Mulberry plantations, densely wooded spurs, and open moorland alternated, until at last in the cool of the afternoon we pulled up at Tokimata at the Ume-no-ya, a lovely little inn close to the starting-point of the boats that make the "shoot" of the rapids on their voyage to the sea beyond.

No experience of travel could have been more delightful than the journey which occupied the whole of the following day, and we were up at an early hour to take stock of the interesting craft that are especially built for this purpose.

The boats themselves are made nearly all on the same pattern, measuring 45 feet long, $3\frac{1}{2}$ wide, and $2\frac{1}{2}$ deep. They are constructed of long planks of cryptomeria ingeniously dovetailed into each other and fastened by nails driven through vertical slits, which are then filled up with wooden plugs. The whole is so cleverly fitted together that though perfectly firm enough to resist a tremendous pressure, it is at the same time so elastic as to bend and give freely as it dashes through the rapids or bumps over the shallower parts of the river's rocky bed.

Each of the four oarsmen that constitute the crew handles
a paddle made of evergreen oak, three of these being 9 feet
long, while that used by the man who steers is half as long
again.

The cost of the boat, with oars, etc., is about $40 (£5),
but the wear and tear is so great that it only lasts 3 or 4
years, whilst the bottom, which suffers so much from
constant scraping on the rocks, is renewed every 12
months.   The hire of the vessel and crew for the trip to
the coast, a distance of 90 miles, was on this occasion $20.
At first it sounded excessive, but we discovered that
though the " shoot " down takes but the inside of a day,
the return journey is ten times as long, as the boat has to
be slowly and laboriously towed or punted, or occasionally
sailed against a current sometimes of tremendous force,
especially after heavy rains.   The trip, however, is one that
would be cheap at any price, and, after having had experience of nearly all the most famous rapids of this land of
swift streams, I can safely affirm that all others are tame by
comparison.   We made the start, on a perfect morning, at
7.45, the farewell bows directed to our friends ashore being
at once abruptly repeated as an iron rope stretched across
the river, a few feet above the water, at a ferry, warned
us to make a lowly obeisance to avoid disaster.

For the first six hours the long lithe craft speeds swiftly
on its way down a constant succession of races and rapids ;

sometimes through grand, wild, rocky cañons, that shut
out all but a narrow band of sky of deepest blue, or, again,
between the bases of forest-clad heights. Its behaviour, as
it dips and plunges through the surging waves, is almost
that of a living thing. Every time we approached a rapid
or a river-bend the bow-man slowly and solemnly banged
the gunwale with his great paddle, partly, he said, to wake
up his companions to extra watchfulness, and partly to
warn the crews of boats that might chance to be coming
up the stream. On a subsequent occasion I was told it
was also meant as a signal to woodmen, who are sometimes
engaged in felling timber and shooting it down the slides we
sometimes noticed on the steep sides of the narrow ravine.
Others maintain that it brings good luck, and drives away
the evil spirits that lurk in dark and dangerous spots.
The same belief is held amongst the Ainus of Yezo, as
related in Batchelor's " Ainu of Japan." Whatever may be
the reason, the effect is weird in the extreme, as the hollow
reverberations echo through the lonely cañon, and even the
chattering boatmen cease their talk, as if they felt a
subduing influence in their surroundings. Gradually the
current's speed increases—one headlong plunge into a
seething cauldron, and we feel the floor of the boat literally
throbbing again as it grinds over the rocks of the river-
bed, from which only an inch of wood now separates us—
one short, sharp struggle with angry waves that dash over

the gunwale in an effort to swamp a boat that will neither
collapse nor capsize—and then comes sudden rest and
peace, as we once more find ourselves gliding along without
an effort on the unruffled bosom of the stream. The skill
of the boatmen at these times was really wonderful, and
only equalled by their coolness and nerve. Again and
again it seemed impossible to escape crashing into some
projecting headland, or to steer a clear course in a maze of
ugly rocks that lay ahead; but just as we were almost on
the obstruction a quick turn of the steersman's wrist gave
the very touch that was needed, and the danger was behind
us almost before we knew we had reached it. After some
six hours of such a passage through the great chasm rent
in the mountain mass, the cliffs on either hand began
insensibly to slope more gently to the river's margin, and
signs of human life and activity grew more frequent, as
here and there a few cottages appeared in nooks and corners
on the shelving shore. Occasionally we met a boat being
laboriously pulled or poled against the stream, whilst as
we drew nearer the coast, others found progress easier, as
their white sails caught the breezes from the Pacific. As
the day wore on the river grew wider and shallower; our
boat travelled slower, and the crew had to work their
hardest unceasingly. Sometimes, in the deepening dusk,
we went aground, or found ourselves taking the wrong
channel, and so had to retrace our course. By-and-by the

Ichida, phot.

KŌBE, FROM THE WEST.

[*P.* 59.

moon rose, and shed a lovely soft radiance on the scene. At last the lights of the village of Nakanomachi began to twinkle like glow-worms in the distance, and then the long bridge that spans the river loomed up against the sky like some dark gigantic centipede. By eight o'clock the nose of the boat was hauled up at the landing-stage. The voyage was over, and after a cheery word of farewell greeting with our men we jumped ashore, bundled our baggage into *jinri-kisha*, and soon were bowling along the old Tōkaidō road to Hamamatsu. There we said "good-bye" to the freshness and freedom of mountain and stream, and after a restless night, with the thermometer at 90°, we unwillingly entered the train once more. A journey of 12 hours landed us—as we had started—dusty and perspiring at Kobe, just in time to experience the most frightful typhoon with which that beautiful seaport has for the last score of years been visited.

CHAPTER IV.

THE delightful experiences of our tour of 1891 only
served to whet my appetite for more, and the desire to
penetrate further into the recesses of the range that forms
the "backbone" of Japan induced me the following
summer to make plans for attacking the mountains from a
different side. My cheery companion on former expeditions was now on the other side of the globe, but his
place was filled by a mutual friend, who was anxious to
compare with the peaks and passes of Hida his recollections of Scottish highlands, and some of the hills and
valleys of unfamiliar Cathay.

Our programme was to enter the province of Hida from
the south, and then to get at the range from the west,
climbing some of its highest peaks, and ultimately crossing
over to Matsumoto in Shinshū. This would help us to
gain a better general idea of the southern and central

portions of the chain, and also afford me a chance of
completing the ascent of Yarigatake, in atonement for
the failure of the previous attempt. Accordingly, the
afternoon of August 1st saw Dr. Miller and myself
leaving the railway at Gifu for an eighty miles' journey to
Takayama, the capital of Hida. The secluded position of
this province, consisting as it does of a great plateau walled
in on nearly every side by lofty mountains, has gained for
it the name of the "Island Province." It is, moreover,
the only one in the Empire which, in the old days of
feudalism, could boast of neither *Daimyō* nor *Samurai*.
Not only is it noted for the grandeur of its scenery, but
also for the primitive habits of its people, who are more
untouched by Western civilisation than those of any other
region in Japan. As we stepped outside the station at
Gifu a white-clothed policeman advanced and politely
requested a sight of our passports. The inspection proving
satisfactory, we told him of our plans, which he did his
best to further by negotiating with a *jinrikisha* man for
the transport of our baggage. A walk of ten miles over
a terribly rutty road, that wound in and out of sandy
pine-clad hills, took us no less than four hours. In many
spots the holes were so deep and the ground so rough that
there was a call for every shoulder to the wheel, and we
had literally to carry the vehicle along. At Seki, our
stopping-place for the night, we were hospitably enter-

tained at the Yorodzuya. Increased attention was shown
as soon as Miller's therapeutic powers became known.
The landlord happening to have a sick friend in the house,
he brought him in for treatment, after which he treated us
to a special performance of the ceremony known as *cha
no yu*. The following morning, as we got into our *jinrikisha* for a 12 hours' ride towards Takayama, he surprised
us each with the present of a lovely little fan, whilst to the
doctor he also gave a handsome stiletto as a special mark
of gratitude.

For the first seven miles the road fully bore out the bad
character we had been given of it, and even with two men
to each *jinrikisha*, our progress was painfully slow. Then
came one of those curious contrasts sometimes met with on
the highways of the interior, for between Tonomura and
Kanayama, a distance of nearly 15 miles, the surface of
the road was smooth enough for a bicycle-track. Near
Kanayama the character of the scenery underwent a
striking change. The low sandy hills, bare, or only
thinly clad with pines, gave way to richly-wooded
heights, and our route then entered the walls of cliffs
that hem in the swift waters of the Hidagawa. This
fine river is one of the chief affluents of the Kisogawa,
and the road followed its banks for nearly 40 miles after
joining it close to Kanayama, where the borders of Mino
and Hida meet. Outside that village it receives the

Mazegawa, and grand are the precipices that rise above the confluence of the waters.

Beyond Shimohara the ravine opens out for a while into a pleasant vale, on the far side of which a fine old Buddhist temple, belonging to the Zen sect, looks out from a dark grove of noble cryptomeria. Then it closes again, and we pass along on the edge of a precipice, 500 feet in depth, looking down on a group of pine-clothed islets rising above the rapids of the torrent. The roughness of the road prevented us from covering more than 32 miles before darkness came on, so we put up for the night at Hoido, where a few scattered cottages dot the fields that spread in an open valley down to the water's edge.

Beyond Hoido we found the pathway cut into the face of wild cliffs that overhang the torrent, and whose fearsome aspect has gained for the locality the title of *Jigoku* (hell). The climax of the scenic beauty for which this route is remarkable was reached at Osaka (not to be confounded with Ōsaka, the great "Manchester of Japan"). A turbulent mountain torrent, born far up the rugged western side of Ontake, dashes down a dark ravine and joins the main stream at the base of rugged cliffs. A rocky promontory at the meeting of the streams supports a fine cryptomeria grove, whose recesses shelter a little shrine dedicated to Kwannon, "the goddess of Mercy."

Beyond this point, apparently without the least reason,

the river changes its name, affording an instance of one of the puzzling practices adopted by the Japanese in their geographical nomenclature.   At the birth of the stream in the green tarn $\overline{O}$-*ike*, high up on Norikura, it receives the name Adanogōgawa.   As it grows bigger, between Kukuno and Osaka, this is changed to Masuda-gawa. But, oddly enough, it is not until it leaves its native province of Hida and passes into Mino that it takes the title by which it is best known, of Hidagawa.   Finally, on reaching the Nakasendō, near Ōta, it ceases to have any individuality at all, as its waters are there merged into those of the Kisogawa, not far from the outlet of that river in the Gulf of Owari.

At Kukuno our roadway parted company with the stream, and we left the *jinrikisha* without regret.   For, as my friend remarked, though the jolting we had had may be, like equestrian exercise, "very good for the liver, it is uncommonly bad for the troosers."   We sent on the baggage by porters in advance, while we followed leisurely over the frequent zigzags of the Miya-tōge, a pass which crosses over to Takayama.   On the right the broken ridge of Ontake, streaked with snow, stood out boldly, and far up the valley of the stream we had been ascending rose the massive twin summits of Norikura.   On the north side of the pass a majestic grove of cryptomeria overshadow a stately Shintō temple, the *Ichi-no-miya* of Hida.   As its name implies, it is the chief shrine in the province, and though the present buildings are comparatively modern, its foundation dates from prehistoric times. The structure is of plain wood, once white, but now tanned by exposure to a dirty brown. The roofs are covered with a simple thatch, and the *tout ensemble* is thoroughly in keeping with the straight massive trunks and dark foliage that surround the enclosure. It is a fact worth noticing that the Japanese almost invariably seem to have chosen the loveliest spot on hill-side or in valley for their places of worship. It is especially true of the Shintō temples, the earliest erections, meant to serve as a meeting-place for man and those powers without him, of whose aid he feels the need, and whose favour he wishes to invoke. In many a place much of the beauty of the landscape has been sacrificed on the altar of ruthless, though practical utility, yet the one thing spared is the clump of tall trees whose recesses shelter some rustic fane. Its sacredness alone has saved its guardians from falling beneath the woodman's devastating axe, and their preservation ensures the supply of timber that is needed to rescue it from falling into dis-repair and permanent decay. That the sublime to the ridiculous, however, is but a step we felt as we left the shrine and caught sight, in an adjoining shed, of a group of tawdry wooden horses, gaudily painted, in ludicrous contrast to their sternly plain surroundings.

F

Through the valley, at the bottom of the hill on which the temple stands, the Miyagawa flows gently towards the hill-girt plain in which the town of Takayama lies.

Whilst we ourselves were strolling along the banks, our coolies went on in advance to announce our coming and to leave our baggage at the Tanekaya inn. As we drew near the entrance to the town a dancing spark of light in the far distance grew into the red glow of a native *chōchin* (round paper lantern), and a profound obeisance on the part of the holder next told us a welcome was waiting for us at the inn from which he had been sent to meet us. May Takayama long be preserved from the visits of that species of globe-trotter whose ravages have as yet been chiefly confined to the show places of the treaty ports and their neighbourhood. There he is known, unfortunately, too well, and his selfish carelessness, or worse, has already gone far to teach a nation of gentlemen to despise the manners of the country of which he is supposed to be a fair representative. You may know his haunts by the deterioration of the manners of the people with whom he has had most to do, for of him it may, with all too much truth, be said, *nihil tetigit quod non contaminavit.*

As the road leaves the east end of the town it passes by the cremation-ground and through a narrow valley, where a rice-straw rope bears witness to a curious superstition. It acts as a sort of barometer, and according to the date at which the weather increases its tension to snapping-point, omens, bad or good, are drawn of the coming crops. A grand view of our mountains rose up as we topped a low hill called *Tetezaka*, and almost made us shout again with exultation at the glorious prospect. The fresh clear air of the early morning was marvellously exhilarating, and our spirits rose as we wound in and out among the hills that form the lower spurs of Norikura's massive western flanks. For a dozen miles our track kept company with the dark stream of the Niūgawa, which we followed nearly up to its source in a deep emerald lake on the mountain. Picturesque little bridges crossed its impetuous rapids, and led us from side to side of a narrow defile between richly-wooded hills. Near the hamlet of Hiomo we stopped to take some barometrical observations, and as we turned to look down the ravine a lovely picture, as striking as it was unexpected, confronted us. Vignetted in an angle of the nearer hills, the shapely cone of Hakusan reared its 9,000 feet westwards beyond the borders of the Hida plateau, 60 miles off as the crow flies. Close at hand the green hills slope till their outlines meet, and then nothing intervenes to catch the eye till the great "white mountain," scarred with a thousand wintry watercourses, stands clearly outlined in white and purple against the sky of a perfect summer's day.

In four hours from the start we pulled up at Hatahoko,

a little collection of cottages at the foot of a range of steep
hills that cut us off from the valley of Hirayu, for which
we were making as our head-quarters. The coolies we had
brought with us had now to return, and as the morning
was well advanced it was not easy to replace them. The
peasants in these mountain valleys turn out to their work
at an early hour, and the head man of the hamlet hesitated
a good deal at our request for help. Whilst he was
grumbling at the inconvenience it caused, we sat down and
proceeded to dine.   By-and-by it leaked out that my
companion was a " medicine man," and a complete change
came over the spirit of our crusty friend. Not only did
his manner soften, but his demands at once dropped, as he
trotted out all the sick folk of the village with a petition
for professional advice.   The sight of the front verandah of
the poor little cottage, transformed into a hospital ward,
was as ludicrous as it was pathetic.   For, as one has well
remarked, " Humour was born a twin, and the name of her
sister was Pathos."   One person had a pain in the stomach,
and wondered if it was not heart disease, there being a
popular belief that the seat of the affections resides in that
region.   Another was anxious to take half a dozen doses of
pills all at once in the hope of hastening the cure.   A
sturdy woodcutter showed a frightfully gashed leg, the
result of an accident when felling timber.   He smiled as
he noticed my involuntary look of pity, for these curious

Japanese have themselves such an astonishing insensibility to pain. No doubt it is largely explained by their totally differently constituted nervous organization. A *jinrikisha* man whom I once saw in Tōkyō afforded a curious instance of this. As I passed by his "stand" I noticed him intently engaged in examining a wound in his foot. Presently he took, with a pair of iron tongs, a red-hot piece of charcoal from the *hibachi* (brazier) by his side. He then proceeded to press it on the injured spot until the flesh began to sizzle, but all the time he showed the most perfect unconcern. As I watched the smoke of his burning flesh slowly curling up, he was attracted by an exclamation of surprise I made, and burst out into a roar of laughter at my astonishment. I have witnessed scenes of suffering in Japanese hospitals keen enough to move any heart, but the sufferers themselves rarely murmured. Shortly after the earthquake of October, 1891, I was one day going the round of a temporary hospital in a village near Gifu in company with a friend, who was engaged in distributing relief to the sufferers. I shall never forget the way in which one poor old lady, with a badly fractured leg and other injuries, insisted on trying to get up in bed to bow her grateful thanks in appreciation of our visit, apparently insensible to the pain one would think it must have caused.

By midday the patients had all been dealt with, our porters were forthcoming, and we were off. A steep ascent through a forest of beeches, oaks, and firs, with here and there a clearing for a charcoal burner's hut, brought us to the top of the Hirayu tōge, about 5,500 feet above the sea. A decaying hut, inhabited by a few dilapidated stone images of Buddha, crowns the summit, which is densely wooded. A quick descent of less than an hour took us down to the baths of Hirayu, which nestle in a green hollow, walled in almost on every hand by tall mountain sides, the only natural outlet being by a narrow valley to the north. Until the last few years the hot mineral springs (chalybeate) formed the chief attraction of the isolated little spot, but recently other sources of prosperity have been opened up in the mines on the western side of Norikura. The first-named, however, now claimed our immediate attention, and we were soon sitting up to our necks in the grateful warmth of a semi-private bath, near the little inn of Yomosaburō, with whom we were to stay. The spring from which the waters flow lies a couple of hundred yards away, and supplies the water, which leaves it at a temperature of 190°, for the public baths close by. These are of a very primitive kind, consisting simply of roofed-in tanks, some 10 feet square, quite open to the public gaze. The heat of the water is moderated by a stream of cold, conducted also through bamboo pipes. Men and women bathe together, and the behaviour of one and all is beyond reproach. At one time, in some of the larger

towns, which foreigners sometimes visited, and at the
Treaty ports, a police regulation ordered that at the public
baths the sexes should be separated. The order was
obeyed in letter if not in spirit, and many places where the
prowling policeman was not too strict in his interpretation
of the rule, saw reformation in a barrier, which consisted of
a piece of string stretched across the bath to denote " This
side for ladies, that for gentlemen."

In one out-of-the-way place I have heard of* the people
will stay in for practically a month at a time, and usually
sit with large stones on the knees to keep them from
floating or " turning turtle " in their sleep. The caretaker,
Mr. Chamberlain states, an old fellow of three score and
thirteen, stops in the water almost the whole winter through.
At another place the villagers apologized to my friend for
being what they called " so dirty," " for," they said, " we
have only time to bathe twice a day, because it is the
summer-time, and we are so busy." " How often, then,"
asked Mr. Chamberlain, " do you bathe in winter ? " " Oh,
we then have less to do, and can get four or five baths
a day, and the children get into the water whenever they
feel cold." Those who are familiar with the habits of the
Chinese in this respect will readily endorse Mr. Chamberlain's remark that love of bathing is one at least of the

* Cp. Chamberlain's "Things Japanese." The name of the village is
Kawanaka, near Ikao, in the province of Jōshü.

original items of Japanese civilisation. Tubs the Celestials have certainly not been responsible for introducing into Japan, "for," they say, "only dirty people like foreigners need to wash so often!" The mineral waters of most of the thermal springs are held to cure an amazing catalogue of diseases. Those of Kusatsu are said to be able to conquer all distempers but one, and that is—love! Of whatever fickleness the Japanese may have been accused in other matters, it is certainly a fact that their love for hot water has never grown cold.

The immediate object of our visit to Hirayu was the ascent of Norikura from the west. Several ascents had been made, we were told, from the east side, but hitherto the few foreigners who had passed through Hirayu over the range had not turned their thoughts to the exploration of the great mountain from the Hida side. From a Government official who happened to be staying in our little inn we learned that we could spend the night at the mines high above Hirayu, on a north-west spur, which would make matters a good deal simpler. During the evening after our arrival this gentleman came in to visit us, and showed us some sectional maps he had been making of the lower parts of the mountains in the neighbourhood, in connection with a report he was preparing for the Agricultural Department. He had been unable to do much, he said, in the higher regions, as the climbing was too hard, but he would be grateful for any information we could give him on the subject after our explorations. Each day saw him and his assistant sally forth, clad in semi-military uniforms of bottle-green, armed with swords (for ornament only), and laden with sketch-books and instruments. Early one afternoon Miller and I quitted the inn in company with a couple of porters for the climb to the mines. At the foot of a steep hillside above the south-east end of the village we reached the smelting works connected with the mine above. The ore (silver and copper) is brought down in baskets and rough sledges, and the track thus used was the one by which we ascended. A stiff walk of half an hour brought us to the top of a grand cascade, Hirayu-no-taki, which a little while before we had been admiring as a soft silken ribbon streaming through the trees of a picturesque ravine. Now it falls in a broad white sheet, with a thunderous roar, into a rocky basin 200 feet below. The rough path ended, at a height of 7,360 feet, at the entrance to the miners' settlement, which is built on the steep hillside in which the galleries are pierced. Two long lines of low huts, protected by a wide verandah, accommodate the miners, who are at work the whole year round. Until the mines were opened, even Hirayu itself was in the winter months deserted, and its inhabitants removed to Ōtani, in the Takayama plain. But the new industry provides them with continuous occupation in supplying the wants of the 150 men and women up at Kōzan, as the mines are called. As we appeared, wet and muddy, at the door of the overseer's hut, a hospitable welcome greeted us, and we entered a cosy little room, occupied by the manager and his half-dozen assistants. Dry *kimono* (native garments) were brought to replace our rain-soaked things, for our porters had fallen far behind. A sumptuous meal of octopus and slices of sweet potatoes fried in oil was specially cooked, and then a cheery chat about our surroundings soon made us feel at home.

The mines, the manager said, had been only working for about four years, and the average output of copper is 140,000 lbs., that of silver being 2,500 lbs. or less annually. A similar mine was once worked on the eastern spur of Norikura, and traces of the old buildings, furnaces, &c., are still to be seen above Ōnogawa, on the Shinshū side. It is 30 years ago since operations ceased, and the works are now entirely deserted. In the winter time the whole valley and hillsides are covered deep in snow, and special footgear is worn by the workmen on their journeys up and down. For hard snow a sort of *crampon*, made of a flat triangular piece of iron with three points, is tied on beneath the straw shoes that encase the feet. For softer snow a light circular frame, made of a sort of creeper called *kadzura*, enables the wearer to pass safely over the deepest drifts.

The room we and our hosts occupied was between the two huge dormitories where the miners themselves slept. Just as we were lying down for the night a commotion in one of these announced the arrival of a peripatetic story-teller and his assistant *samisen*-player. As the workmen cannot go down to the valley for their evening's amusement, the entertainers have, Mahomet-like, to come to the mountain, and, unluckily for us, on this occasion chose this particular evening. One could hardly expect that, when the miners had once got their mountebanks, they would let them go without getting their money's worth. The Japanese are too well versed in making a business of pleasure, and the performance went on until midnight. Consequently, it was 6·30 on a damp grey morning before we got away, and only then in spite of the grumblings of our coolies. "The weather isn't fit," they protested. "It will be too risky, and we may get benighted," and so forth. In the midst of all this we were agreeably surprised by the unexpected arrival of an addition to our party. This was a cheery, grizzled old hunter, who had come up from Hirayu that morning, and wanted to learn the way. He said it would be useful in case any other stray foreign traveller might wish to follow in our footsteps. His cheerfulness of mind was only equalled by his astonishing activity of limb, and his presence, by raising the spirits of our porters, assisted materially our ascent. A descent down a steep talus of shale took us to the bed of a torrent, which we crossed at a point where we had to scramble up a precipitous bank on the opposite side. In the dense forest beyond, tree stumps, hidden in the long wet grass, tripped up the unwary one. Then, whilst looking out for these, an unobserved branch above knocked him over the head. The least shake to bush or bough brought down an impromptu shower-bath, and the slippery grass brought down the climber himself.

After an hour's work, two of the "guides" wanted to give in and go back, but we made them stick to it, and at length got out of the forest and descended an awkward little precipice into a second torrent bed below. Far off on the right, the lowest slope of snow, about 7,000 feet, showed up dull and cheerless in the cold rain, but we turned our backs upon it and mounted to the left up the rocks of the ravine. This did duty for the convenient couloir, and brought us to the top of a ridge where we found recent traces of a bear. Passing over slopes of snow we reached a second ridge from which a lovely view was gained of the dark green waters of the lake Ōniū-ike. The torrent which descends from the lake is the one that comes out at Hatahoko, and is there known as the Niū-gawa. We next descended a stretch of spiky *haimatsu*, an involuntary sitting down on which occasionally produced most painful results. A long snow slope led us up to a saddle, where we overlooked another lake some 400 yards in length, surrounded by a fine amphitheatre of sharp rocky peaks.   At an altitude of 9,000 feet we found a natural cave in the rocks just beyond the lake, and after breakfast there had a grand scramble up to the crest of the ridge.   Away to the left lay an empty hut, called *Murodō*, used by those who make the ascent from Ōnogawa on the Shinshū side.   A traverse across the rocks above put us on a sharp *arête,* which we followed to the northernmost and highest (10,160 feet) of the twin summits that give to Norikura its name of the " Riding saddle mountain."   A magnificent view of the finest peaks of the Japanese Alps is the climber's reward. Close at hand on the north rise great towers of rock and precipitous ridges from a mass of shifting vapour, but the cloud curtains that veil their lower slopes only enhance their grandeur.   On the south, the tall form of Ontake with its crater-indented summit rises in a bold sweep beyond a low wide saddle.   Beyond Komagatake and the mountains of Koshū, the never-absent form of Fuji greets us familiarly.   At the base of the precipice on the edge of which we stood, the round pool of Ō-ike gives birth to the Hida-gawa, the stream of many names.   The nature of the rocks, the peculiar form of the highest ridges, and the traces of lava flows in the direction of Ōnogawa, tell us that Norikura is an ancient volcano.

On the east side extensive beds of shale are overlaid in the most curious way by a stream of lava, but no eruptions seem to have taken place in historic times. A little shrine of storm-bleached wood on the summit is dedicated to the " God of dawn."

The descent was enlivened by a ptarmigan hunt, in which the preserver of lives spent much energy in frantic but futile efforts to slay the bird that popped in and out of the low level clumps of *haimatsu* in the most provoking way. Though I have seen many stones hurled at this bird I have never seen one take effect, and yet no game ever gave so many chances to its pursuer. The Japanese call it *rai-chō*, or " thunder bird," as it is supposed to be responsible for the thunderstorms which, though infrequent in the lowlands, are constantly experienced in the higher regions in central Japan where the ptarmigan is oftenest found. Its feathers, especially when found on Ontake, are much valued by silkworm breeders for use in brushing off the silkworm eggs from one paper to another.

A pouring rain overtook us long before we could get back to the mines. The ascent had occupied five and a half hours, and the care needed on the steep smooth rocks in the highest ravine forced us to take nearly as long in the descent. Hearty congratulations welcomed us on our arrival, but our wet condition deterred us from the further stay we were begged to make. We were the first foreigners this hospitable folk had seen, but should others come after us they will find themselves " in clover " at this interesting spot. It was 6˙45 as we, with night, came down on Hirayu a second time. Great was the interest shown, when, after dinner, we and our coolies gathered with our host and his family round the fire that blazed in the middle of the great smoke-blackened kitchen to talk over our expedition.

The rest of the following day would have been spent in peace but for the mob of rustics who gathered round our corner of the house repeatedly to gaze in at our open *shōji*, like the curious crowds that throng the cages of a wild beast show. Not that there was anything objectionable done, for the staring multitude was all perfectly quiet, and no rudeness whatever was shown. The fact was that they never dreamed of causing us annoyance, nor could they even have understood our finding their attention distasteful. No sooner, however, did either of us chance to get up than the whole company would literally jump with surprise and scatter like the mists before the rising sun. In the larger towns it is quite common to find the shop front one may have chanced to stop at, quite darkened by gathering dozens of natives who show a much greater interest in inspecting you than you yourself find in the shopman's wares. Under these circumstances, the best remedy for dispersing them is to quietly turn round and gaze intently at their feet. You will then notice them stealing uneasy sidelong glances at each other, shuffling about almost as if they would like to hide their feet in their pockets, and finally, as they feel this is impossible, with an uncomfortable grin they will gradually disappear. This simple but ingenious device was first recommended to me by an English lady, and I may add that I have never found it to fail.

The evening of Sunday was spent in trying to help the sick folk staying in the village. Many of them were visitors from adjoining valleys where, in their isolation, they never see a medical man once in their lifetime. Their chief remedies for their ills are herbs or strange reptiles, whose flesh when dried and cooked is credited with the most marvellous curative properties. Apart from these, their main chance lies in the waters of the mineral springs. On this occasion, the advent of a foreign doctor, the first they had ever seen, was too great an opportunity to be lost. Long before our dinner that night was done, a continuous stream of would-be patients came pouring in at the entrance to our inn. Far into the night the work went on of interpreting their symptoms to my good-natured friend, who not only had to prescribe but also to provide the means of cure. Every item of advice, even each bitterest pill, was received with the most touching tokens of gratitude. The only hesitation at accepting anything was that which followed the assurance that there really was nothing at all to pay in return.

CHAPTER V.

As we looked down the narrow valley that forms the
only natural outlet from the secluded little plain in which
Hirayu lies, a grand rocky peak closed in the distant
prospect. It owes its name Kasadake ("the umbrella
peak") to the supposed resemblance of its great buttresses
and snow-filled couloirs to the ribs and hollows of a half-
open native umbrella. On Monday morning we set off to
explore the neighbouring valley which runs up to the
southern base of the mountain, in the middle of which
we found a cluster of cottages surrounding a hot spring
strongly impregnated with iron. On appealing to the
kuchō ("head man") of the primitive hamlet of Gamada
for information and help, a wet blanket at once stifled our
hopes.

The appearance of a couple of foreigners was in itself a
sufficiently astonishing event, but why they should want
to climb a mountain where neither silver mines nor crystals

G

were to be found was quite unintelligible to him. As I
subsequently found out, there were other reasons that
deterred him from furthering our plans, but until a couple
of years later these did not transpire. He ended up a
profusion of polite apologies with the statement that
recent storms had burst the banks of the Gamada-gawa
which it would have been necessary to cross and recross
higher up, and no hunters could be found willing to
attempt the ascent. The positive manner in which the
kuchō gave his dictum, showed that beyond it there was no
appeal ; so, finding it, as the Japanese phrase expressively
puts it, a case of *shikata-ga-nai* (" doing side does not
exist "—" there is no help for it "), we retired to drown our
disappointment in the thermal waters of the village baths.
There is no inn at Gamada, but a kindly old farmer named
Jimbei took us in for the night. It was a case for him of
entertaining a good friend unawares, for Miller found out
the old man was suffering from a serious internal
complaint, and was not only able to treat him there and
then, but also a week later sent him fresh remedies when
our arrival at Matsumoto brought us within the reach of
medical supplies.

Two days later we left Hirayu at 6 A.M. for the passage
of the Abōtōge, which crosses the main chain at a height of
6,400 feet, over the northern shoulder of Norikura, and
affords during its length of 25 miles between Hirayu and

T. Hori, phot.

BATH-HOUSES OF SHIRAHONE ONSEN, AT THE FOOT OF NORIKURA.

[P. 83.

Hashiba views of the finest scenery of its sort in Central Japan. A narrow track led us up a densely-wooded defile, now and then crossing the débris of a landslip where tall fir trees had been uprooted or snapped in twain like so many matches. Only the distant murmur of a mountain torrent, or the full liquid notes of the *uguisu* (nightingale) broke on the ear as we mounted the steep ascent, and the stillness of the sweet-scented shade was restful beyond description. As we descended from the top of the pass, where a small post marks the boundary between Hida and Shinshū, and wound round the spurs on its eastern side, a lateral valley on the north suddenly disclosed a beautiful vignette. In an angle formed by richly-timbered hill-sides appeared the grey granite towers and snow-seamed flanks of Hodakayama. Further on the forest trees gave way to stretches of grassy slope gay with flowers, and affording abundant feasts of wild strawberries of enormous size. Then a thin column of steam far down on the right told us where the hot springs of Shirahone lay solitary in a narrow ravine. The spot is out-of-the-world to a degree, but a few dozen rustics visit it every summer and shelter in its picturesque châlets for the sake of taking the healing waters. Below the springs a torrent is crossed by an elementary bridge, which consists merely of a couple of pine trees stretched from a tall mass of rock to the opposite bank. The slippery poles swayed and bent

cheerfully as we gingerly shuffled across, and the flashing
waters dazzled the eyes distractingly the while.   At noon
a quaint little cottage on the top of a ridge mutely
invited us to rest.   A bent and wrinkled old lady appeared
and put the invitation into words, though no more solid
food could she supplement it with than a little hot water
and abundance of dried peas.   Potatoes there were, it is
true, but they were raw, and several dry withered snakes
that hung their grey lengths from the beam indoors were
not sufficiently tempting to our tastes.   As the porters with
our baggage and provisions were lagging far behind we
had to content ourselves with the peas.   They may be, as
we were told, sustaining, though to a hungry mountaineer
they are far from satisfying.   But the sight of bunches of
mistleto that showed thickly through the delicate green of
some small oaks below the summit of the ridge afforded
abundant food for reflection upon some of the contrasts the
Japanese present to ourselves.   This interesting parasite,
which here makes its home not only in oaks but also in
beeches, willows, and maples, has for them none of the
associations with which it is often connected in the West.
Moreover, the custom it so frequently suggests at an
English Christmas-tide is regarded by these far Orientals
as both barbarous and unhygienic.   A Japanese school-
boy I know of, one day brought his English teacher a
spontaneous effusion prompted by the behaviour of an

engaged couple in a certain little American community in the interior of Japan. It was entitled "KYS," and he began by censuring kissing as a most disgusting practice. After then endeavouring to prove that it was not only lowering to the dignity, but also dangerous, as being a means of communicating disease, he crowned his arguments with the sarcastic query—

"And is this *civilised nation's* custom?"

A series of ups and downs over thinly wooded ridges led us, by 2 P.M., to Ōnogawa, a finely situated village whose cottages cling to the steep sides of a rocky bluff that pushes itself out into the broad waters of the short but swift Mayegawa. The hour and a half we had to wait for our coolies was passed pleasantly at the house of the headman. A bathe in the rapids just below was followed by a lunch of fresh trout, tea, and cakes of pink, white, and green ground rice. The meal was served with the most charming attention by our host and his wife. As the former squatted on the mats by our side he told us a little about himself and his concerns. The baths of Shirahone belonged to him, and to his other duties he added that of a local official of the Agricultural Department, in witness whereof his dark green uniform with its tarnished gilt buttons hung up conspicuously on the front verandah. Just now, unfortunately, he wasn't very well, he said, but what ailed him he could not tell, and there was no doctor within

many miles. His joy at learning Miller's profession, and
his subsequent gratitude for a diagnosis and a prescription,
knew no bounds. A result was that by the time our
porters straggled in, a fresh trio of much stronger fellows
were ready to relieve them, and we proceeded without
delay.

Never will the memory of the last 12 miles of that day's
walk lose its charm. For the greater part of the way tall
cliffs rose stern and forbidding right from the water's edge,
only here and there sloping more gently to afford a footing
to dark pines and fresh green shrubs. In many places the
pathway is cut in the living rock. In others it has been
built up round the smooth vertical face of the ravine, and
is supported on struts of timber from below. These have
been frequently swept away by landslips and avalanches,
so that the track has disappeared bodily in the rushing
torrent far beneath. In such places we enjoyed delightful
scrambles, scaling the cliff and then traversing above so as
to descend to the path beyond the gap. Here and there
the shattered timbers that once held up the road hung in
ragged festoons down the face of the cliff, and made it
ticklish work to trust to their precarious support. At
every turn in the winding valley, which in itself is a
grand example of erosion, fresh beauties claimed attention.
Near the junction of the Mayegawa with the Azusagawa,
a curious waterslide slips, like a broad sheet of liquid

glass, over the polished surface of a dark rock face on the left bank of the latter stream. Further on, to the right, a cascade falls almost on the pathway, and scatters its spray in iridescent showers before the mouth of a cave that opens in the base of the precipice. Picturesque bridges lead the road across from side to side and afford variety to the view. At Inekoki the valley expands to allow the cottages to spread themselves over a pleasant cultivated vale. The peasants here use storehouses consisting of holes hewn in the rocks called *kaze-ana* ("wind-caves"), where they can house their little crops in safety from winter storms. By half-past six the narrow valley was already in twilight, and the yellow rays of a swinging *chōchin* were our guide to Hashiba. Boulders and hollows in the path that are unnoticed in broad daylight then are magnified astonishingly, and the darkness that envelopes the surroundings doubles the length of the journey. By 7·30 P.M. a few scattered points of light began to glimmer fitfully through the trees on the river's right bank. The path suddenly took a turn to descend abruptly to the massive bridge, and then a few steps up the steep and stony ascent at the entrance to the silent village brought us to the door of the hospitable "Shimidzuya." In response to the hollow rattling of the outer shutters a door was slid aside, and a pleasant greeting, "Many thanks for last

year's visit," welcomed us in.   The ever-grateful bath was
succeeded by a substantial meal—and then came a council
of war.   One of the hunters I had last year appeared from
a remote corner of Hashiba, to tell me that he and his
two brothers will gladly do their best to complete this time
the expedition that last year so narrowly failed to succeed.

A rising barometer, a cloudless sky, and the best trio of
hunters I had yet employed as guides, all helped to raise
our spirits high as the next morning saw us re-crossing
the Zōsui-bashi *en route* for Yarigatake, the miniature
Matterhorn of Japan.   The air of the valley was fresh
and pure, and the dewdrops trembled like diamonds on
every leaf.   The sweet scent of the tall straight pines that
shaded our path, the murmuring torrent below and the
deep blue vault that spread a narrow canopy above the
tall sides of the now familiar ravine, made even existence
itself a delight.   Truly we were in Nature's Academy,
hung with some of the choicest of the Creator's master-
pieces.

Three miles out from Hashiba we were greeted with the
sight of an innovation in the secluded valley.   A chalybeate
spring had since my former visit been discovered on the
left bank of the stream, and its waters are now utilised
for mineral baths.   They are conducted in bamboo pipes
to the opposite side, and in a wooden bath some 6 feet

·square are heated for the use of the dozen or so of country folk who come from Hashiba and Shimajima. The custodian, a dear old gentleman (for his manners were perfect though his garments were poor and threadbare), was sitting on his heels in a little shanty by the wayside. He begged us to stay and have a cup of tea with him, and then to test the wonderful powers of his novel *furō* (hot bath). His kindly importunity could not be resisted as regards the drink, but the long day's march before us compelled us to leave the bath to the little group, of both sexes, that reclined in various attitudes on the scantily matted floor of the adjoining dormitory. As we passed by the Dashinosawa hut, we saw it was closed, and the recollection of the fleas that probably still disported themselves within made me glad to be outside. Interminable seemed the steep zig-zags up the Tokugō Pass. The afternoon was terribly hot, and scarcely a breath of air stirred the bamboo-grass through which the track was cut. At the summit we flung ourselves down in the shelter of the trees and enjoyed a well-earned *hiru-ne* (siesta) until the dry bark of the thirsty little half-wild dog our hunters had with them waked us to bid them follow our example. The road up the valley we had just traversed had been a good deal improved since the previous year, but at the top of the *col* all work had ceased, and the path down the northern side soon lost itself hopelessly in the broken rocks of the

now half-empty watercourse. As the grand mass of Hodakayama again rose up on the opposite side of the valley
we were strongly tempted to transfer our affections from
Yarigatake, but the longing was sternly suppressed, and
after a rest at the Tokugō hut we forded the river and made
the best of our way through a corner of the forest beyond.
Three miles up the Azusagawa we encamped for the night.
Wood there was in plenty, and of water an unlimited supply.
Whilst some of us set to work to get it, others went off to
fish, and a dozen delicious trout were speedily landed.
The hunters made themselves a shelter of branches on the
edge of the forest which comes down here to the water's
edge, and Miller and I slung our hammocks between
convenient trees. Over each hammock we spread a sheet
of native oil-paper, for the night was fine and clear, and
we knew the dew would fall heavily. By the time these
preparations were completed a grand fire lighted up the
dark forest around, and all was cheery and bright. Never
was trout so dainty, nor curried fowl more appetizing.
Then the stars began to light the sky, and clear and cold
the moon rose over the dense pine forest on Nabekamuriyama's rounded top before us, whilst, behind, the pale
granite cliffs and snows of Hodakayama loom ghostly and
grand. Even the hunters themselves smoked their pipes
more stolidly than usual, and one was loth to break the
solemn silence.

How Bret Harte's lines bring back the scene :—

> " Above the pines the moon was slowly drifting,
>   The river sang below :
> The dim sierras, far beyond, uplifting
>   Their minarets of snow.
>
> The roaring camp-fire, with rude humour, painted
>   The ruddy tints of health
> On . . . face and form . . . "

As we tumbled out of our hammocks in the grey light of early dawn a shower of wet from above told us how tropical dews can fall. The hollows in our oil-paper roofs were as full as if a heavy rain had beaten down during the night. As soon as the sun had brought light into the valley we left the camp as it was, and strode up the stony river-bed in eager anticipation of the day's climb. Our route was the same as that by which Belcher and I had descended from Yarigatake twelve months ago. Passing on the left the Yokoōdani we kept to the course of the Azusa-gawa on our right, scrambling through dense thickets, and over broken rocks on the mountain side above the torrent, or crossing and re-crossing its turbulent waters by jumping from boulder to boulder as before. Some miles up the stream, near the foot of Chōgadake, a tall wooded mountain on the left bank, a narrow valley on the other side opens up our first view of Yarigatake's aiguille-like summit, and spurs us on more keenly still. Occasionally a torrent feeder joins the main stream on right or left, and has to be forded or scrambled across. At one of these points I had an impressive reminder of the fact that *waraji* (straw sandals) give better hold on water-worn boulders than hobnailed boots. An awkward jump from one smooth surface to another just missed the proper mark, and the next moment found me cooling my heated frame in the foaming torrent, in which I had sat down with great emphasis, after the manner of the commencing skater in his earliest attempts. Three hours of hard work with jungle and stream took us at length to the Akasaka no iwa goya, "the red cliff cave," so called from the colour of the rocks at the foot of which it lies. The familiar slope of snow opposite still furnished an unmistakeable landmark, and the whole scene recalled the pleasantest of memories. After a halt underneath the shadow of the great rock wedge, we set off at noon in real earnest. An hour's scramble up the bed of the stream placed us at the foot of broken slopes partly covered with grass, but ending higher up in bare loose rocks. Yarigatake now came in full view from base to summit, and we felt that victory was assured. Long slopes of snow gave a pleasing variety to the climb, and we were sorry to leave them for the wild confusion of the broken moraine-like steeps above. The "aspect of destruction" about the whole scene vividly recalls the noble passage in Ruskin's 4th volume of 'Modern Painters' on the Aiguilles of Chamonix : "Those waste leagues around its feet are loaded with the wreck of

T. Hort, phot.

YARIGATAKE, FROM THE N.E.

[P. 92.

what it was. On these, perhaps of all mountains, the characters of decay are written most clearly : around these are spread most gloomily the memorials of their pride, and the signs of their humiliation."

Two hours' steady climbing from the torrent bed was enough to place us in the narrow gap in the ridge from which the pinnacle of the " Spear Peak" abruptly rises. Then we turned northwards and soon succeeded in passing the spot at which Belcher and I had turned back. The smooth steep slabs, dangerous enough in wet weather, were now perfectly dry, and convenient cracks and ledges gave good hand- and foothold everywhere. For 400 or 500 feet we kept to the edge of the *arête*, but then a curious twist in the upper part of the peak forced us to turn sharply to the west.

A dozen steps more, and we were overlooking all else. Yarigatake is ours, and save for Fuji the peerless, we stand on the loftiest point of the whole surface of this mountain empire. The peak consists of an intensely hard weather-resisting brecciated porphyry, which is traversed by numerous foliated silicious bands. These bands are inclined at high angles, and are frequently contorted. To the hardness of the rock it owes its height, and to the silicious bands its jagged spear-like shape. Its altitude is 10,300 feet. The actual summit is a narrow platform a few yards long, dropping on the east and west in perpendicular cliffs, and affording a prospect grand and impressive in the extreme. To the north stretches the long line of rugged peaks that separates the province of Etchū from parts of Echigo and Shinshū. The wild valleys that radiate from their bases are very little known, excepting to an occasional hunter of chamois, boar, or bear. Westwards, across the valley of the Gamada-gawa, Kasa-dake promises a splendid scramble. Far over its northern shoulder a glittering band of blue beyond the Toyama plain is radiant with the " many-twinkling smile of ocean : "

> . . . . ποντίων τε κυμάτων
> ἀνήριθμον γέλασμα . .—ÆSCHYLUS, *Pr.* 90.

Due east the triangular form of Jōnendake is sharply out-lined against the sky. Asama Yama's smoke rises in the far distance. Southwards the eye ranges over the nearer giants of the main chain, Hodakayama and Norikura, with Ontake beyond them. To the south-east Komagatake, and further still, the Koshū peaks stand up boldly. But stateliest of all, the symmetrical cone of Fuji rises from the Pacific shore, separated from us by a distance—as the crow flies —of nearly 90 miles. To enumerate all the vast sea of summits that lift their swelling crests within our view would be to give a list of all the grandest mountains in Japan. Nearly the entire width of the central part of the mainland is embraced by the magnificent prospect.

A good deal of care was needed on the descent of the

smooth slabs of the "spear" of the mountain, and down
the loose sharp rocks at its base. Once on the snow glissades made progress easy, and by half-past six, as night fell,
we were back at the "red cliff cave." Tired we were, for
the 20 miles of rough work up and down had been broken
by few rests during the 13 hours we were on our feet.
But elated with the successful issue of our climb, we could
well enjoy our bivouac, and of provisions this time we had
no lack. Leaves and ferns provided us with a bed under
the lee of the rocky wedge, and with shawls for coverings,
and rücksack and camera for pillows, we made all snug for
the night. An umbrella open at our heads warded off the
keen night breeze that pierced a crevice at that end, and a
cheerful fire blazing near our feet left nothing further to
be desired. The return to Hashiba was accomplished
without mishap on the following day. The distance of
30 miles took twelve and a half hours, but it was only
by dint of a spurt during the last few miles that we gained
the "Shimidzuya" before darkness set in. The hunters,
who had worked splendidly throughout the expedition,
were only an hour or so behind us, and deserved every
credit for the way they performed their task.

A Sunday's rest was spent pleasantly at Hashiba, but
Monday found us sweltering in the hot close air of
the Matsumoto plain, with a temperature at noon of
90° indoors. Some compensation was afforded by the

nearness of the delightful baths of Asama no yu, a little village nestling on the slopes of a hill north-east of the town. Each of the various inns that flourish on the visitors who come to the thermal springs, possesses its own private tank, but the best and biggest are those of the Ume-no-yu. There one may either join the public at a penny a head, or for fivepence one may get a private room. The water of the springs, which is partly impregnated with sulphur, is stated to be efficacious in no less than 28 specific complaints. The list begins with brain disease and ends with paralysis.

MATSUMOTO CASTLE.

CHAPTER VI.

AT Matsumoto I had to part with my genial companion, as he had an engagement to keep near Karuisawa, while I was bound in nearly the opposite direction. Of all the peaks I had viewed from the summit of Komagatake the previous year, none had more taken my fancy than that of Akaiishi-san, one of the tallest of the mass that separates the Tenryū-gawa from the well-known Fujikawa. So far as I could ascertain it had never been visited by foreign travellers, but the one or two who had been anywhere near it spoke of it with the greatest admiration. On hearing of my plans the ever-obliging landlord of the "Shinanoya," Sasai Motoji, at once begged me to let him share them, an offer I gladly accepted. Apart from the peaks ascended yearly by the white-robed pilgrims, whose travels are little more than a continuous religious picnic, few mountains are climbed by the natives for the pleasure the expeditions

H

afford. The country folk can rarely understand why a man
should undergo discomfort and toil for the sake of climbing
where neither silver mines nor crystals are to be found.
Though one's reasons may be accepted with the politest
outward assent, the questioner always reserves his own
opinions as to the truth of them. The majority are of the
same mind as a European lady whom I once heard remark,
"Well, you know, for my part, I always consider
mountaineering a mild form of madness, and you can't
make me believe it is anything else."

I was glad to find a native keen enough to take a long
journey to an unknown district solely for the sake of the
pleasure and interest it might afford. From Matsumoto to
Shiwojiri on the Nakasendō we jolted in a *basha*, to whose
tender mercies I once more had the temerity to commit
myself. Having safely accomplished this dozen miles or
so, the driver said he would go no further, so an hour was
spent in wrangling, *de more Japonico*, over the hire of
another vehicle. The experience is absurdly funny when
time is no object. The arguments the driver uses in order
to extract from you three times the sum he expects you
will give are often curiously Japanese. He, however,
generally ends by coming down (as you yourself are
running the risk of doing literally later on), and whether
he or you have come off best in bargaining, he is equally
cheerful as he leaps up on the box and whips up his steed

for a start. From Shiojiri a well-made road led by gentle gradients to the top of the Motoyama-tōge (2,800 feet), a pass which crosses the hills separating the basin of the Saigawa from that of the Tenryū-gawa. We then descended a pretty little valley by the side of a stream that near Miyaki falls into the Tenryū. Further on we also nearly did the same, owing to the harness suddenly falling to pieces and nearly pitching the *basha*, baggage, and ourselves on the top of the unfortunate horse. By using the term "harness" I do not wish to mislead the reader. The attachment of the horse to the carriage is no stronger literally than I should imagine it to be figuratively. It usually consists of a mixture of string, straps, and sometimes the driver's *obi* (girdle). Traces of proper leather are seldom seen. The result, as on this occasion, often is that when a strain is put on it a rupture with more or less startling consequences occurs. On arriving at Matsushima, we gladly quitted our "jaunting car" and crossed by a bridge over the Tenryū-gawa, whose course we then followed for some six miles, with grand views of Komagatake (of Shinshū) on our right, and of its Kōshū namesake on our left. By 7·15 P.M. we were at Takatō, a busy little town that stands high up on the right bank of the Mibu-kawa, the chief tributary of the Tenryū, in a valley on its east side. To our astonishment, on proceeding to the Kisoya inn, to which we had been

H 2

recommended, we were refused admittance, as they said they were full.   A second attempt elsewhere met with a similar result.   In despair we then went to the police station, and invoked the help of the sergeant in charge. He most politely came with us to a third inn, the Ikegami-ya, where we were received with doubtful pleasure, though with all politeness.   The landlord said he had never entertained a *gwaikoku-jin* ("outside-countries man," *i.e.*, a foreigner) before, and feared he would fail to give satis-faction, though he would do his best.   And so he did, for supper, bed, and breakfast in comfortable quarters, and with unremitting attention, only amounted to sixpence a head.

For half the following day our route kept company with the Mibu-kawa, through a narrow picturesque valley on the west of Komagatake (of Kōshū).   Occasionally some lateral ravine opened up on the left and disclosed a dark vista of the rugged cliffs and wooded slopes of the lower part of the mountain.   At Ichinose (sometimes also called Entsuji) we halted for lunch and for a change of pack-horse, as our coolie wished to return to Takatō that day. There was no inn at the little village, but on appealing to the "head-man" he kindly undertook to give us what we wanted, adding that the substitute would appear *tadaima*. This word is popularly *supposed* to mean "immediately," but in actual fact it is best translated " some time between

now and Christmas." In this case it had to be rendered
"two hours and a half," a serious matter where the swarms
of flies were a perfect plague. Wherever silkworm culture
is carried on this pest is sure to be found, and though at
Hirayu and elsewhere we had found them bad enough,
Ichinose was superlatively prolific in them.

A great surprise awaited us as we stepped inside the
open space beyond the door of the head-man's house.
Sacks of charcoal, agricultural implements, native saddlery,
bundles of vegetables, all were mixed up in confusion on
the floor. The rooms adjoining were all innocent of mats,
but guilty of a good deal of dirt and smell, the frequent
adjuncts of the industry named. But on passing these and
penetrating to the innermost apartment at the back of the
house, we found ourselves in one of the loveliest rooms
I ever entered. Spotless mats of unusual quality made
soft the tread, and dark polished woodwork, carved with
exquisite taste, surrounded the walls on every side. When
the long wait was ended by the arrival of the relay for our
baggage, we were indeed loth, in spite of the black swarms
of flies, to turn out of the cool retreat. But time, like the
policeman, was bidding us move on, and we fairly gasped
again as we stepped out into the blazing sun that beat
down pitilessly on the close valley we had now to traverse.
Three miles beyond the village the narrow track crossed
the Ichinose-tōge, 4,440 feet above the sea, and here an

abundance of delicious wild raspberries tempted us to
linger inordinately long. The path still pursues its course
due south, and only leaves one torrent-feeder of the
Tenryū-gawa to join another at its very source on the
opposite side. Welcome shade was now afforded by the
forest of firs and maples and *Sawara* (*arbor vitæ*), which
supply the timber for the saw-mills that give employment
to most of the peasants in the valley. The wood is chiefly
made up into bowls and sweetmeat boxes. An odd little
cluster of houses on a steep hill-side attracted attention
by its strange name—*Onna-taka* (the "women's hill").
Report explains it to refer to the fact that it is *women* who
here occupy the position of heads of families. Should a
stranger aspire to the hand of one of them his days are
said to be henceforth numbered, so heavily does the yoke
press on his shoulders. The hen-pecked husband is usually
supposed in Japan, if not to be as scarce as the "dodo," at
any rate to be a *rara avis*, and it is astonishing to find, in
this country above all others, a spot where the experiment
of "woman's rights" has been so completely carried out.
The "new woman," after all, would seem to be older than
has been generally supposed.

By six o'clock we came to a halt at Ichiba (20 miles
from Takatō), where scattered cottages are dotted about
the sides of the picturesque ravine, through which the
Kashio-gawa flows. Crossing the long bridge that spans

the stream, we put up at a modest inn called *Dai-maruya*
(" the house of the great circle"). As usual, the pack-horse
was well in the rear, but as it was still quite early, I
preferred to wait for my own provisions, which the
baggage contained, and meanwhile accepted an invitation
to " deign to enter the honourable hot water." To one
unaccustomed to Japanese country ways the position would
have had its drawbacks. The oval bath-tub stood in a
conspicuous place outside the front verandah, and in full
view of the villagers as they passed up and down the
narrow stony path. Possibly, as I have often seen elsewhere, it was so arranged in order to allow the occupant to
see and chat with his friends as they ambled to and fro.

Many and long were the hours that dragged on as I
afterwards waited, Micawber-like, for "something to turn
up" in the shape of my baggage and the food it held. It
was all in vain, though, and, after once declining the
proffered dinner of native food, I had to eat humble-pie
and recall the rejected meal. Only a little rice, however,
was left, as the rest had been devoured in the kitchen.
When midnight arrived I was compelled to turn in, or
rather simply to turn over on the *futon* on which for the
past five hours I had been reclining in fruitless expecta-
tion. Misery is commonly supposed to acquaint a man
with strange bedfellows, but those who shared my couch
that night were all too familiar to be agreeable. I was

faint enough for want of sustenance myself, but the fleas had certainly no cause for complaint.

The sun was already well up in the sky on the morrow when the truant pack-horse and his laggard leader appeared. On demanding the reason for the 14 hours' delay, I was told the horse had suddenly "become weak by the way." The excuse could deceive no one, for on going out and unloading the animal I found that the rascal had piled up a large burden belonging to some one else he had met *en route*, and he expected to get payment from this person in addition to the liberal price I had already promised to give.

Opposite our inn a narrow ravine on the left bank of the stream is the site of some salt springs, which rise up in wells a hundred feet or so in depth. The water is pumped up on to the top of layers of bamboo leaves and stems, which form a sort of sieve, through which it trickles into a pan below. It then goes through a process of boiling and subsequent evaporation. Beyond Ichiba our torrent joined the Koshibu-gawa at right angles, just where that stream takes an abrupt turn westwards to join the Tenryū, near Iida. Grand bluffs rise straight from the water's edge at the bend, and higher up the Koshibu valley the brown cottages of the hamlet of Ōkawara nestle cosily amidst well-cultivated fields. On the hill-side above, a picturesque temple peeps out from its security under the protection of a grove of splendid cryptomeria. In spite of the remote situation of the village, its inhabitants are evidently thoroughly go-ahead folk. A primitive belfry stands in the middle of the fields to summon the peasants together whenever common consultation is desirable. It consists of a flat board of very hard wood, in shape like the ordinary notice-boards of the country, suspended between a couple of tall posts. When thwacked with a stout truncheon that hangs by the side, the board gives out a note that resounds far and wide up the valley and in the hills. In contrast with this relic of bygone days, now rarely seen but in the most primitive spots, stands the village school, recently erected in "foreign style," with glass windows and whitewashed walls. Kindness itself was the treatment accorded on seeking out the little, so-called " inn " of Imai Takijirō, and so zealously did he and his whole family run about and otherwise exert themselves on my behalf, that I fared better here than anywhere else on my tour. A desk and a table were, spontaneously, sent for to the school. The policeman in charge of the district, who had come with us from Ichiba, set out to search for someone who could pilot me up Akaiishi. Soon he returned with the very man I needed. This was a hunter who a year ago had succeeded in reaching the summit with a War Office surveyor, and who now was ready to guide me also. A walk of six miles up a wild gorge that leads out of the prosperous valley took us to a *yuba,* or bath-house, standing on a steep slope above the bed of the torrent, known as Koshibu-no-yu.   Rustics resort hither for the sake of the sulphur springs, which are conducted into two large tanks standing on a platform in front of the rough châlet which does duty for an inn.   In one tank the water is heated to nearly 120° Fahr., in the other to about 65°.   From hot to cold is, therefore, but a step, an advantage not to be neglected.

The fortunes of this out-of-the-world establishment are presided over by a grey old patriarch of three score and thirteen.   How politely he received me, full of apologies for the dirt and discomfort he said I should find so trying ! With modest pride he presented me with a packet of *yubana* ("hot-water flowers"), the solidified deposit of the solfatara, which he assured me would make me a grand bath when I got back home beyond reach of the real thing. The way he skipped about was astonishing for one of his years, and no effort did he spare to make me comfortable.   To my subsequent regret, he turned out, un-known to me, a party to whom he had given the best room (such as it was), and begged me to only grant him one favour in return for his humble efforts—that I would allow him to see me eat in " foreign style."   Never shall I forget the wonderment with which he watched me performing on a tin of curried fowl, supplemented with rice and jam, helped down with cocoa.   As he sat down deprecatingly on the top step of the rough stairs, he might have been a visitor at the "Zoo" watching the wild beasts feeding. Yet never, in or out of Japan, have I met a truer gentleman than this poor "untutored rustic," who had spent all his days in one of the remotest valleys in the Empire.

On the following day I left at 6 A.M., in lovely weather, for my climb. From the bathhouse a faint track descended the steep side of the ravine, and then lost itself in the bed of the stream. For the next $2\frac{1}{2}$ hours the perpendicular cliffs on either hand forced us to keep to the torrent bed entirely. On the right bank a fine cascade, called *nana kama* ("the seven cauldrons"), falls in a succession of leaps into the main stream, which a score of times we had to cross and recross by flying leaps from rock to rock, or by wading through the cold rushing water. Occasionally it filled its channel deeply from side to side, and then we had glorious scrambles over the face of the cliff that overhung clear green pools. The coolies, unfortunately, disliked this method of advance, and on the descent avoided such places wherever they could. At length the ravine forked into two branches. One gradually fades in the wooded slopes in front, and the other opens out into a still grander defile running far into the western base of Akaiishi on the left, and forms the source of the Koshibugawa. The meeting of the waters is called Hirokawa ("the wide river"), and the steep pine-clad ridge that fills the angle afforded us a way to the western slopes of our mountain. Through the shady pines, as we mounted up, the sunlight shot in golden bars, and far away to our left the tall granite cliffs above the stony bed of the Koshibu gleamed dazzlingly white below a band of clear blue sky. A dip in the ridge, called *Fune-kubo* ("the hollow like a boat"), afforded a capital lunching place, and immediately afterwards we were out of the forest shade, and scrambling up the loose red rocks that give the mountain its name. Three hours' easy ascent sufficed to land us on the sharp northern ridge of Akaiishi. From this point we looked eastwards over desolate valleys, partly filled with snow, beyond which rose the triple peaks of Shiranesan, whose highest point ranks next to Yarigatake in altitude of all the mountains in Japan. This is called Kaigane, and reaches 10,200 feet. Once on the *arête*, we turned to the south, till we reached the summit, 10,140 feet, at 4 P.M., or 10 hours from the start. Masses of dark cloud now gathered about us, and shut out nearly all the surrounding prospect. Occasionally the cold wind tore a sudden rent in the misty curtain, to disclose a fleeting glimpse of some neighbouring peak, but that was all—" we viewed the mist, but missed the view." Huddling together for warmth, we sat down on the top by a little cairn of rocks, erected by the surveyor who last year made the ascent. A long hour passed, but we waited in vain.

Then a mingled storm of rain and sleet began to come down. At this we gathered together our belongings, and fled from the spot. Eagerness to avoid getting benighted on the exposed west face of the mountain contested with the prudence that dictated care to escape a tumble over the deep precipices on the east. But by six o'clock we were off the ridge, and hurried with all speed to the spot where we had left most of our baggage on the ascent.

This was in some rocks near the head of a narrow defile in which my hunters had promised we should find water, and wood, with shelter in a "grand cave." Quite suddenly a pall of black vapour swept up the mountain, and by 6·30 P.M. we were nearly in darkness, almost without a moment's warning. The descent then became very trying. The loose rocks in the steep bed of the dried-up water-course, down which we had literally to feel our way, demanded the greatest care. At length the porters stopped, took off their bundles, and remarked that this was where we were going to bivouac.

" But where is the cave ? " I enquired.

" Oh, it's further down."

" And the water ? "

" That is lower still," was the answer.

Why the men were anxious to stay in such a forsaken spot as this I could not divine, so I gave orders to move on

once more. By seven o'clock our blind gropings came to
an end, as a shout from the leader announced that we had
reached the cave. Considering the way they had praised
it beforehand, I confess to a feeling of disappointment at
the sight. The "grand cave" simply consisted of two
enormous pillars of rock, some 15 feet high, inclined
towards each other, so as to partially enclose a space eight
feet by three, but with nothing to afford the least shelter
overhead. The disadvantage of this immediately struck
us, as the storm that had long been brewing burst upon us
in all its violence, just as we were trying to rig up a roof
of oil-paper to remedy the deficiency. A thunderstorm is
always a grand spectacle, but nowhere so grand as in the
mountains, and even situated as we were, we could not
help realising the magnificence of the scene. In blinding
sheets the vivid lightning lit up the darkness, only to leave
it darker still; then—

> "Far along,
> From peak to peak, the rattling crags among,
> Leaps the live thunder! Not from one lone cloud,
> But every mountain now hath found a tongue."
> BYRON, *Childe Harold*, C. III., 92.

By-and-by the rain began to abate, and, as the sky
cleared, the brilliant stars looked out to answer the light
of the camp fire. The porters produced their rice, and
expressed themselves deeply grateful for the gift of the
leavings of a tin of sardines to help it down. From

the remarks of my companions the next morning I inferred they had not passed a pleasant night. For myself, as I had left flea-infested *futon* in the valley far away, I was not surprised to find I had slept well enough not to notice the behaviour of my cape, which I awoke to discover securely wrapped round my head. The previous night's storm had swept away the clouds to leave a sky of absolute brilliancy. As we climbed up the ravine, and regained the western slope of the mountain above, the long jagged summit of Komagatake started up grandly on the west side of the Tenryū-gawa valley. Over its northern shoulder rose the long line of the Hida range, the sharp peak of Yarigatake overtopping the rest, and standing clear cut against the blue at a distance of over 60 miles.

By 1 P.M. we were receiving the congratulations of the courteous old custodian of the bathhouse. He told me that the policeman, Hasegawa, anxious at our non-arrival in Ōkawara that morning, had come up to ask after us. He was much distressed at getting no news of our welfare, and went back, but great was his relief when, in the evening, we turned up at the village safe and sound. With real regret I bade farewell to my grey old friend at the bathhouse. When I asked him what I was indebted to him for all his kind attention, he shook his head in deep perplexity. "The fact is," he said, " you are the first foreigner I have had to stay with me, and I really don't know *what* to charge." Finally, with much hesitation, he stammered out, as if half ashamed at the exorbitance of the demand, "Do you consider five *sen* (three halfpence) would be *too* much?" And then when I pressed on him a *chadai* (the extra "tip" usually added when paying the ordinary charges) he was overwhelmed—and, I believe, sincerely—with gratitude.

At Ōkawara I spent a delightful Sunday on my return journey. My landlord there sent a special messenger to a village some distance off to bring in a curious "stone" he was anxious I should examine. It was about the size and shape of a turkey's egg, of a buff colour, and quite smooth, excepting on one side, where a piece appeared to have been chipped off. He said it was discovered some time before in the stomach of an *iwashika* (mountain antelope), the chamois of Japan. It proved to be a "bezoar stone," such as Dr. Bonney speaks of in his "Alpine Regions," p. 180. "Owing, probably, to the resin contained in so much of their food, and its fibrous character, a hard, dark-coloured ball, from the size of a walnut to that of an egg, of a bitter taste, but pleasant odour, is often found in their (*i.e.* the chamois') stomachs. This is called 'Bezoar,' and it was anciently supposed to cure all evils, and to be a protection even against musket shots. A sceptical analyst has, I fear, expelled it from the pharmacopœia."

As I said an unwilling farewell to these kindly folk at Ōkawara, the mother of my host insisted on my accepting six potatoes as a token of her friendship. As I stuffed them into my *rücksack,* her gentle old face beamed again with delight, and her satisfaction knew no bounds. At Takatō we spent another night, and then proceeded northwards to the village of Midōgaitō, where we turned to the right and crossed the Kōshū range by the Kanazawa tōge. This leads down to the village of Kanazawa on the well-known road called Kōshū-kaidō, running from north to south through a considerable part of the fertile and prosperous province of Kōshū. Near the top of the pass (4,120 feet) I noticed stretches of short close turf,* strangely unlike the coarse, rank grass so common on most hillsides in Central Japan. As we marched south towards Kōfu, the capital of the province, we found ourselves in scenes of busy life and traffic that contrasted curiously with the quiet solitudes of the valleys on the western side of the range. At one point in the road an odd sight startled me as we passed a cottage perched in a little garden on the top of a bank some 20 yards away. It was nothing less than a human head, with a shock of dark hair standing on end, lying, apparently, on a wooden table in front of the house. The staring, wide-open eyes had a startled look about them that

* This is also to be seen on the top of the Gombei tōge, north of Komaga-take in Shinshū.

compelled me to draw near and examine the thing more
closely. But then the illusion was dispelled. It proved to
be the master of the house enjoying his hot bath in the
cool of the afternoon, and he preferred, like my friends
at Ichiba, to have it where he could also enjoy the

surrounding scenery, and converse with his friends should
they happen that way. The scenery of the Kōshū-kaidō,
in other respects, also, is full of interest, particularly
as the road draws near the eastern base of the wooded
granite heights of Komagatake. Far away to the
south the tall cone of Fuji now and again appears,
but the great mountain has lost its snowy mantle,
and with that its greatest adornment. At Daigahara
an inn, of unpretentious exterior, but exquisitely neat

and pretty within, gave us good quarters for the night. But the fact remains that here, as well as at the other inns on this route, just three times the amount is charged for accommodation compared with the hostelries I had hitherto visited on my tour. It is merely a sign that "civilisation" is passing along this way. The road is sometimes trodden by foreigners, conducted by native "guides," who have their head-quarters at the Treaty ports, and the result is that the prices go up accordingly. It is of course only fair that "foreign" guests, who usually give much more trouble than native travellers, should pay higher rates, but it is curious that on those routes where the "guide" is not known one seldom finds such distinctions made. On this occasion my Japanese companion, Sasai Motoji, had food and lodging similar to my own. When I came to pay the bill for *hatagō* (supper, bed, and breakfast) I was charged more than four times the amount put down to him. On asking the reason, I was simply told it was the "custom." The foreigner is supposed to be richer than the native, more ignorant of the "customs" of the country, and, therefore, far more may be exacted.

As the next morning wore on, the plain that surrounds the town of Kōfu gradually came into view, dotted about with busy villages, and here and there brightened with vineyards interspersed amongst the rice fields and mulberry plantations. It is in this province that the finest grapes in

Japan are produced, and the attempts to make wine for home consumption appear to have met with some success.

A short halt during the intense noontide heat at Kōfu included a visit for lunch to a restaurant known as Chōyōtei. For the second time during three weeks I got fresh meat, and the well-cooked meal, that consisted of omelette, chicken cutlets,* bread, butter, and cake, with two bottles of *ramuné* (the native attempt at " lemonade "), cost no more than 1*s*. 3*d*. From Kōfu a dozen miles' journey took us to Kajikazawa, a riverside village just beyond the south-west limit of the plain. This is the starting point for the boats that shoot the rapids of the Fujikawa, and go down to the Pacific coast near Iwabuchi, on the Tōkaidō railway.

A thunderstorm of unusual violence burst over the plain as we were on our way to Kajikazawa, and, as a consequence, it was prophesied that the voyage would be one of more than average speed. The following day's experience proved the prediction true. The " mail-boat " in which I engaged a place for less than a shilling, gained nearly two hours on its usual time, and landed us, hot, but happy, on the margin of the blue waves of the Pacific in 6¼ hours from the start.

* Familiarly known as " chikkin katsuretsu."

CHAPTER VII.

A mountain railway—Zenkōji—A polite stranger—Wayfarers in distress—
Curious chimneys—Palatial accommodation—Unexpected gratitude—
Interested visitors—The Harinoki-pass—A lonely bivouac—Romantic
route—The hot springs of Ryūzanjita.

In planning for the summer of 1893 another holiday
tour in the Japanese Alps, three expeditions stood out
prominently before my mental vision as affording the
greatest promise of interesting exploration. These were the
crossing of the Harinoki-tōge, in the northern portion of
the range, the ascent of Kasa-dake, in Hida, and that of
Hodakayama, on the borders of Hida and Shinshū. The
Harinoki Pass had not for many years been crossed by
foreign travellers, though I knew of several parties that had
made the attempt.

Kasadake and Hodakayama, also, were still untrodden
summits, as far as foreigners were concerned, and even the
people who knew them best by sight seemed to have such
a wholesome respect for their formidable appearance that
they were not anxious for closer acquaintance. Hitherto
the enjoyment of my expeditions had been enhanced by

the presence of cheery companions to share it, but this time I was obliged to go alone.

The best way of reaching the Harinoki Pass is from Zenkōji on the Karuisawa-Naoetsu railway, and on August 4th, a bright fresh morning, the usual successor here of a wet and cheerless night, greeted me as I stepped into the train at Yokogawa, the station at the southern base of the Usuitōge.   Previous journeys over the pass had been made by tramcar or on foot, but now the railway was open, and I had stayed over-night at Yokogawa in order to see by daylight what this new departure in Japanese railway construction was like.   On the whole it reminded me of a combination of a Swiss mountain line and part of that between Genoa and Spezia.   The twenty-six tunnels we went through gave one the feeling of the passage from end to end of some gigantic flute.   The locomotive pushes up from the rear of the train on ordinary rails for the first mile or so, but then the cogs and rack-rail come into play for most of the remaining distance. The journey—a dozen miles—occupied 70 minutes, and as the engine was behind us we could keep the windows open without risk of asphyxiation.   The average inclination is moderately steep, the greatest gradient being one in fifteen. A sweltering hot afternoon—over 90° in the shade— saw the train rattling down the long incline to Zenkōji after a three hours' run from Karuisawa.   Under the shadow of dark hills the great temple that gives the place its ancient name looks out over the mouse-coloured roofs of the houses to the fertile plain beyond. The word Zenkōji represents the Chinese characters which stand for the Japanese words rendered "the Temple of Yoshimitsu." Its name it gets from the builder of the original shrine, on the site of which the present erection stands. Its *raison d'être* is the preservation of a golden image representing the Buddha and two of his followers, Kwannon and Daishi Bosatsu, which is said to have been fashioned by S'akya Muni (the Buddha) himself 3,000 years ago, from gold found at the centre of the universe. The strange adventures through which the image is said to have passed, begin with its journey from Korea, when Buddhism was first introduced through that country into Japan in the middle of the 6th century A.D. The opposition of the priests of Shintō (the native faith) made it the object of continuous persecution, but each fresh attempt to destroy or make away with it failed. Once an effort was made to burn it, another time to cut it to pieces, and twice it was thrown into the Ajikawa near Osaka. At last it fell into the hands of Yoshimitsu, a native of Shinshū, who carried it off to his native province, where it found a resting-place in the original temple he himself erected. The name Zenkōji thus rather represents the religious associations of the place, whilst the official title of the town, Nagano, has reference to it as the capital of the *ken* or county which is co-extensive with the province of Shinshū. The image is enshrined in a recess, covered with magnificent brocade curtains, at the back of a sort of chancel in the Hondō or main building. No one is allowed to see more than the outermost of the nest of boxes in which it is enclosed, and that only on payment of certain fees. Underneath the " chancel" is a sort of crypt, a subterranean maze, which I was invited to explore. Descending a short flight of steps we were soon in pitch darkness, but my cicerone, an old " verger," took my hand and walked backwards the whole of the intricate way with a confidence only born of constant practice. A thrice-repeated round is held by the many pilgrims who flock to pay their devotions at the shrine to be most meritorious, and the corners of the passage walls are polished smooth by the frequent touch of hesitating hands. The transition from the dense darkness into the dazzling brilliancy of the summer afternoon was almost blinding. The courteous attendants in an antechamber outside invited me to a cup of tea, and then began to discuss the relations of Buddhism towards Christianity. As I rose to depart, my guide in the maze asked if I would not like to make an obeisance at the shrine, but before I had time to reply, the youth who had conducted me from an inn in the town, offered an explanation in an indignant aside, that made the old man withdraw in confusion, to my great annoyance and regret.

In front of the shrine stretches a sort of spacious "nave," where white-winged pigeons flutter to and fro in undisturbed security above the heads of the worshipping pilgrims seated on the matted floor. On a rising knoll near the temple stands the Meteorological Observatory, one of a number scattered about the country, where the courteous officials allowed me to compare my instruments with their own standard ones, with which the place is thoroughly equipped.

From the southern end of the town a rough road crosses rice fields and mulberry plantations to a pretty little hamlet called Shimbashi, perched on the left bank of the broad Saigawa, at the entrance to a picturesque defile. As my porters and I plodded on in the cool of the afternoon along the river's edge, the poorness of the road only reflected the poverty of the scattered hamlets through which it passed. Daylight was dying as we began the ascent of the Yanoshiri tōge that passes over the hills to the valley where Shimmachi lies, my halting-place for the night. A courteous wayfarer, seeing my porters had fallen behind, good-naturedly volunteered to help me out of my difficulties, and whilst I sat down for a moment at a wayside cottage for a cup of tea, he scrambled up the hillside to borrow a *chōchin* from a friend to light me on my road. Nor did he leave me until a couple of hours later on we marched merrily down the long street of Shimmachi to the Miyoshiya, where the kindest of attentions lay in store.

From Shimmachi a picturesque journey of 16 miles took me to Ōmachi, on the eastern side of the Harinoki Pass. The earlier portion of the walk lay along the banks of the Saigawa again, and the numerous boats that were hauled up here and there on the river brink, told of the water traffic that goes on between Matsumoto and Zenkōji. Formerly the whole way between these two places was navigable by craft of the Tenryū-gawa type. But in 1847 a frightful earthquake shook the province, and after wrecking Zenkōji and many of the neighbouring villages, brought down a landslip that dammed up the Saigawa near Shimmachi so effectually that communication has ever since been interrupted half way. At Zenkōji, on that occasion, the earthquake shock was followed by a fire which completed the destruction of the town, and then the floods that came in its wake filled the cup of suffering of the unfortunate peasantry to overflowing. When finally the tale of woe was fully told, no less than 20,000 persons were numbered on the roll of death wrought by earthquake, flame, and flood.

Of the many lovely pictures that fill the gallery of memory on this walk to Ōmachi, the loveliest is that of the hamlet of Hina, which greeted us as we suddenly turned an angle in the hills. There we looked down on a deep valley embosomed in a setting of tree-clad heights, with the emerald waters of the Saigawa flashing far below between the dusky cottages perched in peaceful seclusion on either bank. This was almost our farewell glance of the great river, for it now took a turn southwards, cutting its way through the hills, whilst we proceeded due west over mountains that barred the way to Ōmachi. The noontide sun beat on us fiercely, and made the walk unusually trying. The narrow ravine up which we had first to climb beyond Hina was closed to every breath of wind. Not a leaf stirred, and Nature herself seemed too drowsy for exertion, or as if lulled to sleep by the never-ceasing droning of countless cicada (Jap. *semi*), a noise that suggests a perpetually revolving circular saw. The path to Ōmachi climbed now for several miles over steep shadeless hill-sides towards a narrow cutting in the topmost ridge. Far below, at the foot, stands a fearsome blue-painted image of Fudō-sama (Sanskrit, *Atchala*), who is represented with a sword in his right hand to strike terror into evil-doers, and with a rope in his left to bind them with if detected in crime. The cascade close by also takes its name Fudō-taki from this popular divinity, but now the heat has completely dried it up. On the hill-side below the summit I stumbled across a young farmer, who lay prostrate on the narrow path in a state of absolute collapse. By his side his young wife sat wringing her hands, and gazing helplessly into his livid face. A word of sympathy was gratefully received, and when later on

FUDO-SAMA.

the man succeeded in struggling to the top of the pass, I was able to dose him with Burroughs and Wellcome's tabloids, to his speedy relief. Near the summit of the pass stands a little hamlet called Sō (*i.e.*, grass) in the middle of a slope cultivated with hemp. Beyond it the track passes through a forest of pines, larches, and *nara* (a sort of oak).

ROOFS AT ŌMACHI, LOOKING TOWARDS THE HARINOKI-TOGE.

[P. 125.

From the cutting in the ridge (8,000 feet) we descended quickly towards the plain of Ōmachi through a grand ravine. As this opened out into gentler slopes the dark snow-streaked mountains that rise beyond Ōmachi now lifted their rugged shoulders into view, but their heads were veiled in dark angry-looking clouds that spoke of gathering storm. By four o'clock I was at Ōmachi, a quaint little town, whose houses nearly all bore the wide stone-weighted roofs so characteristic of Alpine Japan. A curious feature is the *shōji* (paper windows) in the chimneys, all facing southwards.

On seeking accommodation at the "Yamachō," the inn to which I had been recommended from Shimmachi, "mine host" received me with some reluctance. He had nothing fit to offer me, he said. At length, however, I managed to persuade him I was not very fastidious, so he led the way to the top storey, where the sound of hammers and saws told of carpenters at work. At the top of the stairs we found a large room being fitted up as a place for public gatherings, but at one end of this was an apartment only just finished, fit for a *Daimyō*. It was the largest I have ever occupied in a Japanese inn, measuring 30 feet by 18, or as the Japanese themselves would say, "27 mats," and these were as spotless as could be wished. On two sides ran a wide verandah of polished dark wood, commanding a grand view of the southern portion of the great mountain barrier, which the people here compare to a row of mighty screens. In spite of the initial unreadiness of my landlord, he certainly did his best afterwards to make me comfortable. Not only did he provide me with a chair and table for my meals, but when bed-time came, he and his attendants appeared with several benches, and an enormous box some six feet square by one foot deep, with which he proceeded to construct a bedstead. He explained that agile as the ubiquitous flea invariably is, the elevation of my bed some feet above the floor, he thought, would place me beyond their reach. The experiment proved a success, and my foes were cheated of their feast.

The next day, which happened to be Sunday, I received a visit from my sick friend of yesterday. He came to tell me that he was feeling better, though rather feverish. After dosing him with quinine I asked him to return in the evening and report progress. Great was my astonishment when he later on reappeared, radiant with delight, to tell me that his " bodily feelings " had vastly improved. He also pressed upon me the acceptance of a lovely *kakemono* (hanging picture) as a memento of our meeting, and a token of his thankfulness. It was no use explaining that no such acknowledgment was needed. The good fellow would take no denial, and I saw he would be quite distressed if I refused his gift. Long shall I value it as a souvenir of sincere gratitude from a chance acquaintance in a land where gratitude is not popularly supposed to be a very strong feature of the national character. During the morning I was attracted by the sounds of singing proceeding from a house on the opposite side of the road. The strains, it is true, were not of a high order, but on going to enquire, I found out that this was the head-quarters of a little body of native Christians; so far is the faith penetrating, often without foreign aid, into some of the innermost recesses of the Empire.

As I was about to retire that night to my lofty couch, my landlord approached me with a message from a number of my fellow guests. "They have never met a foreigner before," he said, "and would be much honoured if they might be allowed to come and see you." Accordingly chairs were brought in, tea, cakes, etc. put on the table, and one by one a company of seven or eight filed into the room. With the usual polite phrases and bows each took his seat upon the extreme edge of his chair, placed his hands upon his knees, and then took a general survey of the room. The strange erection in the middle, partly hidden by a canopy of the native mosquito curtains made of a musty dark-green netting edged with pink, provided them with a complete surprise. To set their minds at rest I explained that it was—not what it looked like, an operating table (at least I hoped it would not be so)—

merely an improvised bedstead. After libations of tea had unloosed their tongues, they began to ply me with questions.

"What is your honourable country?" "Have you come to search for silver mines?" "No; then it must be crystals?" That I was simply climbing for pleasure I found it very hard to persuade them. As I was by this

DARUMA.

time getting sleepy, our conversation soon began to flag, and eventually an unusually "brilliant flash of silence" was succeeded by a general movement on the part of my guests, who rose and took their leave as politely and solemnly as they had come. No sooner had I mounted my throne, however, than another interruption came. One of the gentlemen had sent a domestic to say that he was afraid I might be disturbed in the night, even though sleeping at such an altitude, and he hoped I would do him the favour of accepting a small tin of Darumatian. At first I was a little puzzled. Daruma I knew to be the Japanese name of the old Hindu saint Dharma, who is said to have sat for nine years in profound abstraction till his legs fell off—but that was all. On descending to the floor and opening the *fusuma* (paper sliding walls), I found that it was simply a supply of Keating, or rather of a native imitation, labelled with its less familiar name (in Japanese characters), "Dalmatian powder." Though the gift was a little superfluous just then it came in most useful later on.

On Monday, August 7th, a lovely morning saw me off in company with my two hunters for the crossing of the Harinoki-tōge, the "pass of the Alders." With the help of my landlord I had secured their services overnight, having had to send for them to Noguchi, a little hamlet west of Ōmachi, where most of the hunters of the neighbourhood have their head-quarters. Their late arrival, however—at 8 A.M. instead of 6—combined with other circumstances, made me rather suspect they were not very keen about the expedition. For, as a matter of fact, the pass has long had a bad reputation. Until it was first opened, some twenty years ago, there was practically no means of communication for a distance of fifty miles south of the Sea of Japan, between the provinces of Shinshū and Etchū. During the first few years after the path—such as

K

it was—was opened, several parties of foreign travellers, including Satow, Chamberlain, Atkinson, and others, crossed the pass without much difficulty. Soon, however, the ravages of those influences we call the tooth of time began to tell; avalanches and landslips, with the heavy autumn rains, before long had battered the track out of all recognition, and the Harinoki-tōge became a mere wreck of its former self. For practical purposes it was soon abandoned, and it is now dead—indeed, almost buried—and its epitaph has been already written *Tōge fuit*. An American traveller, Mr. P. Lowell, in his book on "Noto, an unexplored corner of Japan," describes an attempt he made to cross the pass in the spring some seven or eight years ago, from the west, or Toyama, side. The four chapters he devotes to the expedition, however, only bring the reader to the beginning of the pass proper, as on reaching Ryūzanjita, at the foot of Tateyama, he found himself unable to proceed further and had to return. Earlier than that another traveller, the late Mr. Francis, of Shanghai, in 1885, tried it from the east or Ōmachi side, but met with little better success. He reached the top of the pass, after having nearly been killed through a slip on a steep talus of earth high above a torrent bed, but was then obliged to turn back. His guides told him the expedition had not been made for some years, excepting by occasional hunters. "One year," they said, "two native travellers did make the attempt, but when they got to the steep slopes of snow in wild gullies that had to be traversed, one of them began to cry, and they had to come back."

On none of these occasions was the roughest part of the route reached, namely, that between the summit of the pass and the Ryūzanjita bath-houses on its western side. In "Murray," 2nd edition (1883), it is stated that "the route had become almost impassable;" and in the 3rd (1891), we read that "none but the most experienced mountaineers can hope to succeed in forcing a path for themselves."

These considerations, however, only helped to give a spice to one's anticipations, as we strode across the level stretch of plain that lay between Ōmachi and the distant mountains. At Noguchi my hunters begged me to let them engage a companion, to which I agreed. Passing through a scattered forest of birch and larch, we came to the last inhabited houses that we saw for three days at Oide, a little hamlet on the left bank of the Takasegawa. Beyond this, a shrine in a shady grove, and the primitive torii that spans its approach are decorated with iron swords and spear heads, votive offerings to the gods of the great mountains whose tall forms now tower darkly above the valley we are ascending. The wild swift torrent that dashes down is the Kagagawa, and our route lies on either bank or up its rugged bed to its very source. Dense

K 2

forests clothe the hills that shut us in on either hand.
Far in front rises the great rocky barrier whose snow-filled
ravines now come well in sight.   The nearer we get to
them the less my companions seem to like them.   They
begin to express their doubts as to the possibility of the
expedition, and the unexpected sight of a couple of hunters
fishing in the stream, constrains them to halt to discuss
the situation.   In the end this resulted in engaging a
fourth man, for though my coolies' loads were by no means
heavy, their minds were burdened with a growing anxiety
that seriously threatened the success of the climb, and I
was quite prepared to witness a burst of tears.   The loss
of time involved in palaver and rearranging the packs was
more than compensated for by the gain in strength, moral
and physical, that our new friend added to our party.   He
was a cheery person, who had been a wrestler in his
younger days.   Now, however, he possessed more muscle
and less fat than when he trod the sanded ring, and his
good spirits helped the rest to move along more cheerfully.
For some hours we pushed our way through dense thickets,
or scrambled over loose rocks high above the right bank of
the torrent.   At 3 P.M. we descended to its bed, which we
crossed by leaping from rock to rock at a point once
known as *Maruishi-bashi*, "the bridge of the boulders."
In the palmy days of the pass, a wooden bridge existed
here, but though the boulders remain in abundance,

all traces of it have long years ago been swept away. Immediately from the valley in front of us rises a fine granite peak, Jiidake, some 9,000 feet high. Its lower flanks are densely wooded, but the shoulders and summit are bare, streaked here and there with slopes of snow. The granite is exceedingly close grained, and bears traces of garnets. Half-an-hour's scramble up the broken rocks on the left bank brought us to the foot of a magnificently wild ravine, hemmed in on either hand by grand cliffs that rose steeply 2,000 feet or more above. As we saw the work that now lay before us, we began to doubt the possibility of reaching the summit of the pass before nightfall. These doubts were speedily settled by a sudden and violent thunderstorm, such as one rarely meets with at a lower altitude in Japan. We fled for shelter under the rocks without delay, and having got there we had to stay so long as to make it useless to think of moving on again. The incessant growls of thunder that had been warning us what to expect, now gave way to ear-splitting crashes that reverberated from crag to crag, and rolled down the valley we had ascended. When the downpour of rain had abated a little we set to work to prepare a shelter for the night. The alder trees that grew here and there within easy reach provided us with branches and leaves with which we made a "lean-to" by the side of the biggest rock at hand. Over the branches we spread the sides of my oil-paper tent

My waterproof ground sheet came in handy as a protection
against the damp ground, and by the time a fire was
blazing at the open end of the shanty things began to look
more cheerful.   The altitude of the spot, which the hunters
called *Ushigoya*, " the cow cave," proved to be 5,500 feet,
and this, combined with the fact that the tall cliffs shut
out nearly all the sun's genial rays, made our situation a
chilly one.   The tone of my companions' conversation was
by no means reassuring.   Two of them were for going back
home.   The other two, however, were more hopeful.   The
efforts of the quondam wrestler to cheer up the melancholy
ones were backed up by the youngest member of the party,
who said, in effect, that *nil desperandum* must be our
motto, and insisted on making a bold bid for victory.
Still it was not until 7 o'clock the next morning that we
turned our backs on our bivouac, and mounted by a curious
ridge of rocks, exactly like the lateral moraine of a glacier,
to the bottom of the lowest snow slope which forms the
birth-place of the wild torrent of the Kagagawa.   Here,
at a height of 6,000 feet, the great gully contracts to its
narrowest width, and mounts up in a succession of snow
slopes, here and there broken with rocks, to the crest of the
ridge.   In the crevices of the rocks a few plants appear.

In one spot an unexpected feast of delicious wild strawberries invited attention.   The angle of the snow, the

surface of which was smooth, now steepened to nearly 38°, at which my coolies expressed the strongest disapproval. Their straw sandals gave little hold, so they flatly declined to touch it, and took again to the precipitous rocks at the side of the ravine. My way, however, proved more expeditious, and by 9 A.M. I was standing in the gap in the ridge by the small wooden post that marks the boundary between Shinshū and Etchū, and the summit of the Harinoki-tōge itself.

An hour passed all too quickly as we discussed breakfast and took observations of altitude and surroundings. The height of the pass is 8,120 feet, but the distant view is much shut out by the neighbouring cliffs. Southwards, though, the aiguille-like form of Yarigatake rises imposingly, and then to the south-east, at a distance of nearly 100 miles, the ever-present cone of Fujisan thrusts itself up between the sharp tops of Yatsugatake and Komagatake of Shinshū. In the near foreground, on the north, the eye plunges down the dark ravine we have ascended, with its glittering stretches of snow overshadowed by towering cliffs whose scarred sides show many a trace of the power of avalanche and storm. Southwards dips the valley we have to descend, the nearer slopes covered chiefly with the alder trees (*harinoki*) that give the pass its name, and with the low-creeping branches of the *go-yo-nomatsu*, " the five-

needle pine." Very little snow lies on this side, and here
and there faint traces of the old path peep out of the
undergrowth near the upper part of the pass. The
projector of the original enterprise died in 1884, and since
then no further attention has been given to the work.
Dropping down quickly into the ravine below, we soon
reached the torrent of the Harinoki-gawa, and then the
descent became extremely rough, occasionally calling for
the use of the stout line I carried in case of emergencies.
The bed of the stream was so precipitous and the rocks so
large that every care had to be exercised, and there was
little chance of doing justice to the grandeur of our
surroundings. Occasionally a halt for breathing space
enabled one to view the mighty castellated granite cliffs
that rose wild and bare for several thousand feet above our
heads, whilst in the distance the imposing form of Tateyama,
"the beacon mountain," its rugged sides streaked with
snow, beckoned us on. Wild raspberries lower down, by
the torrent bank, invited us to pause, and then the descent
gradually grew less steep, as the gorge opened out into the
more level valley of the swift Kurobe-gawa, which here
sweeps by on its way to the Sea of Japan. As we looked
across its broad stream we saw, perched on a steep bank on
the opposite side, the last survivor of the rest-houses of
Kurobe that once gave shelter to travellers over the pass.
We forded the river, and had a delightful scramble up

the steep face of the rocky headland below the hut, and at
3·15 we were standing under its decaying roof. Like the
pass itself, its best days had long gone by, and its actual
aspect of desertion and ruin presented a mournful contrast
with what its well-built walls and substantial beams showed
it was meant to be. Part of the building had done duty for a
spacious kitchen, whilst the remainder was divided into two
good-sized rooms. By the time we had got settled down
the usual thunderstorm broke on us, and I did not regret
my decision to halt here for the night, though the day
was yet young. The hunters had assured me that the
most difficult part of our work still lay before us, so I
determined to give them every chance by getting under the
only possible decent shelter now, and securing plenty of
daylight on the morrow for the route beyond. My evening
meal was enhanced by the addition of some delicious trout,
some as much as 1lb. in weight, taken in the Kurobe-gawa
by the cheery person of my quartette. I slung my pocket-
hammock between two of the stoutest posts in the walls
and turned in.

At 6·30 A.M. we started on a stiff climb up the Nukui-
dani-tōge, the first of two passes between Kurobe and
Ryūzanjita. The moisture-laden bamboo grass and tall
luxuriant docks through which we had to fight our way
soon soaked us completely through, and made the steep
ascent still harder. On the other side of the pass the

grandeur of the scenery increases. Descending the broken face of the precipitous hill-side we found ourselves in totally different surroundings. The densely-wooded slopes and bamboo thickets now give way to a valley filled with shining slopes of snow guarded by ruddy-tinted granite cliffs which here and there give footing to the dark foliage of silent pines. The glorious Japanese Alpine bell (*Schizocodon soldanelloides*) and many a familiar flower gives brightness to the enchanting scene. At the top of the second pass, the Zaragoe (7,300 feet), which we reached at 10·30, I was able to take off my sodden garments and dry them in the genial sun. The scene westwards, whither we were bound, was wonderfully impressive. The rocky sides of the savage gorge present an aspect of destruction that makes one wonder not so much that the route has been abandoned, but that anyone ever dreamed of opening it up at all. On every hand the débris of avalanche and landslip are scattered. Masses of rock hurled down from the cliffs to the bottom of the gorge below lie piled upon one another in unutterable confusion. It is a positive relief to look beyond all this wild chaos still further westwards and let the eye rest on the peaceful fertile plains of Toyama, intersected by the silvery windings of the Jinzūgawa, and bounded on their northern shores by the blue sunlit waters of the Sea of Japan. For a few yards below the summit of the pass a bit of the old

track is visible, but this vanishes abruptly into nothing-
ness, and we had to cross the face of a slope of brown
earth at an angle of 60°. Even now I can recollect the
unhappy expression on the face of the mournful member of
my party as I approached the landslip and began to cut
steps across, inviting him to follow. Further down the
gorge, a protected angle in the hill side sheltered the
remains of an old rest-house. The bleached and rotting
timbers looked like the bones of some dead creature of long
ago. Progress downwards was unavoidably slow, but some
of the scrambles over the more difficult rocks were intensely
exhilarating. After descending to the torrent, the
Yukawa, we passed on its left bank a curious lake of
boiling water, about 300 yards in circumference. Its
brilliant blue waters, which leave a deposit of sulphur
round the edges of the circular basin, are said to have been
quite cold until the great earthquake which in 1858
devastated this neighbourhood. Half an hour lower down
the valley we saw before us the open space by the side of
the torrent where stand the curious collection of huts known
as Ryūzanjita, or Tateyama Onsen, *i.e.*, the hot springs
below Tateyama (4,150 feet). Although the caretaker was
extremely astonished to see us, he gave me the kindest of
welcomes, and in a few minutes I was enjoying the
softening influences of his " honourable hot water." What
a curious establishment it was! At one end of the clearing

stood an unpretentious building containing the caretaker's office, a sort of kitchen, and a few private rooms for the better sort of visitors.   At right angles to this stand several rows of huts occupied by the poorer guests, who bring and cook their own food in the little room, some eight feet square, which serves as bed- and dining-room together.   The sitting-room is the bath itself.   Each guest pays about $\frac{1}{2}d$. per day for the use of the room and the privilege of bathing.   The bath-house itself stands at the far end of the compound, and consists of a large shed, partly open at the sides.   The bath consists of a huge wooden tank divided into four compartments, each about twelve feet square, the temperature of the water varying from 105° to 125° F., the hottest being that which receives the water first.   The bathers chiefly consist of peasants from the villages near the upper waters of the Jōgwanji-gawa.   Both sexes bathe together, sometimes as many as fifty being in the bath at once, but the behaviour of one and all is perfectly modest.   During the time I spent at Ryūzanjita, 200 guests were staying in the place.

To the south rises the broken mass of Ō-tombiyama, "the great kite mountain."   In the awful earthquake of 1858, a large portion of its north face fell away and dammed the waters of the stream.   Later on, when the winter snows had melted, the imprisoned torrent burst its barrier and scattered wide-spread destruction far down the valley.

The view of the mountain, as I stood on the verandah outside my little room, was enhanced by the usual thunderstorm that burst on the valley soon after my arrival. Rugged bare red cliffs, now dyed with a deeper hue in the soft rays of the setting sun, stood clearly outlined against an opalescent sky, contrasting finely with the gentler slopes of hills clothed with dark pines and vegetation of every shade of green.

CHAPTER VIII.

TOWERING to a height of more than 5000 feet above
the baths of Ryūzanjita stands the famous peak of
Tateyama, from which the place gets its name, and whose
sacred character attracts hundreds of white-robed pilgrims
to its summit every summer. The "climbing season" is
only supposed to last six weeks, and is inaugurated by a
ceremony called *Yama-biraki* or "mountain opening," on
July 20th. Then the *Kannushi* or "god guardian," who
has charge of the little shrine that crowns the highest
point, leads a procession of pilgrims up to invoke the
blessing of the *genius loci* on all who shall follow in their
steps.

The ordinary Japanese name Tateyama ("beacon
mountain") is owing to the fact that the peak is visible
as a landmark far out on the Sea of Japan. The more
classical Chinese title is Ryūsan, or "Dragon Peak," the
mythical monster being frequently associated in legend

with mountains in the "Land of the Rising Sun."
Tateyama is not, strictly speaking, a member of the long line
of giants that form the main chain of the Japanese Alps ;
it belongs, geologically, to a volcanic range on the west
that at first runs parallel to its central portion, and then,
eventually, turns in to join it south of Yarigatake. It is
thus connected with Norikura and Ontake by means of
lower and less known volcanic peaks.

After a day's rest in the romantic surroundings of the
Onsen, I started in the small hours of the morning for the
summit of the "Dragon Peak." Rising and breakfasting by
the dull glow of the *andon*, I stealthily crept out on the
verandah to pull on my hob-nailed boots beyond the limits
of the soft-matted floor. A native porter was at hand
waiting with his *chōchin* to light the way, and together
we stumbled drowsily across the rough compound towards
the torrent. The long line of low huts lay dark and
spectral on either hand, and the music of the 200 sleepers,
more or less, snoring as one, made harmony with the boom-
ing of the Yukawa in its rocky channel. We crossed by the
rickety plank bridge that looked alarmingly narrow in the
surrounding gloom, and soon began to scramble up the
rough broken hill side that rises 2,000 feet above the
stream. An hour's hard going placed us on the top,
where we found ourselves on the edge of a wide grassy
plateau called Mida-ga-hara. In the middle of this we

joined the track that ascends from Ashikura, a village fifteen miles below Ryūzanjita in the valley of the Jōgwanjigawa. Ashikura is the orthodox starting point for the pilgrim mountaineers, and one of these whom I met plodding wearily up the greasy muddy track told me he had then been climbing all the night, and didn't know when he would reach the top. A scramble up the beds of several torrents, which we ascended by jumping from boulder to boulder in the usual way, came to an end near a point where a curious stone, called *Oba-ishi*, " the old lady stone," forms the subject of a remarkable legend. The first mountaineer to achieve the ascent of Tateyama was one Ariyaka Saemon. After death he was, so to speak, canonized, and his body lies buried close by a temple built to his memory near Ashikura, at the foot of the peak. The form of the grave is somewhat uncommon. It consists of a sort of tumulus eight feet square and five feet high, the sides being faced with stone. On all the great sacred mountains of Japan a limit has, until the last few years, been placed to the height up to which woman-kind might climb. This limit is called *Nionindō*, " woman's way," but naturally enough it varies a good deal on different mountains. The wife of Ariyaka Saemon, however, was either so impelled by curiosity to see what was at the top of the wonderful peak, or so desirous, " new-woman " like, of emulating her husband's feat, that she transgressed the bounds of *Nionindō*, and essayed to reach the actual summit. Her rashness met with its due reward, and she was immediately transformed into the *Oba-ishi*, which still bears witness to her sacrilege.

Lower down the mountain some well-formed hexagonal columns of andesite on a magnificently timbered slope are the subject of a similar legend. Once upon a time when a shrine was being built to the *genius loci*, a number of trees were cut down and prepared at this spot. A woman who had wandered up heedlessly, stepped over the prostrate trunks, and as her touch meant desecration, they were forthwith turned into stone. From this event the place received its present title *Zai-moku-zaka*, " the timber hill." Above the highest of the torrent beds we emerged on a broad plateau, girt on three sides by a magnificent " cirque " of peaks, and commanding an extensive view. Westward lies the broad plain of Etchū with its winding streams, and with the promontory of Noto thrusting itself far out into the Sea of Japan. Due east, amongst its gaunt rocky neighbours, Tateyama raises its graceful summit. At the foot of its actual peak I stopped for breakfast at a pilgrim's shelter called *Murodō*, the " Club hut " of Alpine Japan. From here the ascent lay diagonally over seven or eight slopes of snow, and then up rough and fairly steep rocks to the highest point. Here and there on a rocky ledge a miniature shrine stood

L

sentinel, and received the offerings of the pilgrim climber. Sometimes these consisted of a pipe-case (without the pipe), a piece of paper inscribed with prayers, or occasionally a few *rin* (pieces of money of small value), or a rosary. Near the top some iron chains hang down the steepest rocks to assist the weary. On the summit of a sharp rocky cone a picturesque red-painted shrine overlooks all else, and marks the topmost point (9,200 feet). Whilst trying to take in something of the marvellous view, which almost rivals that from Yarigatake itself, my attention was attracted by the arrival of a band of pilgrims escorted by the *Kannushi*, the Shintō guardian of the sacred mountain. With reverent ceremoniousness he drew aside the gorgeous little curtain of crimson brocade, stamped with crossed eagle feathers in gold, that hung before the shrine. He then opened the doors and took out a number of relics which he exposed to the wondering gaze of the pilgrims, whose rapt attention and almost awe-struck faces, as they crowded round and listened to the stories of the old heroes, were a picture worth seeing. Amongst these articles of veneration were an arrow-head and spear-point that once belonged to Ariyaka Saemon, and some coins and a mirror said to have been the property of the renowned Yamato-dake, husband of Oto-Tachibana-Hime, the Alcestis of Japanese romance (*vide* an interesting note in "Murray," p. 134). The *Kannushi* next brought forth some beautifully lacquered *saké* bottles and cups, adorned with the eagle-feather crest, from which he dispensed welcome refreshment to the pilgrim mountaineers. Nor did his courtesy stop short of the solitary foreigner, for I, too, was given a polite invitation to share in the libations.

Of all the remarkable solfataras in which Japan abounds, some of the most interesting are those that lie half a mile to the north of the Murodō, in a valley that is reached by a path passing between the two green tarns near the hut. Seen from the top of a little hill above, the whole valley is alive with seething and bubbling pools of sulphur and boiling mud. The name of Ō-jigoku ("Great Hell") tells what the country people think about it. The same name used once to be applied to a similar remarkable spot in the Hakone district, well-known to foreign residents. On the occasion of a visit paid by the Emperor some years ago, however, his Majesty changed the name to the more euphonious *Ō-waki-dani*, "the valley of the great boiling."

Descending from the hill-top to the valley floor, the crumbling honey-combed earth demands the greatest caution. The little hummocks of sulphur are intensely hot, and a careless step will plunge one into the depths of the boiling liquid that lies concealed beneath. From clefts in the sides of mounds composed of a mixture of sulphur and white rock, jets of steam and sulphuretted hydrogen burst out with a deafening roar, and carry lumps of solid

sulphur deposit to a distance of five or six yards.   From
some of the pools boiling water of a dark-green or yellow
colour shoots up to a height of several feet, and only
falls down again to be shot up with equal. violence.
The temperature of some of the pools is almost 200°
Fahrenheit.

By three o'clock we were back again at Ryūzanjita,
and by the time the inevitable thunderstorm burst over
the valley I was enjoying the luxury of the Onsen baths.
One of the oddest features of these cosmopolitan "tubs"
is the grave behaviour of the bathers.   However much
the grateful warmth may soften stiffened limbs, mutual
courtesies are never relaxed.   I know of a foreign traveller
who, on entering an Onsen bath after a mountain expedition, was somewhat startled by an affectionate greeting
from a yellow-skinned *vis-à-vis* in the same compartment.
It proved to be a Japanese friend, who had brought his
wife and family to the mountain resort for the sake of the
waters, and one by one he now proceeded to introduce
them *in puris naturalibus* to his foreign friend.   Although
the latter was naturally somewhat disconcerted, the whole
thing was done with such good taste that it was impossible
to take exception to the proceedings.

On Saturday morning (August 12th) my porters and
I were tramping down the ravine on our 30 miles march
to Toyama, in the great Etchū plain.   For some hours our

surroundings were of the grandest. Mighty walls of castellated cliffs rose threateningly on either hand, here and there rent and torn by avalanche and landslip into scenes of wildest confusion. *Oni-ga-shiro* is the suggestive title for this spectacle—"the devil's castle." On the left bank, some miles down, a subsidiary torrent bursts down a dark ravine, and mighty boulders tossed hither and thither attest the force of autumn storms. The bridges that cross such spots are necessarily of the simplest and flimsiest sort. However substantially the peasants attempted to build in such a spot, the life of the best of bridges would be but short. Two kinds are generally employed. The more solid is called *man-nem bashi.* It consists of a long narrow plank tied at each end to pieces of timber projecting from the banks, or lashed to boulders on either side. The structure is so slight and insecure, and withal bends and sways so cheerfully, that one can quite appreciate its name of "the bridge of ten thousand years." A more curious device still is the *kago-no-watashi.* A stout hawser, sometimes of hemp, or occasionally made of the *Kurogane modoshi,* "iron creeper," which is in more primitive regions used as a substitute for ropes, is stretched from bank to bank. On this, suspended by a large noose, a *kago* or basket of bamboo or twisted creepers runs to and fro. The simplest method of crossing is to get into the basket and let coolies haul one over. If the coolies, however, are not forthcoming, the transit requires considerable skill and nerve on the part of the traveller himself. On getting into the cage, he grasps the hawser with both hands, presses the feet firmly on the bottom of the cage, and then by a succession of frog-like jerks, performs the voyage over. The great thing is to keep the basket under the control of the feet, otherwise he is apt to find himself hanging in mid-air with the basket behind, and a boiling torrent below.

At one point in the descent of the ravine, the track crosses the face of a steep buttress of smooth rock, where rickety broken ladders call for the balancing powers of a Blondin. Further down, the path is carried high up above the stream on a narrow line of pine logs, that cling precariously, without any very visible means of support, to the face of the cliff. A landslip here had carried away a long stretch of the flimsy platform, and left a hiatus that has to be circumvented by a descent to the torrent brink. The bare rocky walls that hem in the stream, now insensibly fall away into tree-clad slopes, and here and there a little clearing with a solitary charcoal-burner's hut, shows signs of life. A dozen miles from Ryūzanjita comes Hara, a hamlet remarkable for the curious construction of its cottages. An abnormally steep thatched roof is continued in a flat eave, heavily laden with stones, that shelters a wide verandah. This is a necessary precaution in a district where snow often lies to a depth of over 10 feet. Early in the afternoon the daily thunderstorm overtook us just as we had started after lunch from the village of Omi, and the sheets of rain that came down in true tropical style, drove us incontinently back to our resting-place. In a lateral valley on the left near here, the village of Arimine shelters inhabitants credited with the most primitive customs and stupidity phenomenal, owing to their only inter-marrying with the same families. In money matters, however, they are found to be quite "civilised," and well able to hold their own. Beyond Omi the river widens, and the clear-cut outlines of the terraced hill-sides between which it flows, show unmistakeable traces of its former bed. Five o'clock found me resting on the cool soft mats of a pretty little inn at Kamidaki. This is the principal village on this side of Toyama, and lies at the foot of a bold bluff that looks out over the flat plain of Etchū, just as the promontory-like form of Stinchcombe Hill juts out over the valley of the Severn west of the Cotswolds.

At Kamidaki I had been told I should get *kuruma*, but a search all over the village revealed but one, and that the owner declined to let me have, owing to its need of repair. Finally a *ni-guruma* (a sort of hand-cart, with four wheels) was produced. On this my baggage was tied, and, by way of variety, I mounted on the top of all. In state I bade

farewell, and started on the final run-in of seven miles
to Toyama.   Half-an-hour's tedious jolting over a rutty,
cobbly road soon rubbed off the novelty of the situation,
and it was with intense satisfaction that I hailed a passing
jinrikisha, bound, without a fare, for Kamidaki.   After
transferring the baggage, one of my coolies trundling the
cart turned in his tracks and gaily cantered home again,
whilst the other buckled to on the *jinrikisha*, and so I
drove speedily tandem-fashion across the rice-fields into the
busy streets of the capital of Etchū.

After a week in the wilds, a quiet Sunday at the pretty
" Kiya " inn was welcome, though the intense heat, a damp
92° in the shade, proved less agreeable than the cool clear
air of the mountains.   As my stockings had suffered a good
deal from wear and tear since leaving Ōmachi, I asked one
of the maids of the inn, a shiny-faced, red-cheeked, dumpy
little personage, if she could kindly mend them.   " Oh,
yes," she said, " quite well," and ambled away with a tread
that shook the house like a small earthquake.   As I was
leaving on the Monday morning I enquired if the stockings
were mended.   With a roar of laughter at having forgotten
to bring them, she tumbled down the slippery stairs, and
soon returned, with modest pride exhibiting the proofs of
her skill—she had mended the holey soles by sewing over
the gaps large pieces of coarse canvas, fit for the sails of a
native junk.

Toyama, a town of 55,000 inhabitants, is only five miles from the mouth of the broad Jinzū-gawa, where its port, Higashi-Iwase, is in steam communication with the principal towns on the Sea of Japan. Its position makes

THE MID-DAY MEAL.

it an admirable starting point for some of the most interesting routes of travel in the least known districts in Central Japan. On this occasion I left it, on August 14th, with the intention of penetrating into the heart of the Japanese Alps, by the valleys of the Miyagawa and the

Takaharagawa. My objective point was Kasadake, the peak from which, unascended, I had been sent away by the villagers of Gamada the year before. The road as far as Funatsu, my first halting-place (36 miles from Toyama), was said to be practicable for *jinrikisha,* so I deposited my baggage and myself in a *saki-biki* (a *kuruma* drawn by two men tandem-wise), and at 7·30 A.M. we were bowling southwards across the sun-scorched plain. Behind me, beyond the northern margin of the wide expanse of paddy fields, lay the Sea of Japan. Far away to the south-west rose dimly through the summer haze the tall, graceful, snow-streaked cone of Hakusan, the "white mountain of Kaga."* Straggling collections of dusky cottages, with rustic shrines and temples half hidden in clumps of fir or bamboo, dot the plain. Interesting methods of irrigation attract attention by their ingenuity. Wherever the roughness of the stone-strewed road made "going" hard for the coolies, as was frequently the case, my descent to walk was the signal for a crowd of old and young to gradually gather round, with polite curiosity, to discuss myself and my

---

* At one time, during the Shōgunate, this famous peak was claimed by each of the three *Daimyō* on the borders of whose provinces it stands. The dispute was at last carried to the Shōgun himself, to whom the *Daimyō* of Kaga applied. "I have come," said the officer, representative of the great lord to the Shōgun, "concerning the matter of the ownership of Haku-san in Kaga." "If," replied the Shōgun, "Hakusan is in Kaga, there can therefore be no dispute about it." Consequently "Kaga no Hakusan" is the title by which the mountain has ever since been known.

probable business in these out-of-the-way regions. Near
Sasadzu, 10 miles from Toyama, the path crosses the
Jinzūgawa by a startlingly modern bridge, built with
white-painted iron girders, painfully out of keeping with
the quaint surroundings. Here the river comes sweeping
through the breach it has burst in the mountain barrier.
By its exit we made our way into a region where every
turn revealed fresh prospects of enchanting loveliness.
Here and there the track leaves the bank and climbs the
hillside, to pass through a cutting, and then drops down to
rejoin the swift green waters beyond. The stream abounds
in fish of various kinds. *Masu* (salmon trout), sometimes
weighing eight pounds, are harpooned with a four-pronged
fork, while *ai* and *iwana* (species of trout) are taken with
nets. The seasons for fishing are the latter part of spring
and the beginning of autumn.

Near Inotani the road passes through open fields, cultivated with tobacco and potatoes, and reaches the boundary
of the provinces of Etchū and Hida. The prospect at this
spot, where the Takaharagawa and the Miyagawa unite to
form the Jinzūgawa, is of the grandest description. The
river is crossed just below the point of junction by a
bridge that springs from the luxuriant foliage on either
bank, and hangs far above the rushing current, here
hemmed in by tall, densely wooded hills. Taking to the
right bank of the Takaharagawa, we soon reached another

lovely spot, where a wild mountain torrent, the Tanigawa, dashes down a picturesque glen on the right, whilst on the left a cascade falls in a succession of leaps and bounds over a precipitous cliff. For the greater part of the distance the road is so atrociously bad that I had to leave the *jinrikisha* and walk. Beyond the neat little hamlet of Modzumi its character suddenly changes, and for several miles is fit for a bicycle track. At Domura, however, it abruptly ceased altogether, for we found that the melting of winter snows had not only damaged the path, but had also swept away the bridge by which the Atotsugawa, a tributary of the Takahara, is crossed. The situation afforded a pleasant diversion, as we shouldered the baggage and jumped from rock to rock across the boiling, eddying torrent. The spectacle of one of my coolies with the *jinri-kisha* topsy-turvy on his head, gingerly picking his way over, created considerable amusement. On regaining the road on the opposite bank, we passed on high above the Takaharagawa, under magnificent bluffs that reminded me of Matlock Bank and the river Derwent, but on a far grander scale. Just before reaching Funatsu a fine new bridge crosses the river to Kanayama, where we noticed the busy smelting works of the Shikawa mine. The mine itself is in the hills far above the village, and is one of the most productive in Japan, large quantities of copper, as well as a certain amount of silver, being put out annually.

Darkness overtook us as we straggled up the narrow main street of Funatsu, our journey of 36 miles having taken just 12 hours to accomplish. At the house of one Watanabe San, the usual kindly welcome, hot bath, and, later on, a good Japanese dinner were waiting, and the *jinrikisha* coolies came to pay their respectful farewell before I turned in for the night. My journey on the following day gave me a still closer acquaintance with the beautiful mountain stream of yesterday afternoon. A sturdy coolie shouldered some of my baggage, and with the rest I started at 6·50 for a twenty miles' tramp to the secluded valley of Gamada. The sight of a foreigner produced the usual amount of polite astonishment, as I passed the country folk coming in from the scattered hamlets that dotted the river's bank, or nestled under the cool shadow of the grand pine-clad hills further back. My morning greeting, however, invariably produced a kindly smile and respectful bow, and the little children trotting in to school showed that already they had, at least, learned good manners, as they abruptly halted and made their bobs and curtsies spontaneously. An hour away from Funatsu, in a broad, bright meadow on the right bank, stand a group of newly-built cottages, whose familiar form makes one rub one's eyes to make sure that Sugo is not in Switzerland. The low, wide-spreading eaves, weighted with white boulders from the river-bed, overshadow broad verandahs. The fresh, sweet-scented pine wood of which they are built is not yet tanned by exposure, and the whole scene looks as if it has been bodily transported from some Alpine valley. Occasionally the narrowing track passes through a grove of giant cryptomeria, in whose dark recesses stands some simple shrine, hard by a great oval stone, that bears the ever-recurring invocation : *Namu Amida Butsu* (" Hail, Eternal Buddha "). Picturesque bridges of simple but ingenious construction span the noisy torrents that dash down the lateral valleys on either hand to join the main stream, and here and there a cascade falls over the cliff, and scatters its spray over the dusty path with a refreshing coolness that nearly takes away one's breath.

By the time I got to Taore, six hours beyond Funatsu, the pangs of hunger called a halt for lunch. Unfortunately, I had left my own food in the *kori* (basket) carried by my coolie, who was now far behind, and my application at the house of the head man of the little village at first met with a chilling reception. The place was in charge of an old dame, who was much concerned with a bundle lying by the fire in the middle of the spacious kitchen. Sundry movements and grunts on the part of the bundle proved it to be the headman himself, who was sick, but, on my apologizing for my interruption, the old lady relented, and produced some rice and dried fish about the size of large minnows, flavoured with *shōyū*, a sauce made chiefly of fermented wheat and beans. The resources of the valley of the Takaharagawa, like most country districts in this secluded " island province " of Hida, are unusually slender. Before reaching Taore, I had asked for food at several places on the road, but no one could produce more than a little seaweed or pickled octopus, neither of which is either appetizing or satisfying till one acquires the taste. Tea was not to be had, its place being taken by stuff brewed by pouring hot water on barley. Mindful, however, of the delights of Gamada, with its hospitable headman and its sulphur springs, I shouldered my rücksack again, and pushed on. At Imami, grandly situated at the confluence of two wild mountain torrents, a little group of cottages proudly gather round a new and diminutive Post-Office. Here I had to say good-bye to the beautiful stream whose companionship for these two days had afforded so much pleasure. My route now lay up the valley of the Gamada-gawa, on the left, as the track on the right leads to Hirayu, near the source of the Takaharagawa, on Norikura. A kindly welcome greeted me as I halted before the wide verandah of the house of Jimbei, my host of last year. Kicking off my boots, with the white dust of a twenty miles' tramp glittering thick upon them, I stepped up on to the soft mats of an inner room, where the adopted son of my old host beckoned me with many bows to enter. To my regret I learned that Jimbei San had died since my last visit, but the recollection of my former companion's kind attention on that occasion prompted a polite enquiry as to the "august health of the honourable Mr. Doctor." Whilst waiting for the arrival of the coolie and my baggage, I was hospitably entertained by a visitor occupying the room next my own.   This was the drawing-master of the Middle School (*Chu-Gakkō*) of Takayama, who had come from the hot plain to these cooler solitudes for rest and inspiration.   At my request the *Kuchō* (village head man) was sent for, and once more a council of war commenced as to the possibilities of an attack on Kasadake's grey peak.   From the hesitation with which the *Kuchō* took his seat on the floor, the many rap-taps needed to empty the ashes of his diminutive pipe, and from the owl-like way in which he screwed his head from side to side before approaching the subject, I at once realized my case was a hopeless one.   "The fact is," he said, "though the mountain can be climbed, there is no one who can be induced to make the ascent with you."   "But why, they can't be busy in the fields at this season, surely?"

"No, just the contrary.   The fact is that the drought of these last seven weeks is killing the crops, and the hunters, who are the only men that venture on the higher peaks, are all away on *amagoi* expeditions themselves."

Amagoi! ("praying for rain").   I had often heard of

the custom before, but had never so practically come across it. At Ōmachi a fortnight earlier I was told the peasants of the district were already sending out *amagoi* parties through the distress the drought was causing them. The most favourable spots for the ceremony are held to be the summits of the highest peaks accessible. The grandest spots are usually credited with sheltering the mightiest powers for good or ill, and these, then, are oftenest visited with prayers for rain. When climbing Jōnendake subsequently, I was told by my hunters that that peak was a splendid place for *amagoi*. The rite is carried out as follows:— A party of hunters, selected for their activity and power of lung, as the representatives of the suffering villagers, make their way to the little shrine of the *tengū*, the *genius loci*, on the summit of the peak. With branches of the *haimatsu* (creeping pine), brought up from below, they make a bonfire before the shrine, and then proceed to give a mimic representation of the storm they have come to pray for. Primed with *saké* (rice beer), they fire off their guns, and, with unearthly yells, roll down from the topmost ridge great blocks of andesite. As these go crashing down the cliffs the hunters loudly invoke the attention of the *tengū* to their prayers. "And," one of my men added, "after a *very* long drought, rain nearly always follows within a few days."

Sometimes, however, hope deferred renders the men

M

desperate, and a deputation has been known to go to destroy the shrine in disgust. This also sometimes happens in the plains. In one village the guardian divinity had so long been deaf to the peasants' prayers that at last they threw down his image from its stand, and with imprecations loud and long pitched him head foremost into an evil-smelling paddy field. "There," they said, "you may stay yourself for a while, to see how *you* will feel after a few days' scorching in this broiling sun, that is burning the life from our cracking fields."

In another district a party of villagers go in procession to the bed of a mountain torrent, headed by a priest who leads a black dog devoted for sacrifice. At the chosen spot they tether the animal to a stone, and forthwith make it their target for bullets and arrows. As soon as the poor beast's life-blood is seen to bespatter the rocks, the peasants throw down their arms and lift up their voices in supplication to the dragon divinity of the stream, exhorting him to send down forthwith a cleansing shower to purify the spot from its defilement. Custom has prescribed that on these occasions the colour of the sacrificial animals shall be black, symbolical of the wished-for storm clouds. In the neighbourhood of Lake Biwa a deputation is sent to fill bamboo tubes with water from the lake. They then run home at full speed. As the rain desired is now expected to fall only at their first stopping-place, they forbear to halt by the way. Should home be reached without a rest, the party proceeds to some neighbouring hills to drum and shout vigorously by way of calling the attention of the god to their desires.

If fine weather, however, is wanted, the offering must be one of spotless white. When on a visit to Korea during the recent war, I learnt that similar customs are in vogue in the " Land of the Morning Calm," to those already noticed in the " Land of the Rising Sun." The following extracts are taken from a translation of the " Daily Gazette " of the Korean capital, for 1892.

July 24th: " The Board of Ceremony states that as there has been no rain for a long time, and as it is getting late to transplant rice, an inferior officer should first be sent to the South and to the North Mountains (close to Seoul), and to the river to pray for rain. Granted."

July 27th: " The Board of Ceremonies asks that an officer of the 3rd rank be sent to Yong-San at the river, to pray again for rain. Granted."

August 7th: " The Board of Ceremonies announces that the Bo-sa-chei ceremony, thanking Heaven for rain after the recent sacrifices, will take place on the 28th of this moon."

August 8th: " His Majesty the King rejoices that the anxiety caused by the recent drought is over ; and orders that a deerskin be given to each of the officers who went to pray for rain."

But this is a digression. The *Kuchō's* pronouncement about the *amagoi* completely threw cold water on my schemes, and it was quite plain that beyond his dictum there was no appeal. Compelled to accept the inevitable, I again departed to drown my disappointment in the comforting waters of the village thermal spring. The next morning, as the sun looked over the great ridge south of Yarigatake, it saw me trudging back once more, disconsolate, to Hirayu. Down the beautiful glen I went, across the quaint *mannembashi* bridge, over the intervening spur between the Gamada valley and the ravine of the Takaharagawa, and finally up to the secluded hollow where Hirayu lies, sheltered by the dark form of Norikura's twin-topped mass. At the house of Yomo Saburō I was again received with cordiality. After the usual greetings, my first enquiry was as to the fate of a certain pair of trousers I had left behind the previous year, and which subsequent letters had failed to recover. Yomo Saburō was away from home, but his deputy rose to the occasion.

"Oh, the honourable trousers, is it ? Oh, yes ; they're all right."

"But did you get my letters asking for them to be sent on to me ? "

"Well, yes ; but the fact is, we were too busy to send

them. But, still, here they are. We have been keeping them for you all the time."

The way he said, "Keeping them all the time," sounded very odd, almost as if I was so "wrapped up" in the garments that I was sure to return for the sole purpose of recovering them! When they were produced, I found them just as I had handed them over a year ago to be dried and brushed, after a scramble down from the Norikura *Kozan* in mud and rain. A year's delay in getting things from the laundry, and then getting them in *statu quo*, was quite a "record."

On the arrival of the landlord later in the day, he had no sooner made the usual salutations than he abruptly disappeared again. He was soon back, however, and produced with pride a pocket-knife I had given him, and a doll I had presented to his little eight-year-old girl, acknowledging with the profusest obeisances these trifles of twelve months ago.

A walk up to the smelting works just above the village, showed clearly that the prosperity of the mines was on the increase. On what was last year a piece of waste ground near the furnaces, there now stand a number of houses built in a sort of quadrangle. Some of these are used as offices, whilst others are shops for the sale of provisions, etc. amongst the workpeople at the mine.

CHAPTER IX.

THE morrow's walk of 30 miles over the Abō-tōge to Hashiba, whence I proposed to start for the ascent of Hodakayama, demanded bed betimes. The landlord and the *Kuchō* between them promised I should have a couple of coolies for the passage of the mountains waiting for me at 3·30 A.M., for a start at dawn was most desirable. Just as I am dozing off, a rattling is heard at the *fusuma* (paper doors) of my room, and as they slide open a husky voice whispers—

"Danna San ! Danna San !"

"Well, what is it ? "

"The coolies refuse to go at the price the *Kuchō* settled, and say they won't start unless you pay them at the rate of three *sen* (three farthings) instead of two (a half-penny) a mile ! "

"All right, *shikata ga nai* ('there is no help for it '), good night ! "

" *O yasumi nasai* " (" honourably deign to rest "), and then the *fusuma* are slid to, and I turn over again. But sleep would not come. The fleas came, however, and made matters still livelier. However tightly I shut the mouth of my sleeping-bag sheet, they burrowed their way in, and only after getting up to sprinkle fresh libations of " Keating " over bedding and mats, could I hope to rest. Once more I sank into blissful forgetfulness of landlords, fleas, and similar interlopers, when a new but more hopeless terror seized me. Some native travellers here to " take the waters " were getting up steam in their noisy carousals in the next room. As they conduct them-selves in the silly childish way that only a Japanese reveller in his cups knows how to behave, I know I am in for it with a vengeance. Regrets, remonstrances are useless, and only after five hours' restless tossing did sleep, through sheer weariness, visit my eyelids.

Yomo Saburō had faithfully promised to call me at 3·30, but at 3·45 I awoke to find the house resounding with snores, and my landlord still blissfully buried in *futon* and forgetfulness. At 5 o'clock, however, my coolies and I were on the march. The younger of the two men, who turned out to be a farmer from the Takayama plain, was the speedier, and treated the long tramp through the pouring rain as a huge joke. I asked him the name of a particularly fine variety of wild raspberries which I found near the top of the pass. He called them *uma-ichigo,* "horse strawberries." To further enquiries about botanical subjects, his invariable reply was " *Wagi wa shiranosu,*" a very oddly-sounding corruption of *watakushi wa shiranu* (" I don't know "). The pronunciation of some of the words used by the Hida mountain dwellers is very curious, and I have sometimes found myself, after several seasons' travel amongst them, called upon to interpret between them and their own fellow-countrymen from distant parts. A perversion of the vowels is very common, *nü rü* (two *ri*), for instance, being frequently heard for *ni ri.*

By 9 o'clock we reached the Azusagawa, and crossed the pair of long, thin, barkless pine poles that serve for a bridge. Previous recollections of this Blondin-like passage had made me cautious, and I successfully slid over the wet, slippery, swaying trunks (after the manner of an acrobat on a slack wire), with *waraji* tied beneath the soles of my boots. On the top of the *Hi-no-ki-tōge* (" the pass of the pine trees ") I found the withered old dame who had charge of the little rest-house had improved her resources, and now added tea to her store of dried peas. With delightful anticipations of a rest at the house where last year my companion's medical help was so much appreciated, I clattered down the stony declivity on which the cottages of Ōnogawa are perched. Gratitude, however, is sometimes short-lived. The master of the house,

H. J. Hamilton, phot.

POLE-BRIDGE AT THE FOOT OF THE ABŌ-TŌGE. [P. 168.

who last year was ill, turns out now to be well, and away
on business, whilst his wife is entirely engrossed with the
attentions of two gay young sparks, who are making
themselves agreeable in the room where last year Miller
and I were so hospitably entertained, and she refuses to
pay the least heed to my enquiries. With a feeling of the
keenest disappointment, I turned slowly away, mentally
contrasting this reception with the experience of the rustic
I had met on the sultry slopes of Sō-no-sawa a fortnight
earlier.

At the house of Okuta Kiichi, however, I fared better,
and was enjoying a substantial lunch when my coolies
arrived. The older man avowed he was unequal to going
on, but the cheery person offered to relieve him of his
pack and to come with me to my journey's end. After
sharing the baggage between us, we gaily strode on down
the grand gorge of the Mayegawa towards Hashiba. By
the time the path reached the banks of the Adzusagawa,
we found the heavy rains had already begun their work
of destruction. Frequent landslips had torn away the
track, and the greatest care, heavily laden as we were, was
needed in crossing the rents in rock and soil to prevent us
from a sheer fall into the foaming torrent. All went well,
however, and by 4·45 P.M. I was again at rest under the
hospitable roof of the " Shimidzuya " at Hashiba. I found
the landlord a good deal exercised by the fact that, for the

first time in the history of the village, mosquitoes had made
their appearance. As no one was provided with nets, the
visitation was a real affliction. Amongst the greatest
proofs of filial piety in Japan is said to be the readiness
of a son to attract mosquitoes to feed on his own person,
in order to free his parents from the scourge, where no
other protection is available. For a widow to mention
to a suitor that her mosquito net is too large, is equivalent
to expressing her willingness to " name the day."

Before starting on the expedition to Hodakayama I
had occasion to go down into the Matsumoto plain for
letters and provisions which were waiting for me at the
house of Sasai Motoji, the ever-obliging young landlord
of the " Shinanoya." That worthy I found full of plans
for the erection of a wondrous hotel, the like of which
Matsumoto had never seen. The pleasure my friends and
I had found in our visits to the neighbourhood, combined
with the fact that in a few years' time the town was
expected to become a terminus for a railway connecting
these parts with the Tōkaidō line, had apparently given
him the impression that crowds of foreign travellers
would soon flock to the place. The hotel, therefore,
was to be a regular castle, with five storeys, one of
which would be reserved exclusively for the use of
foreign guests, and be furnished in foreign style. The
decorations of these rooms would consist exclusively of

the portraits of his visitors, to each of which was to
be attached a short autobiography of the original. He
invited me to inaugurate the series with my own. Next
he began to expatiate upon the beauties of a tea-service
of Kaga ware which he was anxious to give me. His
habit of flitting about, butterfly like, from one topic to
another was interesting but confusing. Suddenly he came
down from the realms of fancy in which he had been
soaring, and astonished me with an abrupt request for the
loan of 25 *yen* (dollars).

"But how," I asked, "are you going to build your five-
storeyed hotel next year, if this year you have to borrow
25 *yen* for your current debts ?"

"Oh, that's all right," he replied ; "I shall borrow a few
thousands from a friend ! "

"But supposing your friend hasn't the money to
lend ?"

"Oh, there won't be the least difficulty about it. If
he hasn't the money himself, I shall simply get him to
borrow it from *some one who has !* "

From this conversation it may be safely inferred that the
erection of the pagoda-like structure proposed by my host
is likely to be long deferred. And in my own mind I
shall not fail to locate in the same latitude the Matsumoto
"hotel of five storeys," and the proverbial "Châteaux en
Espagne."

On unfolding my plans for the expedition to Hoda-kayama to Sasai Motoji, he at once volunteered to accompany me.   On the Monday morning, however, just as I was about to start he came to me, apparently in considerable amusement, to say he could not come.   " The fact was," he said, with a grin, " he had just heard of the death of a friend, and he must go to the funeral."   The curious laugh which so frequently accompanies announce-ments of this character, is a constant puzzle to the European who is unfamiliar with Japanese thoughts in such a connection.   It is nearly always taken as an indication of want of feeling, and yet many a time the laugh only hides a breaking heart.   On one occasion a friend of mine was calling on some of his Japanese acquaintances whom he had not seen for some time.   After the ordinary greeting, he enquired particularly after their little boy, an only child.   He was just joining in the burst of laughter his question had produced, when it was followed by the an-nouncement, " Oh, he died a few days ago ! "

And yet these parents idolized their boy.   But apart from other considerations, the Japanese, those Spartans of the far-East, do not usually consider it good manners to betray considerable emotion under circumstances where more demonstrative Europeans would make little or no attempt to hide their grief.   And consequently we are too apt to think that because they do not show their deepest feelings in quite the same way as ourselves, they are therefore lacking in them.*

On my return to Hashiba, I found the prospects of my climb of the dreariest. Rain was falling heavily. Hour by hour the swift waters of the Adzusagawa rose higher as they roared past the rocky headland on which the little inn was perched. My hunter, Kamonji, to whom I had been directed as the best man to take as guide, said an immediate start was impossible. The fulness of the streams meant abundance of fish, and he could make more money by fishing than by guiding. " Besides," he added, "we could not yet possibly get across the broad turbulent stream that has to be forded before the base of Hodakayama can be reached. The rocks, too, on the peak are steep and smooth, and an attempt in wet weather would be unjustifiably risky." A fortnight before, he and another hunter had been with a Government official (a surveyor in the War Department), who then succeeded in making the first ascent of the highest point. At a difficult spot near the top the man slipped and was sent flying downwards for sixty feet, bumping from rock to rock with a violence that made his survival a matter of marvel.

Whilst waiting for the weather to clear, I occasionally

---

* Interesting remarks on this characteristic will be found in the chapter entitled " The Japanese Smile," in " Glimpses of Unfamiliar Japan," by Mr. Lafcadio Hearn.

donned my mackintosh and prowled about the village in
search of variation from long hours of sprawling on a flea-
infested floor.　On one occasion I found myself in
the garden or courtyard of a house of such spacious
proportions that it seemed quite out of place in such a
forlorn little collection of cottages as Hashiba.　As I
approached the front verandah I saw a trio of weather-
beaten hunters sitting on the mats of a wide lofty room
making a fishing net.　The delicate silken meshes, loaded
at the extreme edge with slender cylinders of lead,
contrasted curiously with the big horny wrinkled hands
that so deftly wove them.　One of the party, whose face I
thought I recognised, proved to be a young hunter who
had acted as one of my coolies last year on the ascent of
Yarigatake.　So I was at once welcomed and treated
with as much courtesy by these unschooled peasants as
if I had been an honoured guest at a Tōkyō villa.
Over the doorway of an adjoining cottage I noticed a
pair of child's *zori* (straw shoes) hanging up.　I was told
they were meant to ward off the ills of childhood from the
juveniles.　And yet many English folk who laugh at such
a "superstition" as this are uncommonly keen believers in
the efficacy of an old cast-off horse-shoe when nailed over
the lintel of their civilised English homes !

During my enforced inactivity at the inn, Kamonji
regaled me with some yarns of bygone experiences.　One

ZOSUI-BASHI, A BRIDGE AT HASHIBA.

H. J. Hamilton, phot.

[P. 175.

story he told was by way of explanation of the curious name of the village bridge, " *Zōsui bashi,*" " the bridge of the mess of pottage." *

" *Mukashi, mukashi,*"—the little hunter began—" Once upon a time, before ever a bridge was built between Hashiba and Shimajima, a man of the latter place named Abe fell in love with a certain O Setsu (*Anglicè*, ' Miss Constance '), of Hashiba. It was a case of love at first sight, and at a rather long range, for they were separated by the width of the stream from closer contact. A device, however, suggested itself to the lady's wits, and somehow she managed to communicate it to her lover, and forthwith they proceeded to carry it out. By forswearing such luxuries as *daikon* (a sort of large radish) and rice, and by confining themselves to a diet of *zōsui*, they contrived to put by enough money to enable them each to purchase a pine tree. These they stripped of their branches and fixed to their respective banks of the river. By causing the poles to overlap in mid stream a means of passage was provided, and the bold Abe went across to claim his constant bride. In commemoration of this romantic episode, an orthodox bridge was afterwards built, whose successor to-day hands down the story in the title *Zōsui bashi.*"

On Thursday morning the weather cleared, and we were

* *Zōsui* is a coarse food composed of scraps of herbs, vegetables, &c., and is only eaten by the poorest of the people.

able to make a start. But from our observations of the
rocks and river banks we saw the stream had risen for the
time being at least a dozen feet. Several weeks afterwards,
on my return to the coast, I learnt how heavy was the
destruction these almost tropical downfalls had caused.
On the east coast the Gifu plain had suffered terribly from
the overflowing of the Kiso-gawa, which rises near Norikura. On the west the plain of Etchū had been inundated
by the Jinzūgawa. In each case the damage to life and
property was very great. And even as I write news
comes to hand of the same districts being once more
visited by a similar catastrophe. The harm wrought far
afield, however, had no counterpart here at Hashiba.
The harvest of the full waters was so great that a special
matsuri (feast) to the river-god was proclaimed for
Wednesday night. A number of youths, taking advantage
of the occasion, unfortunately chose my inn (as a matter
of fact the only one in the village) as the scene of their
carousals. For hours they made night hideous with their
insane revels. And what was worse still, by way of
adding insult to injury, I found, when calling for my
kanjō (bill) a few days later, that they had caused me to
be charged with the *saké* they had swilled !

Thursday morning (August 24th) found my two hunters
(Kamonji and a companion) and myself on our way over
the Tokugō tōge to the foot of our peak. As we passed by

the queer little bathhouse at Furōtaira on our way up the valley from Hashiba, I found the damaged surveyor resting after his accident. From his account of his climb I gathered my own was likely to be interesting. When I asked him about the altitude of Hodakayama, he could tell me nothing—he had only been using theodolite and compass, and a mercurial barometer or aneroid was not included in his equipment.

Early in the afternoon we descended on the now decaying hut, with which I was already familiar, on the left bank of the Azusagawa. One of its dilapidated rooms was occupied by a couple of herdsmen, who had driven over their cattle from Matsumoto for the sake of the pasturage. The grass is much better than the coarse, rank stuff found 3,000 feet lower down in the plain. Indeed, pasture land in Japan is almost as scarce as fallow land, though in two of the places in the northern part of the Kōshū mountains I have found turf fit for the finest lawns. The herdsmen gave us a cordial welcome, but could offer nothing more. I managed, however, to obtain the loan of a cotton quilt for the night. My dinner was improved by the addition of a dozen fine trout Kamonji caught soon after we arrived. As he told me he had a "hunting box" of his own (a shanty built of bark and twigs) on the opposite bank, I allowed him to go over to sleep in his own home. He promised, however, to be back at dawn,

N

so, after making up the fire in the *iroriya* (an open space
in the middle of my portion of the hut), he made his
obeisances, and, with his friend, withdrew. The morning
broke dull and cold, but for long after I had breakfasted
and packed my *rücksack* with instruments and provisions,
no signs of my men were visible. A couple of hours
dragged slowly by before the stunted form of the sturdy,
queer-visaged little hunter was descried pushing through
the trees on the opposite stream, and cautiously making his
way across the ford. His explanation of the delay was
that, as the weather looked so bad, he didn't think we
ought to start. After some time had been wasted in
useless argument, however, he gave in. At 7·45, in spite
of his protestations that we should be, if not killed, at least
benighted on the mountain, we started. Crossing the river
at the ford, we quickly sped through the lower part of the
forest which covers the level ground on the right bank.
For a couple of miles we held on to the route which I
had previously taken towards Yarigatake. Then a sudden
turn to the left introduced us to a small mountain torrent
hidden in the thick undergrowth at the east base of our
beautiful peak. Judging by the way Kamonji forced the
pace, he evidently had no intention of spending that night
on the inhospitable cliffs of Hodakayama. With his heavy
knife he hewed his way through the dense brushwood on
the torrent bank with grim determination. On we went,

HODAKAYAMA FROM THE S.E.

[P. 178.

now plunging through the icy cold water, jumping from
one slippery, moss-grown boulder to another, or scrambling
over fallen tree trunks that lay on the banks. The closely
interlacing undergrowth, whose cord-like creepers persisted
in tying themselves bewilderingly round one's ankles,
wrought much confusion. Fortunately this struggle only
lasted about an hour. We then emerged from the denser
part of the forest, near whose upper limits we parted with
the stream. Then came a battle with a steep stretch of
tall bamboo grass, which transferred to us as much of the
morning's rain as our already sodden clothes would hold.
A long scree, stretching down from the base of a fine cliff
in front, at last gave better going, and afforded a suitable
spot for breakfast. Beyond this I was suddenly greeted by
a familiar scent, suggestive enough, indeed, of an English
fruit garden, but quite foreign to those of Japan. The
source of the fragrance was not made clear until, a few
yards higher up, I found myself face to face with the
unwonted sight of a clump of black currant bushes. The
find was as welcome as it was unexpected, nor did I move
until after a satisfying feast. So far as I have been able to
gather, this is the first occasion on which the black currant
has been found growing wild in Japan, or at any rate south
of Hokkaidō (Yezo), though it is known to flourish unaided
in some parts of Russia, &c. Efforts have been made to
cultivate it in Yokohama gardens, but I am told it rarely

lasts long. Near Hakodate, in a colder climate, it thrives, but whether it grows uncultivated I have been unable to discover. The altitude at which I found it was about 7,500 feet, and, further on, I gathered a rich feast of the finest wild raspberries I have met with in all my wanderings.

The perpendicular cliffs in front of us now forced us to the right, where we climbed to the top of a sharp ridge, on the east side of which lay a small pool. Peering over the edge of the ridge, we found ourselves overlooking a mighty *couloir*, or gully. Its western end stretches far up to the main *arête* of Hodakayama, whilst on the east it ends abruptly in a precipice, over the edge of which a fine cascade, fed by the snows high above, falls into a rocky basin with thunderous roar. To reach the floor of the gully we had to descend from the crest of our ridge transversely across a nearly perpendicular rock wall. The rocks were rather rotten and loose, and one had to depend chiefly on the hand-hold afforded by the creepers that festooned themselves over the face of the cliff. As we started on the passage Kamonji turned anxiously, and asked, "Dare you come ? It needs great care." Reassured by my answer, he proceeded, and a delightfully exciting scramble took us slowly but surely to the *couloir* floor. We then turned our faces towards the main north *arête*. A rapid climb up big, loose rocks led us, at 10·30, to the base of an over-

hanging cliff in the right wall of the *couloir*, where
a halt for " second breakfast " was called, and all
superfluous baggage was deposited in a sheltered spot.
Another ascent up great granite slabs brought us in
an hour to the first slopes of snow at an altitude
of 8,500 feet. The inclination of these by my clino-
meter was about 40°, as steep as any I have met
with on the peaks and passes of Japan. A few
hundred feet over the snow brought us again to steep
rocks, and from here to the summit proved the most
enjoyable part of the whole expedition. The rocks were
steeper and firmer than any we had yet encountered, and
the call for our best energies made the work the more
exhilarating. By 12·45 we were standing on the sharp
arête from which rise the great towers of granite that give
the peak its appropriate title—" the mountain of the
standing ears of corn." Before 1·30 we were on the highest
pinnacle. Driven into a crack in the rock I found a small
stake, which marked the visit of the War Office surveyor
some weeks before. As I looked down the rocks, where
Kamonji pointed out the line of his fall, it seemed
incredible the man could have survived. The marvel was
that the aforesaid stake did not mark the double event,
and stand as a memorial of his destruction as well as a
token of triumph. From the summit, which my R. G. S.
mercurial barometer made 10,150 feet, the distant prospect

resembled that from Yarigatake, its northern neighbour. The nearer view, however, was more impressive still. The jagged *arête*, broken into its fantastic spires and towers, fell down westwards in precipitous depths and snow-filled *couloirs*, which loomed wild and desolate through wreathing veils of mist. But a cold wind was blowing from the south-east, and the ragged state of my knickerbockers now hanging partly in ribbons and fluttering wildly in the breeze, rendered a long stay undesirable. At 1·45 we turned away from the top, and sped downwards to the foot of the cliff, where we had left our things. Immediately on our arrival we were assaulted by a host of small gnats, that hung about the spot in a dense cloud. The hunters told me they were particularly fond of worrying the chamois on these peaks, and it is near the haunts of those animals that they are generally noticed. For some hours after our encounter with them they pestered us unmercifully. Several times they got into one's eyes at such inconvenient moments, when we were descending steep rocks, as to bring one within an ace of serious disaster. The lower we got on our descent the higher our spirits rose, and even Kamonji began to exult at the falsification of his melancholy prophecies earlier in the day. However, as the French proverb has it, it isn't well to whistle till you are out of the wood. We had just entered the forest near the base of the mountain when the truth of the adage was vividly

THE 'THUNDER GOD' AT THE MAUSOLEUM OF IEMITSU, AT NIKKŌ

[P. 188.

brought home. Kamonji, who was just ahead of me, had stopped to make a remark about a prostrate tree trunk that lay in our way. Suddenly his quaint features underwent an extraordinary change. His face assumed the aspect and his form the attitude of the "Thunder God" who stands guard before the great shrine of Iemitsu at Nikkō. At the best of times Kamonji would be ugly, but on this occasion his appearance was uncanny. He began to leap about with the wildest antics, and, for a moment, I feared he had taken leave of his senses. On hurrying up closer, a moment's observation disclosed the truth. Kamonji had stepped upon a wasps' nest—hence his activity. The creatures were rising in their fury as I approached him, and soon I, also, began to dance an involuntary, and, withal, ungraceful hornpipe. Kamonji's tight-fitting, tough, hempen garments protected most of his person from the onslaught of the wasps, but the great rents in my thin flannel knickerbockers, and the exposed condition of my bare neck and arms, gave them a grand chance. In a few moments I found myself the selected target of a dozen stings. Only by dint of much painful self-flagellation, aided by well-meant violence on the part of Kamonji, was any relief obtainable. At intervals, however, I still continued to feel from hidden corners of my loose unmentionables painful proofs of the presence of the enemy. I felt much like that creature of whose habits Mark Twain tells us that "when the

musing spider steps upon the red-hot shovel he first
exhibits a wild surprise and then shrivels up."

The incident served as a vivid illustration of a Japanese
proverb that is the counterpart of our own adage that
" troubles never come singly." The proverb runs, " *Naku*
tsura wo hachi ga sasu " ("It is the weeping face that
the wasp stings "). A few minutes earlier I had been
mourning over the rents in my garments, and the loss of
the heel of one of my boots during the rough descent. So
the Japanese version of the old saw seemed to hit off
the situation with singular appropriateness. Shortly after
leaving the scene of the disaster we reached Kamonji's
shanty, picturesquely situated by the still waters of a
secluded mere, whose glassy surface mirrors the form
of the giant cliffs at whose foot it nestles so securely.
Crossing the river ford once more, we reached the Tokugō
hut at 6·15 P.M. The most curious experience of the whole
day was yet to come.

On our return to the hut Kamonji had a good deal to
say about our adventures, particularly as to the wasps,
which in more ways than one had produced such an
impression on us both. Amongst many remedies suggested
for my wounds was *kuma no i*, " bear's gall." No bears,
unfortunately, were handy, and I could hardly afford to
wait till the winter hunts began. There was, however, a
Japanese in my party who knew quite well what was

needed, though for the moment, like Uncle Remus's "Brer Rabbit," he "lay low and say nuffin." Later on in the evening as I stood by the fire in the middle of my room drying some of my sodden clothes, Nakazawa, the person in question, stealthily crept in, and said, "Will you please show me where the wasps stung you?" Pointing out the wounds, I went on unconcernedly with my drying operations. At length I chanced to turn round. To my astonishment I saw Nakazawa squatting on the floor behind me, making a series of mesmeric passes and finger twistings over the injured spots. This over, he arose, went to the open door of the hut and turned his face reverently towards the sombre cliffs of Hodakayama, now looming up grand and ghostly in the light of a brilliant Oriental moon. He then clapped his hands to summon the spirit of the mountain to his aid, and bowed his head in the attitude of prayer. As soon as his supplications were over, he again clapped his hands, and quietly returned to where I was standing. In a deep sepulchral voice he said, "This is what we call *majinai* (exorcism or sorcery); you will be all right in the morning!"

The explanation of this curious incident, in view of the attitude of the peasants of Gamada towards the great mountains lifting their tall dark forms above the valley, is not a difficult one. As a foreigner I had, according to Nakazawa's belief, offended the god of the mountain by trespassing on his sacred precincts.   What looked (and certainly *felt*) like wasps were simply embodied spirits of vengeance sent forth to punish me for my act of desecration.   As Nakazawa, however, possessed the power of exorcising them, I thus became an involuntary sharer in the extraordinary pantomime I have described.   The experience was such a strange one that on my return to Kōbe I at once turned my attention to its investigation, and my enquiries resulted in the discovery of the most curious practices and beliefs amongst the lower orders of the Japanese.   As a rule though, the people are so shy at telling a foreigner what they know, for fear of ridicule, that it is difficult to "draw" them.   The results of my investigations I must defer until later.   In the meantime I may add that Nakazawa's promise was *not* fulfilled. The intense pain and stiffness from the stings entirely banished sleep that night.   As I lay awake watching the bright flames fitfully leaping up from the burning logs, I fell to musing on the memories of other bivouacs in bygone days.   Sometimes the picture that seemed to shape itself in the glowing embers showed a benighted party under the great rock at the foot of Yarigatake's monolithic peak.   Again, it resolved itself into a weather-bound trio sheltered for two stormy spring nights during a typhoon that roared fiendishly round a solitary shanty in the great forest that clothes the lower slopes of Fujisan.   And the bright recollections of those cheery trusty comrades in my present solitude made me realize how much the enjoyment of these wanderings is enhanced by the presence of congenial companions.

A determined effort on the following day enabled us to gain my inn at Hashiba early in the afternoon. My hunters were too done up with their exertions to accompany me into Matsumoto, and I had to take advantage of a pack horse that happened to be going into Matsumoto to send my baggage on whilst I followed at leisure. My sturdy little companions had done their work well, and their pay, of $1 (about 2s. 6d. in English money at that time) each, per day, was thoroughly earned. My chief care on reaching a centre of comparative civilisation was to first call on the local barber and then to call in the itinerant shampooer. With the latter I was already well acquainted; the former in Japan I had never employed. On entering the little shop, denoted by the orthodox European barber's pole, I was seated before a big staring mirror which had probably been brought from Yokohama. The barber, without any preliminaries, at once began on my beard of a fortnight's growth (and an unusually stiff one at that) with a tiny razor minus a handle. At my suggestion that he should use soap and water he was at first rather taken aback, but by way of humouring a foreign idiosyncrasy he complied. The water was, however, quite cold, and my request for hot was only granted with a look that betokened much inward scorn.   The Japanese beard, and there are millions of Japanese who cannot grow them, is usually scanty and soft, and those aids to the barber's skill common amongst ourselves are unneeded and almost unknown.   After luke-warm water and bitter soap of native make had been brought, my friend set to.   For a quarter of an hour I literally held on to my chair in silent agony.   I should have writhed but dare not.   At last I took advantage of a moment's pause which my tormentor made to survey his work, and dashing down my *sen* upon the chair I fled.   I finished the work in a dark corner of the verandah of my inn, and then sat down to my evening meal in peace.   This over, I called in the *amma san*, the shampooer (masseur), whose whistle may be heard in every Japanese town after nightfall.   Next to the delights of the *furō* (native hot bath) no institution I know is so delightful a boon after days of scrambling in the mountains as this. The craft has been limited to the blind from time immemorial, so that these unfortunate ones can often support, instead of being a burden to their families.   Mr. Chamberlain states* that many of them make so much money that they often turn money-lenders—for squeezing literally seems not an inappropriate training for doing so figuratively also.   As soon as it grew dark the plaintive

* "Things Japanese," p. 288.

STREET SCENE IN JAPAN.   (FROM A DRAWING BY A NATIVE ARTIST.)

[P. 189.

whistle of the reed pipe was heard outside my *shōji* at the inn, as with slow deliberation my old friend the blind man felt his way along the busy street, striking the stones with a thin iron rod he carried in his hand. "*Kami-shimo jis sen*" (lit. "Up and down for 10 sen"), is his shrill, melancholy cry, meaning that for 2*d*. he would give his customer a thorough shampooing all over. On sending for him, his shaven pate soon showed itself up the stairs. By the sound of my voice he managed to grope his way to my mosquito net where I lay on my pile of futons, arranged, I must own, uncommonly like a funeral pyre. Under the operation of his firm sensitive touch a delicious sense of repose was induced. Only the rapid thumping of his clenched fists all over my body at the close woke me from the slumber in which the operation nearly always leaves its subject. The next day's rest was spent at the lovely little village of Asama-no-yu, round whose thermal springs a class of inns has sprung up such as Matsumoto cannot boast.

On Monday morning I was up at 3 A.M. to catch the *basha* that crosses by a *shindō* ("new road"), over the hills near the Hofukuji-tōge to Uyeda on the Karuisawa-Naoetsu railway. Sasai Motoji, my landlord, had begged me to allow him to come with me, as he was anxious to climb Asamayama, whose famous volcanic peak he had often seen smoking away from the hills surrounding the

Matsumoto plain. To my astonishment, however, when we reached the *basha*, he said he couldn't come. The reason never transpired, but it was probably owing to my having hurt his feelings by demurring at his charge for getting some of my garments washed by the local " washman," at what I happened to know was seven times the orthodox rate. But, after all, that summer was an unusually memorable one in the annals of the laundryman's craft. For it was in this connection that one of the most extraordinary documents I have ever beheld went the round of the foreign settlement at Kobe. It is so good a specimen of what Mr. Chamberlain has termed " English as she is Japped," that I shall venture to reproduce it unmutilated by correction.

It was occasioned by a strike on the part of the native washmen* of Kobe, who demanded an increase in the rate of pay.† Their demands were not acceded to by their foreign employers, and an opposition company or guild was started by other Japanese washmen. Their circular soliciting support ran thus :—

" LADIES AND GENTLEMEN,

" We the washer of every kind of clothes, blankets, and " so, newly established the company and engaged the

---

* The laundry work in Japan is almost entirely done by men.

† Washing is paid for at the rate of so much per 100. A higher price sometimes is charged to ladies, as summer dresses give more work than the collars, etc. usually forming the masculine portion.

" business at no. 2582 Hachimancho, Rokuchome, Ono,
" Kobe. Contrary to our opposite company we will most
" cleanly and carefully wash our customers with possible
" chief price as follows—

 " Ladies $2   100 per.
 " Gentlemen $1.50   100 per.

 " Certain due to the day transacted : if we will mis-
" conduct for washing we will manage with equal kind or
" reasonable money for it.

 " To our earnest request & honour we wish to have
" your pleasure to let us wash your clothes & so on.

 " With your wages we will work the business.

 " The opposite company of every clotheswasher.

    " August 5th.   Meiji 25."

CHAPTER X.

The "Matchless Mountain"—Up the Nakasendō—Collapse of the *basha*
—Nakatsugawa—Ena San—"Over the hills and far away"—Tokimata
—The Tenryūgawa—A typhoon on Fuji—Over the mountain—The
policemen and the passports—An ingenious device—Reading our own
obituary notices.

To sing the praises of the "Matchless Mountain" [*] so
dear to the heart of every Japanese would be akin to
an endeavour to paint the lily or gild refined gold. So
impressed is the artistic instinct of the people of Japan—
and every individual of them is more or less of a born
artist—with its beauty of colour and of contour, that at
every turn of life the articles that are in most constant
domestic use serve as so many occasions for a reproduction
of its charms. Fans, screens, tea-things, lacquer-ware of
all sorts, the carving that adorns the interior of the house,
and the corner of the landscape garden outside, even the
clothing (of the women) worn every day, all bear some

[*] An interesting little monograph on Fuji will be found in Professor
Chamberlain's "Things Japanese," p. 178 *et seq*. This book is a remarkable little encyclopædia of useful and entertaining information on every
imaginable subject connected with the people and their land. Its com-
prehensiveness is equalled by its accuracy.

silent witness to the affectionate admiration of this nature-loving nation for one of the most striking peaks in the world. To dream of Fuji, if that vision include two cranes and three *nasubi* (egg-plants), is a sign of good fortune. As with the representation of a carp ascending a waterfall, so that of a dragon climbing the volcanic ridges of this sacred peak is an emblem of successful effort and prosperity.

The snow that covers its shoulders between the summers with a dazzling mantle rarely sullied by the foot of man is the symbol of the perfection of whiteness. For though the mountain is annually ascended by some thousands of pilgrims bent on pleasure, combined with religious zeal, it is for ten months in the year shunned with unanimous consent. The climbing season only lasts from July 15th to September 10th. During the rest of the year the pilgrims' huts are closed, and it is often almost impossible to induce any of the peasants who act as "guides" to set foot on the mountain when once its cone is enshrouded in white. A curious superstitious awe then places a cordon round its flanks, and woe betide the audacious intruder who shall dare to pass the lines!

In spite of this ban, however, occasional expeditions have been made at quite unorthodox seasons. The editor of the "Japan Mail" speaks of a party which climbed the mountain in the spring-time some five-and-twenty years

o

ago. But the experience is one that appears to be seldom repeated. Shortly after the great earthquake of October 28th, 1891, a report was spread abroad by an excitable Teuton that a vast chasm had suddenly opened in the eastern slope, about two-thirds of the way up, and great was the excitement caused among the foreign population of the country. It was, however, only a case of *"parturiunt montes, nascitur ridiculus mus."* As a matter of fact, there had been no alteration of the shape of the mountain at all. When on my way to visit the celebrated cascade of Shiraito-no-taki, at the western foot of Fuji, in the following December, I induced a "guide," much against his will, to ascend the mountain with me from the western (Murayama) side, to examine the alleged subsidence. Only by dint of making him hold on tightly by the belt of my Norfolk jacket could I manage to get him up and over the snow to the edge of the "great chasm." When we arrived there we found it was simply the old hollow at Hō-ei-zan, which had been in existence since that great excrescence was formed by the last eruption in 1709. When first the report was circulated about the "subsidence," recent falls of snow had had the effect of throwing up this hollow and the great dark lava cliffs above it, in striking relief against the surrounding white. This was observed by a party on their way to the central scene of the destruction wrought by the earthquake. The sight

H. W. Belcher, phot.

SHIRAITO-NO-TAKI, AT THE W. BASE OF FUJI-SAN.

[P. 194.

of the mountain itself naturally would suggest an enquiry as to whether Fuji herself had not been affected by the shock. And the appearance of the old hollow, which generally would have been passed by unnoticed, was now seen in a new light by persons on the look-out for proofs of the far-reaching effects of the catastrophe. Telegrams were immediately despatched to Yokohama for photographers to come and take the mountain in its new aspect. A comparison, however, of these views with others by a friend of my own (Mr. Belcher), from the same side the previous winter, showed that no change whatever had taken place in the neighbourhood in question. The peasants and priests at the villages round the base of the volcano knew nothing of any alteration, and were astonished to hear that a pamphlet had been written, *with illustrations,* describing the subsidence alleged to have been newly caused. For not only was the report current in foreign communities in Japan, but even the journal of one of the leading European Geographical Societies contained the following statement : " The sacred mountain of Japan, Fusi Yama (Rich Scholar's Peak), 14,000 feet high, ever figures in the background of Japanese scenes, but is now despoiled of much of its symmetry and beauty owing to the slipping of a huge portion of its graceful cone due to the recent earthquake."

The ascent of Fuji during the summer months is a

matter of neither danger nor difficulty, and a fairly active walker in good condition may reach the top from Suba-shiri in seven hours, inclusive of halts, whilst the descent, a good deal of which lies over the loose ashes of the southern slopes, can be accomplished in less than half that time. An objection to summer ascents is the great heat, which makes the long climb exhausting on the way up; also the haze which too often shuts out the view when one reaches the top.

Nothing, however, can be more delightful than an unorthodox scramble in the clear days of middle spring-time. My first of such ascents was made in May, 1892. Mr. Montague Fordham (of Trinity College, Cambridge) and myself made our way, with a trio of coolies, direct from Gotemba station to the Tarōbō hut, so-called from a certain goblin formerly worshipped by pilgrims at a spot in the forest at the base of the peak. From this hut to the lower edge of the snow, about 9,000 feet above sea level, all went well. The coolies, it is true, continued to scoff at the idea of our reaching the summit. They had, nevertheless, been quite willing to come (at the rate of $1 a man per day) for a certain distance (pre-determined secretly by themselves) to help us to fail. When the snow was reached, however, they flatly refused to proceed further. Seating themselves on the roof of the hut at the 6th station, they lighted their pipes and

settled themselves to watch our discomfiture, prepared
to extend us a speedy welcome back. Much to their
surprise they were able to watch us ascending nearly the
whole way over the snow, and then, after an interval,
standing on the top of the crater lip. Greatly relieved
were they when, an hour and a half after we left the top,
they were able to greet us again and express their satisfaction that their prophecies had not come true.

It was with the recollections of these delightful scrambles
that the spring of 1893 (May 8th) saw me once more,
during a ten days' holiday tour, *en route* for the matchless
mountain, fortunate in the companionship of Messrs. Noel
E. Buxton and H. W. L. O'Rorke, both of Trinity College,
Cambridge. Our plan was to pass along the southern end
of the Nakasendō; to explore an interesting mountain,
Ena San, south of the Komagatake of Shinshū, and then
to cross the range between the two. This would bring us
down to the valley of the Tenryū-gawa, which we could
descend to the coast, and so proceed eastwards to Suzukawa for our ascent of Fuji's snows. At the outset,
however, we were brought face to face with a difficulty,
habited in the dull, dark-blue uniform of a Japanese
police constable. We had left the Tōkaidō railway at
Gifu station, and were about to engage *jinrikisha* to
take us as far as Ōta, where we were to spend the
night. On emerging from the station, however, the stolid

guardian of the peace politely demanded our passports, and after a careful examination, handed them back with the remark that he couldn't allow us to proceed. " Why not ?" we asked. " Because your passports only entitle you to travel in the *Fuji-mi-jū-san-shū.** The province you are now in is Mino, and as Mino is not one of the ' Thirteen ' round Fuji, you may not travel in it."

This was a crushing blow. As soon, however, as we had recovered ourselves a little we tried to gradually draw off his thoughts into a somewhat different channel. We asked him if he had ever climbed Ena San himself. No ? Then had he any idea of the best way of getting near it ? Was the Nakasendō in fairly good condition between Gifu and Ōta ? and so on. Finally the little man's thoughts became so thoroughly diverted from his original contention, that he not only handed back our passports, but actually engaged for us *jinrikisha* (at a much lower price than we could have got them ourselves) to take us in the very direction he had flatly refused at first to let us go !

Soon we were merrily rattling out of Gifu by the road

* *Fuji-mi-jū-san-shū*, " the Thirteen provinces from which Fuji is visible." *i.e.*, Musashi, Bōshū, Kazusa, Shimōsa, Hitachi, Shimotsuke, Kōtsuke, Shinshū, Kōshū, Tōtōmi, Suruga, Idzu, and Sagami. These thirteen provinces until recently constituted one of the divisions for which passports were granted to foreign travellers. As a matter of fact, though it is not generally known, Fuji can be seen, from mountain tops, in several other provinces still further distant, *e.g.*, Yari-ga-take and Tateyama in Hida, Ena San in Mino, Asama-yama (not the great volcano) in Ise, and others.

that joins the Nakasendō near Kanō. Most of the houses
here were new, having been rebuilt after the earthquake
of 1891, from which the great broad plain will yet take
long to fully recover. As we drew near the edge of the
rice-fields the road passed through a plantation of young
pines, whose branches diffused a delicious scent on the
fresh air of the waning spring afternoon. Then on the
right grand bluffs rose abruptly from the green waters
of the swift Kisogawa, overtopped by the pagoda-like
keep of the old castle of Inuyama. At length a three
hours' run deposited us at Ōta, where our pretty quarters
at the Iwaya were soon littered with *kōri* and *rücksacks*
in that hopeless state of confusion to which the foreigner's
advent invariably reduces his room incredibly quickly.

By way of gaining time the next day, we ordered
overnight a *basha* to take us to Ochiai, 38 miles distant,
which we had determined to make our starting-point for
Ena San. It was not until 8 A.M. that the machine was
ready to start. But when once it was on the move, its
behaviour promised well for affording a solution of the
problem of perpetual motion. The appearance of the
basha in general has already been likened to a cross
between a hearse and an ambulance waggon. On this
occasion in particular it came very nearly fulfilling the
functions of one if not of both these vehicles. A horse
of attenuated frame was tied by odds and ends of straps

and strings between the shakiest of shafts. The driver was a smooth-pated old individual of repulsive mien, who, it ultimately transpired, had never held rein before. A small boy of large self-importance performed on a tin horn painfully penetrating of sound, with a view to frightening away any wayfarers deaf enough not to have been already warned by the hideous rattling of the shaky turn-out. A general superintendence of the whole was exercised by a white-haired cur of diminutive size, but of ubiquitous activity. Part of his time was spent in hurrying on ahead to clear the way in case horn and rattle should have failed to do so, the rest in scurrying excitedly back with an air of "Don't be afraid ; leave it all to me, and I'll see you safely through."

Here and there the road crossed the deep current of the swift, silent Kisogawa, or one of its affluents, by picturesque wooden bridges springing from side to side of verdure-clad banks. For the most part the state of the highway left much to be desired, and occasionally long détours by bye-paths were necessary. Near Fushimi one of these was the means of lending additional zest to the proceedings. Our extraordinary "one-hoss shay" had just arrived at an unusually rutty bit of an unusually rutty road. The place, indeed, was so bad that I was obliged, in order to relieve a knee recently injured in a football match, to get out and walk. I thus had an excellent view of the wild gyrations

of the vehicle as it lurched and rolled from side to side.
On the right I noticed the overhanging roofs of some
wayside cottages projecting far into the road. To
my amazement, the coachman drove full tilt at them,
and the roof of the *basha* not being low enough to pass
underneath, was jammed with a grand crash against the
nearest eave. The faces of my genial companions within
the vehicle afforded a delightful study, but only for a
moment. They soon disappeared, for the driver instead of
backing his horse, whipped it up with the stick he wielded,
and did his best to carry away the roof of the house
with that of the cart. For a few seconds there was a
sound of rending timbers, and with a drunken lurch the
vehicle slowly parted in twain. With a violent tug
the horse pursued his course, accompanied by the shafts
and the fore part of the *basha*. The rest of the crazy
structure then slowly toppled over, and my companions
were as completely shut out from view as the light of the
nocturnal candle by the descending extinguisher. In a
few minutes, however, the wreck was resolved into its
component parts. All shoulders to the wheel helped to
reduce chaos to comparative order, and the puzzle was put
together once more. The iron pin that had helped to
fasten the two parts of the carriage together, now lost, was
replaced by a bit of rag, the harness was strengthened
by the addition of the driver's *obi* (a cotton girdle) in-

geniously fixed as a crupper, and this proved to be the most stable part of the whole turn-out.   So much time had now been lost that at Kamado we exchanged *basha* for *jinrikisha*, which just enabled us to gain Nakatsugawa as twilight quickly faded into night.   Our enquiries here resulted in a determination to go no further, but to attempt the ascent of our peak without proceeding to Ochiai at all.   At the "Tamaruya" the landlord received us most cordially, but warned us earnestly against having anything to do with the sacred peak until the *Kannushi*—the guardian of the mountain shrine at the foot—had formally opened it with the usual *yama-biraki* in the month of June.   With a mournful air he listened to our decision that we intended to start without delay, and was astonished to hear that so far from the snow being likely, as he maintained, to swallow us up, we should welcome its presence as an aid to the ascent.   Finding he couldn't dissuade us from the climb, he withdrew and did his best to get us a couple of good coolies to act as our porters on it.   A pouring rain kept us indoors most of the day after our arrival, but the time passed quickly enough nevertheless.   The little garden on which our verandah opened, afforded pleasant food for reflection on the artistic refinement of the Japanese mind.   It was not more than 20 feet square, and yet it was a veritable landscape in miniature.   In a tiny pond a carp and sundry gold-fish

flashed their glittering scales to and fro. A couple of baby
waterfalls, half hidden in foliage, fell with musical splash
into their rocky basin, and a little stream glanced under
the shadow of a diminutive forest of azaleas, maples and
firs. With such a picture as this framed within the limits
of our verandah, no day, however wet, could pass drearily
away. The delightful irregularity was in itself artistic
and forbade all sense of monotony.

The next morning broke brilliant and cool. A cloudless
sky, keen fresh air, and Nature in all the brightness of her
fresh spring attire were ours. A two or three miles march
across the rice-fields to the S.E. of Nakatsugawa took us
past the temple of Hachiman (the God of War), standing,
half-hidden, within a grove of stately cryptomeria. An
hour later we had turned northwards up a valley (the
Shōgwani-dani), and reached the shrine of Ena-jinsha,
where the coolies said a prayer in passing to the *genius
loci* for protection and safe return. We were now at
a height of 2,400 feet, and a clamber up a steep, wooded
spur, inclined at exactly the right angle for quick progress, took us up 1,100 feet more in half-an-hour.
Leaving the deciduous trees below, we pass on through
varieties of pines, beneath whose dark branches tall
azaleas bear a glorious wealth of delicate white flowers.
The undergrowth is chiefly bamboo grass, so the view
between the stems of the taller trees is unimpeded, and

from time to time the grand snow-clad cone of Ontake gleams, westwards, against a sky of deepest blue. Higher up the ridge a pine of yew-like foliage, but like the silver-fir in form, is succeeded by yet another resembling spruce. From far below, on the northern side of the ridge, the dull roar of a mountain torrent is borne up on the still air. Close at hand, the soft coo of invisible doves echoes through the silent forest. No difficulties had barred our progress upwards, though here and there we had to cross or climb the *débris* of a landslip that needed care. The first snow was reached at 5,500 feet, and this soon landed us on the southern *arête* of the mountain, which we then followed to the summit. But the snow was soft, for the angle was not steep, and the last 1,500 feet cost us two hours' hard work. At every step, almost, one plunged in knee-deep, and occasionally deeper still. At length came a marvellous transition. In the cold, silent forest, where the deep snow reached the branches of the tall pines, mid-winter reigned. But as the highest point (7,350 feet) was gained, a few steps took us down, on the eastern side of the ridge, into all the radiance and warmth and freedom of glorious spring-time. The top (which we reached at 12·45) consists of three nearly equal peaks, in an undulating ridge that stretches north and south. The northernmost is the highest, and this and the middle one have each a tiny shrine. A surveying

station also lifts its skeleton-like wooden steeple on the
loftiest point. To the glorious prospect the pen can
do but little justice. In extent it greatly resembles
that from the tall neighbouring peak of Komagatake.*
The eye sweeps over a semi-circle of the giants of Japan,
each still wearing their snowy robes of virgin white on
their massive shoulders. Perhaps the most striking
feature of the whole is the graceful form, due east, of
Akaiishi San, over whose southern shoulder looks the peerless Fuji, a truncated cone of sharpest outline, standing,
snow-clad, against a cloudless sky.

Three hours sped all too swiftly by as we basked in the
warm sunshine and brewed our cocoa over a fire made of
brushwood by the side of a convenient patch of snow.
All the while, at our very feet, spread a boundless expanse
of richly-wooded hills that faded away in the haze of
distance to the Gifu plain. Owing to the descent being
delayed by my injured knee, it was dark long before we
reached the base of the mountain. A solitary farmhouse
on the edge of the forest afforded us welcome rest and
refreshment. One roof sheltered family and flock, for the
building served as home and stable all in one. The farmer
brewed a supply of *tamago-zake*, a sort of " egg-flip," made
by stirring beaten eggs and sweetened *sake* over a slow
fire. Nakatsugawa was reached at 10·30 P.M.

* Cf. p. 49.

The first business the next day was to pay our bill. This was moderate enough in prices, but included an item for 140 eggs. But, then, Japanese eggs are very small, and these had been our mainstay during three days. At every meal (and these, especially on the rainy day, were frequent) they appeared—but as quickly disappeared—in the form of pancakes or of omelettes ; either fried, boiled, poached, or as a substitute for milk. We had brought with us my native cook to save us time and trouble in two important respects—viz., in preparing meals, and in wrangling with coolies, &c., on the various occasions when their services had to be engaged.

From Nakatsugawa we crossed from the Nakasendō to the Ina-Kaidō by the Misaka-tōge (4,975 feet), a pass leading over the northern slopes of Ena-San, and then down to the valley of the Tenryūgawa by one of the loveliest ravines it has ever been my good fortune to traverse. High up, on the eastern side of the pass, a tiny shrine was sentinelled by two giant cryptomeria, one of which measured, at a height of five feet above the ground, no less than 26 feet in girth. Below this, here and there, stood scattered farmhouses, with their gardens radiant in the various tints of cherry-, pear-, peach-blossom, and camellias, here blooming at slightly varying altitudes in the hills as a few weeks before we had seen them in the plains. Little notice was taken of us, oddly enough, by the people. They said no foreigners had crossed the pass before, and they confided to the cook that they thought we were an unusually large variety of their own countrymen not usually seen in this region! One old lady refused to believe we were *gwai-koku-jin* ("outside-countries-men"—*i.e.*, foreigners), as she had never heard that such beings existed. Japan was her only world, good soul. As we passed down the deep valley the afternoon sunlight cast its soft radiance on the wooded hillsides and lit up every shade of green above the turquoise waters of the rushing torrent. The verdure of the banks was picked out with continual blazes of colour from azaleas of every tint, varying from deep pink to snowy white. At 8 P.M. we reached Komamba, where the valley widens and merges into the open plain, within sight of the great mountains of the Kōshū range. Here we failed to get the *jinrikisha* we had been promised, and were reduced to a *ni-guruma* (a coolie's cart with two wheels). After an hour and a half's delay the baggage was transferred from the pack-horse we had brought thus far, and on the top of all I reposed in state, for my knee was now too bad to allow me to walk. With the aid of my stalwart companions, the coolies succeeded in dragging the cart over the rough, stony roads, a distance of five miles further, to Nakamura, where another halt to search for *jinrikisha* was called. Much persuasion (it was now nearly midnight) was needed to induce the village *kurumaya* to leave their *futon*.

First raised his voice in eloquent entreaty the ex-President of the Cambridge Union, seated in a commanding situation on the top of a miniature Fuji of road-mending boulders. To him added judicious reasoning the dignified director of many English institutions, who, though entitled at home to sit on many boards, had on this occasion to be content with another road-side heap of stones. Our combined efforts at last prevailed, and a couple of hours' further jolting over a road that in the pitchy darkness, accentuated by the feeble glimmer of the *chōchin's* yellow light, brought us to the Umenoya at Tokimata. Here, at the unearthly hour of 1·15 A.M., we knocked up the soundly-slumbering inmates of the inn. They received us with no less apparent pleasure than if we had been long-expected friends. A brief rest preceded an early breakfast, and then came the renewed delights of the 12 hours' "shoot" of the rapids of the swift Tenryū-gawa. Borne on the bosom of the great river through the heart of the dark mountain mass, where it irresistibly cleaves itself a passage, we sped onwards to the Pacific shore. Here, at Hamamatsu, we caught the midnight train, and reached Suzukawa, near the foot of Fuji, in the small hours of the morning. Grand and majestic this queen of volcanoes looked in the moonlight on her throne

FUJI-SAN, WITH CLOUD CAP, FROM THE SOUTH-WEST.

[P. 209.

of rock, with her mantle of snow and a glittering diadem
of stars. It is from Suzukawa that the finest near view of
the mountain is gained. The whole 12,400 feet of her
height are seen in one vast sweep from the sands of the
Pacific Ocean. The inclination is quite gradual until near
the top, where it steepens rather quickly to about 35°.

As we lay on our *futon* that morning the maids came
and slid aside the *shōji* to show us, without our stirring,
the mountain in all its glory against the background of a
cloudless sky. By-and-by, however, white vapours gathered
round the summit, and before mid-day these formed themselves into a cap of clouds that fitted the upper part with
perfect symmetry, and then rose high above in widening
spirals, gradually disappearing into space. As we strolled
on to the sea-shore during the afternoon a party of
Japanese officials and their families politely invited us to
share a picnic they were having on the sands, sheltered from
the sun under a temporary awning. One of the village
policemen also made friends with us, and told us he was a
Christian, and that, besides himself, there were some 50
others in the neighbourhood.

Monday morning, May 15th, beheld us at last fairly
started on our climb. A shaky little horse tramway took
us seven miles on to Ōmiya. Here I hired a pack-horse, to
save my knee, and in spite of the evil forebodings of the
villagers and their policemen, we started off for Murayama,

P

the south-western gateway to the sacred summit. An hour and a half over undulating moorland brought us to the great pilgrim's hostelry, kept by the widow Fujimasa, whose husband was the hereditary guardian of this side of the peak. Close by the inn, in a dark grove of cryptomeria, stands the temple of Fuji Sen-gen. This marks the *Omoteguchi*, or " front entrance," for the Murayama route was long regarded as the favourite one, especially by pilgrims coming from Kyōtō and the west.

A couple of hours over moorland, prairie, and forest glades brought us to *Umagaeshi* ("horse send back place "), regarded as the uppermost limit to which horses can be taken. From this hut, at a height of 4,400 feet, we shouldered our baggage ourselves, or rather my friends and the coolies did, and proceeded on foot. At 5,000 feet we passed the remains of the *Nionindō* hut, which, in bygone days, guarded the upper part of the mountain from the desecration of woman's tread. A few bleached and shattered chips lie scattered round in fit emblem of the now—even in Japan—exploded notion of feminine unfitness for mountaineering. Another half-hour landed us, in gathering gloom and damp, at the Ōmomi hut, a somewhat dilapidated shanty in the pine forest that clothes these lower flanks. Since the coolies assured us no water could be got higher up, we decided to spend the night here. As we lifted the section of one side of the building, that did duty for a door, the prospect was anything but inviting. A long room, 20 feet by 15, with a floor some 18 inches above the ground, was all we saw inside. The boards of the flooring had mostly been removed and burnt for firewood by the last occupants some eight months ago. At one end an open space did duty for a fireplace, but no chimney provided an outlet for the smoke. As the roof was the only part of the structure in good repair, this had to make its way out by the cracks and chinks in the rotting walls, but not before a good deal had filled our eyes and noses and lungs. Whilst Buxton and I unpacked the baggage and superintended fire-making, O'Rorke and one of the trio of coolies dived into a steep gully at hand, and, in the darkness, went in quest of water. The expected spring had vanished, and only a little was to be got from tiny stagnant pools. After a substantial meal we settled ourselves for the night. A long log of wood formed a common pillow. A fire at our feet was fed during the night by our coolies, whose ceaseless chatter was of the most doleful sort, full of dire prophecies of coming evil for our presumption.

The next day broke on prospects dismal to a degree. The barometer, the rain, the spirits of the coolies—all were falling with painful steadiness. During the morning a typhoon burst upon the mountain, and (as we subsequently learned) its effects were felt in Tōkyō and elsewhere, and

caused our friends considerable alarm for our safety.
Towards evening the wind dropped, and then our hopes
rose higher, for a spring storm on one day here so often
guarantees a brilliant day to follow. The morning realized
our most sanguine expectations. A cloudless sky looked
through the tops of the tall dark pines, and the air was as
keen and clear as could be wished. The only disappointment was caused by the insane carelessness of the coolies.
By way of drying our boots during the night, they had
stuck them in the burning embers—and left them there
—with very natural results. O'Rorke's had suffered most,
and his prolonged struggles in getting them on only resulted
in rending the uppers from the soles to a degree beyond
the possibility of healing. Strings, travelling cap, *waraji*,
handkerchief—all at intervals during the day came into
requisition. Only the pluckiest perseverance, during 12
hours on snow and rough volcanic ash, enabled our burly
companion to complete the climb with success. At 7 A.M.
we left the hut. In it we also left our baggage, with the
most despondent of the three coolies to act as caretaker.
Above the hut we crossed the track of an avalanche, where
great firs had been laid low like so many matches by its
irresistible force. After a struggle with a stretch of soft
deep snow we quitted the forest and zigzagged through the
stunted larches and alders that straggled thinly above.
Here and there a rib of lava rock thrust itself darkly

through the snow, and offered better going. At a height of
8,000 feet the coolies began to mutter, and almost burst
into tears at the prospect of the great slopes of snow that
stretched above them.

Their *waraji,* they said, wouldn't hold out. They had
only brought an extra pair each, as they didn't expect
we should really try to reach the top. Accordingly, the
feeblest of the pair was dismissed, and sent to keep his
friend company at the hut, whilst his spare sandals were
handed to the last of the trio that remained. Him we
succeeded in taking to the top, aided by the efforts of the
cook, whose spirits were of the cheeriest, for he scrambled
about on rock and snow in sheer lightsomeness of heart at so
novel an experience. No difficulties now hindered our upward way at a single point. By 1·15 P.M. we had reached
the crater lip. Then came a steep slope of snow leading to
Ken-ga-mine (the " sword peak "), and at 1·45 we were on
the actual summit, the loftiest spot in the Empire of the
Rising Sun. No other peak rises within 2,000 feet of this,
and Fuji is so immense relatively to its surroundings that
all else is dwarfed by comparison. From the summit the
view is that of some vast relief map. Varying tints and
shades lie over lake and forest, river, sea, and plain.
Westwards and to the north-west the grandest objects of
the landscape are the snow-clad heights of the Japanese
Alps, with the Komagatake range, and, nearer still, the

Kōshū peaks and Akaiishi, rising up between us and them. Far away east and south stretch the blue waters of the Pacific, whose breakers curl in white lines at the mountain's base, 12,400 feet below. At our very feet the great crater presents an extraordinary sight. Excepting where the inner walls rise too abruptly from the crater floor to allow it to rest, ice or snow spreads a dazzling winding-sheet over nearly the whole mountain top. Here and there huge icicles hang blue against the deep dull red and purple of the rocks inside the crater lip. All is cold and still as the grave. It is soon a positive relief to turn from all this deathly whiteness to let the eye rest on the vast expanse of country clad in all the tender freshness and warmth of colour of its young spring life. The devices of man are remote enough not to disturb, and it is good to be for a while in the pure clear atmosphere of a region where

"Beyond earth's voices there is peace."

Grandly full of meaning come the words of Milton's great hymn of praise :—

> "These are thy glorious works, Parent of Good,
> Almighty. Thine this universal frame
> Thus wondrous fair ! Thyself how wondrous then !
> Unspeakable ! Who sittest above these heavens,
> To us invisible, or dimly seen
> In these Thy lowest works—yet these declare
> Thy goodness beyond thought, and power divine."
> *Paradise Lost*, Bk. V.

As we looked eastwards towards the Hakone hills, and

then on to the promontory of Idzu, stretching far out into
the sea, our minds became possessed with a desire to make
the most of our chances, and to descend on that side instead
of returning by the way we had come. We therefore
sent down the coolie and our cook to the hut, with
instructions to gather up our baggage and bring it round
the mountain to us at Gotemba the next day. We then
applied ourselves to the descent to that village alone. As
the air was brilliantly clear, we could see at the end of the
thin yellow thread, that marked the track in the forest, the
tiny mouse-coloured specks that told us where its cottages
lay in the cultivated fields 11,000 feet below. Straight
down the snow we went. But for my injured knee all
would have been perfectly simple, but a ruptured ligament
caused intense pain at every step, as soon as the hard snow
had been glissaded over, and the soft ashes below had to be
ploughed through. Fortunately we were all three in good
condition, and my stalwart companions were equal to
any amount of work, and with Eton on one side and
Harrow on the other, as supporters or carriers, I managed
to reach more level ground without misadventure. Close
by the Tarōbō hut an aged anchorite sat, silent and
motionless, on a little platform he had erected as a place
for meditation and prayer. He told us, in answer to
our questions, that he had come to gain purity and self-
control, so, with water as his only food, and the trees of the

forest as his sole companions, he had located himself here
as the spot most conducive to these ends. At the first
inhabited farmhouse in the forest we stopped for food, and
joyfully I learned that a pack-horse could be had for hire.
When the animal was produced, a small boy tied a piece of
straw rope round the creature's head, and, with a *chōchin*
to light the way, he bade me mount. It was easier said
than done, however, for as soon as I was being shoved up
by my friends on to the folded *futon* that served for saddle
the charger pranced and pirouetted in an alarming manner.
Then our host came to the rescue. Seizing a foreleg, he
doubled it up, with a view to checking its activity. His
meaning was misunderstood, for my steed began to rear and
plunge in a way that scattered the bystanders in confusion.
Ultimately he reduced Bucephalus to submission and
temporary inaction by tying his forelegs together and
enveloping his head in a large bag. Buxton then took me
on his shoulders, and, with a mighty heave, shot me up on
to the top of the pile of quilts that padded the creature's
bony back. And so the caravan arrived at Gotemba
station inn at 10 P.M. Handing over my passport to the
landlord for police inspection, I departed to the " honourable hot bath " with Buxton, for the tub was of capacious
size. Soon, however, a rattling at the wooden grating
that serves as a window disturbed us. A snub-nosed
red-faced little maid poked in her oily head and re-

quested me to come at once—the police wanted me. After a necessary delay I went and found a couple of constables shaking their heads over my passport. "It won't do," they said; "your passport has expired, you must return at once." I pointed out the rule, printed on the back of my passport, which directs that if the journey be not finished before the date for which the passport is granted has expired, the holder must at once inform H. B. M.'s Minister by post of the fact. This, I said, I had done, and I was now on my way to Miyanoshita, where I expected letters which would set the matter straight. But the worthy officers couldn't see it at all in my light.

For an hour they argued, and only departed at midnight with the injunction that I must take the first train back to Kōbe on the following day. At 5 A.M. I was roused by the maid, who announced the return of the police, and not until 10·30 A.M. did they finally take their leave for good. The way they got out of their difficulty was undeniably odd. They explained that *their* view of the situation would not allow them to permit me to leave Gotemba with my friends by the direct Miyanoshita track. "That wouldn't do," they said; "but what you may do is this— We will order you to go to Kōbe (which lies 300 miles westwards—a nice stroll for a lame man all alone!). Leave the village by its western end, and then when you come to a railway crossing you can go over the line and the path will curve round so that you will meet your friends in the fields beyond." This kindly suggestion was duly followed, and Miyanoshita with all its luxuries received us at the conclusion of a fourteen miles tramp in pouring rain over the *Otome-tōge*—" the Maiden's Pass." Two days later my genial companions bade me farewell at Kōzu station. As I was getting into the train for Kōbe a foreign acquaintance gravely put into my hands a newspaper containing a thrilling account of a disaster on Fuji San. Some foreign travellers, supposed to be British (as they alone take pleasure in such risks), had started from Ōmiya to ascend the mountain. Shortly afterwards a violent storm broke over it, and as days had passed without the travellers returning to the village, they had, without doubt, perished miserably. It was very odd, later on at intervals, to read translations from native papers commenting on the catastrophe, and picturing in thrilling vein the tale of our destruction! Shortly after we separated O'Rorke heard from a Tōkyō shopkeeper *his* version of the accident. In commenting on it the worthy man maintained that it was but a punishment from the goddess of the mountain, and the foreigners thoroughly deserved their fate for their irreverence in presuming to climb the peak before it was duly " opened." The commentator enjoyed a hearty laugh at his own expense when O'Rorke revealed his identity as one of the offenders !

CHAPTER XI.

The Alps from end to end—Earthquakes—Across Japan—Naoetsu—A land-slip—The boatmen of Itoigawa—'Not knowing children nor parents'—A curious inscription—A hospitable headman—An obliging policeman—Primitive bathing-houses—'The Lotus Peak.'

THE programme of my fourth and final summer visit to the Alps of Central Japan, in 1894, was to traverse the entire range from north to south. By doing so, and climbing the chief peaks I had not hitherto ascended, I hoped to gain a truer conception of the main features of the chain as a whole. The issue proved the experiment a great success. It put one in a position to fully appreciate the value of such a work as Sir William Conway's splendid volume on his travels along " The Alps from end to end," and enabled me to realize that an " excentric " mountaineer is not necessarily an eccentric one.

My party consisted of my friends H. J. Hamilton[*] of Nagoya, and Uraguchi Bunji of Kōbe. The former had had plenty of experience of camp life and travel in the Canadian Rockies, and undertook the duties of chief cook

[*] Of the Trinity College (Toronto) Anglican Mission.

and photographer to our expedition. The latter, an archæologist of some experience, proved equally invaluable in other ways, particularly in the investigation of native customs and superstitions, the study of which helped to make our journey doubly interesting.

Our starting point was Tōkyō, where, late at night, after a pleasant interview with the obliging Secretary of the Imperial Geographical Society, we arrived at our hotel— the "Naguraya," near Uyeno station—just in time for a sudden and sharp shock of earthquake. It was the last of the many I experienced during my stay in Japan, but the sensation then was just as odd and uncanny as the first. The foreign resident is generally supposed to pass through a three-fold transition of feeling in this respect. His first sensation is said to be that of amusement, the second of indifference, and the third of a devout desire to never feel another.

The night spent at the "Naguraya" was unusually oppressive, and rendered the more uncomfortable by reason of our being located in the best room; for it is nearly always the chief apartments in the Japanese inn that are situated in the most " smelly " quarters. From Tōkyō we travelled by train right across the main island to Naoetsu —from the Pacific coast to the shores of the Sea of Japan : thus traversing Hondō almost at its widest part within the day. Exclusive of a halt of three hours or

so at Nagano—where, by the courtesy of the officials at
the Observatory, I was allowed to compare my instruments with theirs—the journey occupied exactly twelve
hours, and covered 180 miles. The visit to the "Furukawaya" at Naoetsu was by no means a success. The heat
from the bath-room—which was situated immediately
below ours—combined with the smells outside and the
fleas within, considerably interfered with our slumbers.

At 6·30 A.M. (July 19th) we made our way to the
beach, and amid a crowd of country-folk—bound westwards like ourselves — we boarded a huge *sampan*
(Japonicè *ko-bune,* lit. "baby-ship"), the ordinary fishing-
boat of these coasts, and were pulled off to a small steamer
that runs between Naoetsu and Itoigawa, and now lay
anchored half a mile from shore. On the beach a number
of hawkers offered for sale boxes of *awa-ame,* a much-
prized sweetmeat made of millet. It is regarded as the
meibutsu ("special production") of Takata, a town some
four miles away. Picturesque cliffs, dotted here and there
with tea-houses and country villas belonging to residents
of Naoetsu, rise steeply from the long stretch of sandy
beach where bathers disport themselves in considerable
numbers. Ten miles from Naoetsu the bare face of a
landslip tells where once the village of Nadachi stood.
The place was cleanly wiped out by the catastrophe, but
has now been rebuilt some distance to the west. Far to

the south rises the summit of Ō Renge, "the great Lotus Peak," the highest summit in the northern part of the Japanese Alps, and the first on our list of prospective new acquaintances. By 9·30 A.M. our thirty miles run came to an end at Itoigawa. Sturdy dark copper-coloured boatmen rowed us ashore, and beached their craft for us to land. The get-up of these was scantier than usual, their costumes being chiefly composed—like those of the traditional Irishman—of fresh air. Some had the loin-cloth round the waist, others wore a towel round their head, whilst others wore nothing at all. The paddles they used were enormous wooden spoons with a T-shaped handle. Itoigawa consists mainly of a long line of houses just above the beach, close by the east branch of the Himekawa. A curious effect is produced by the long galleries running in front of the lower storeys of the dwellings. These afford a means of passage from house to house when the streets are, as is often the case, deep blocked with winter snows. The excessive snow-fall in this region, and on the north-western spurs of the main chain of the Japanese Alps, is an interesting phenomenon. The explanation is nevertheless simple enough. As the cold, dry, north-westerly wind sweeps over from Siberia across the Sea of Japan, it there mingles with a warmer and moister air, so that when it finally reaches the western face of the range this moisture is precipitated in an abundant snow-

fall on the west flanks and summits of the range. Consequently, in the winter and early spring an extraordinary
contrast strikes the traveller. On the west the valleys lie
deep in snow under a sky often hidden in a dark veil of
clouds. On the east, however, for months together a
bright sky smiles on valleys and plains comparatively
uncovered. It is to meet the exigencies of this heavy
snow-fall that these galleries are constructed. The
inhabitants are sometimes compelled to live in the upper
storey, and additional light and air are then admitted
through a paper window in a sort of chimney. So deeply
are whole villages occasionally buried that the various
houses can only be distinguished by sign posts stuck in the
snow or fixed on the roofs. The following sort of inscriptions are then employed to point out public buildings :—

"The Post Office is beneath this spot.".

"You will find the Police Station buried below."

In spite, however, of the abundance of this winter snow-
fall no traces of glaciers or of glacial action have been
discovered. No moraines, striated rocks, or erratic blocks
bear witness to the presence of those forces that in many
lands have done, or are doing so much to modify the
features of the face of the country.

But this is a digression. Depositing our baggage at
the "Furukawaya," a modest inn in equally modest

surroundings, we set off westwards, along the coast road, on a trip to the celebrated cliffs that form the northern end of the Alpine chain.* Outside the village we crossed the broad pebbly bed of the Hime-kawa, now almost dried up, though bridges of boats speak eloquently of what the state of the river may be at other times. Three or four miles further we passed the lime-kilns of Ōmi, where limestone is burnt for manure. Beyond this the road rises in the face of precipitous granite cliffs. The blue waves that hurl themselves against their white bases, almost wet with their flying spray the trees and shrubs that clothe their upper slopes. Rocks of fantastic shape lie here and there in the water at their feet, known to the country folk as the "tortoise" rock, the "cat" rock, and so on. The two most noted spots along the whole coast next are reached—*"Ko-shirazu"* and *"Ōya-shira-zu,"* *i.e.,* "not knowing children," and "not knowing parents." Here the tide recedes very little at all. In the days before the road we were now on was constructed, the only means of passage was by the beach. At times, during north-westerly gales, it was only at considerable risk it could be made, and it became a case of *sauve qui peut.* Hence it gained its native name, for it was

---

* The range is of dissimilar geological structure, and its peaks are of different ages. Briefly it may be described as a backbone or axis of granitic rocks, through or over which vast quantities of igneous and volcanic rocks have from time to time been poured.

H. J. Hamilton, phot.

OYASHIRADZU, THE NORTHERN POINT OF THE JAPANESE ALPS. [P. 224.

held that then no one could afford to render aid even to his dearest and best, all energies being needed in "looking after No. 1." The *Ko-shirazu* passage is some half a mile in length, while further on comes the *Ōya-shirazu*,

ON THE SEA OF JAPAN.

which is nearly two and a half miles. It is these granite cliffs that form the starting-point of the range of the Alps, that only sinks down into the plains of Mino, nearly a hundred miles away due south. A grand view of the Toyama Bay, with fishing-boats flashing their white sails

Q

in the summer sun, spread itself below as we reached our furthest point. Here the road is at its best. Level and smooth for some distance, it rises to a height of some 500 feet in the tallest cliff. The spot is marked by an inscription cut in the face of the living rock, " *To no gotoku, ya no gotoshi* " ("As smooth as a whetstone, and as straight as an arrow "). On our way back we stopped at Ōmi, and paid a visit to the maker of the road. He told us the characters which read as above form a quotation from the *Shi-Kyo,* a collection of Chinese standard poetry. He was so proud of his achievement, that when the road was completed he could not resist adding this memorial in praise of his skill.

After the broiling afternoon, a bathe in the sea from one of the fishing-boats near the village was more than welcome. The waters east of Itoigawa are famous for their fish, large quantities being taken of *karei* (a sort of plaice or sole), *hirame* (a kind of brill), and *tai* (sea bream). The last-named is especially esteemed by the Japanese, who have a saying, " *Kusattemo tai* " (*lit.* "Though it is bad even to smelling, still it is *tai*," *i.e.* it is always so good).

The evening was spent in receiving a visit from a couple of policemen. The one came as an official, to inspect our passports : the other as a friend, to give us information (for which I had previously written to the inspector of this district) about our proposed routes. They were both politeness and kindness itself.

The heat of Itoigawa made us glad to flee from the sea, and hasten towards the coolness and shade of the valleys inland. At 9 A.M. (July 20th) we turned our backs upon the village and passed along the right bank of the Hime-kawa to the entrance of the valley whence the river enters the plain. The country side here is thinly populated, and the châlet-like farmhouses and cottages present few tokens of prosperity. The peasants are as polite as usual, and the salute of an occasional grey-headed patriarch is a thing worth coming for. Fifteen miles up the valley we halted at the house of the *sonchō* (head man) of the district, where the domestics, in their master's absence, politely welcomed us. By this time our party had received an addition in the person of one Yamazaki Junsa, the policeman in charge of this region. We had been told at Itoigawa to look out for him, and fortunately caught him up at a wayside cottage. He at once fell in with our plans, and not only did his best to gain informa-tion for us, but insisted on accompanying us during the four or five days we were in these parts. He was imperturbably good-tempered and obliging. When I chanced to fall out of my hammock during the night and landed on him as he lay peacefully slumbering below, he would never refer to the inconvenience he

Q 2

suffered beyond offering a polite and humble apology for being in the way (" *O jama wo itashi-mashita*," " I have caused an honourable hindrance ").

As both Hamilton and myself had suffered the previous day from a sharp attack of fever, our start for Ō Renge— on Saturday, July 21st—did not take place till 10·30 A.M. With a couple of baggage coolies, we went along the left bank of the Himekawa for a few hundred yards to its point of junction with the Ōdokoro-gawa. Crossing the latter by a well-made wooden bridge we turned off and followed the ravine, down which it dashes, for the rest of our walk. As the track mounted the side of the valley we passed the sheds of woodcutters, who make up the trunks of *sugi* (*Cryptomeria Japonica*) trees into planks and shingling. This is the chief occupation of the peasants of the neighbourhood. At the last hamlet on the route an old lady came out, as we passed her cottage door, with a polite invitation, " Since you have got so far, please honourably deign to rest," and forthwith went into her grimy little kitchen to brew us " honourable tea." Still our path ascended, at length passing through a dense forest where magnificent hydrangeas lighted up the gloom with a wealth of blooms, varying in colour from blue and pink to most delicate white. A stiff pull of 1,500 feet up a steep spur known as Hatchōzaka, " the Half Mile hill " (considerably longer, as a matter-of-fact), landed us

H. J. Hamilton, phot.

BATH-HOUSES AT RENGE ONSEN.

[P. 229.

on a ridge commanding a fine prospect of a grandly timbered valley beyond.

A terribly rough track, chiefly composed of mud and slippery stones, brought us, by 5 P.M., to the goal of our walk—the Renge Onsen—where primitive bath-houses cluster round the thermal sulphur springs that gush out from the mountain side at an altitude of 5,000 feet. The arrival of a pair of foreigners caused no little astonishment amongst the three dozen rustics who had come to take the waters, and the caretaker who had charge of the establishment. None of them, we were told, had ever seen a foreigner before, so our ways and doings were watched with interested curiosity. The accompanying illustration gives a good idea of the arrangements of the *yuba*. Three little wooden tanks sunk in the earth, and sheltered by a boarded roof, lie in a row on one side of the inclosure, which is shut in by long low shanties that serve as dining-rooms and dormitories in one. Each dormitory is divided into a number of cubicles eight or ten feet square by partitions that do not quite reach the ceiling. No chimneys give exit to the clouds of smoke from our wood fires, and lowly postures alone give relief to smarting eyes. As the evening wore on the bathers waxed merry, and a party of young men, who continued their soaking until midnight, discoursed dramatic poetry with gusto. The damp air and confined space of the *yuba* are held to be especially

favourable to these recitations.   Instead of the other
bathers objecting to the noise they occasion, I was
assured they look on it as a privilege to be able to
listen !

A number of isolated bath tanks lie scattered here and
there on the hill side above the *yuba* itself, varying in
temperature from 95° to 118° F.   One is said to be
especially good for the eyes, another for headaches, a third
for leprosy.   Fanciful names are attached to them ; one is
Ō-gon (*i.e.* yellow metal = gold).   " *Yakushi* " (the name of
a Buddhist divinity regarded as the patron of the spot) is
the title of another close by the image and shrine erected to
his honour.   A little south of the enclosure many proofs
of volcanic action are in evidence.   Sulphur fumes
issue from the crumbling bare hillside, boiling water
bubbles up in little pools—sometimes side by side with
an icy cold spring.   A thick deposit of sulphur covers
the ground in many places, and, under the name of
yu no hana ("hot-water flowers") is taken home to be
used by the peasants in their own hot baths.   The
water of the baths, conducted into the principal ones
by wooden channels, is changed each afternoon.   The
bathers are expected to bring their own food and
bedding, and pay 4 sen (one penny) for the use of a
cubicle and the baths.   Originally the *yuba* stood in a
different spot, but an explosion of gas some years ago blew

a piece of the mountain side away, destroying the bath-houses, and killing several persons.

The copper-coloured contingent at the hottest bath on Sunday night prolonged their recitations and splashing until the small hours of the morning. In spite of my representations that it was hard on Hamilton (who was, unfortunately, still unwell), they kept up their din till sheer weariness sent us to sleep. And then a hoarse whisper in my ear, " 'Tis already four o'clock," compelled me to turn out.

Leaving Hamilton still slumbering, Uraguchi, Yamazaki Junsa, and myself, with a coolie to act as our guide, quitted the *yuba* by the light of a brilliant moon, and mounted the wooded ridge that rises south of the *Onsen.* Then came a descent to the wild torrent of the *Seto-gawa,* which we crossed by a precarious bridge of tree stems lashed together by tough creepers. Still bearing south-wards, our way lay over thinly wooded spurs with occasional slopes of snow that filled the intervening hollows. The lowest snow was reached at a height of 5,500 feet. A two hours' scramble brought us to the Renge silver mine, where the overseer received us most kindly. After taking me into the galleries now being worked, he presented me with specimens of the ore, and begged me to tell him what I thought of its quality, and whether the veins were likely to prove deep. Besides the

Renge mine two others have been opened in a valley more
to the north, the total output of ore being about 350,000
pounds.   Whether the statement that three per cent. of
silver results from the smelting is correct I am unable
to say.

A scramble up a slippery slope of grass and undergrowth
above the encampment—for the dwellings of the miners
were but shanties of branches and leaves—landed us on a
slope of snow, which, 1,500 feet higher up, was succeeded
by a belt of *haimatsu* (dwarf pine) and rhododendron.
Another slope of 500 feet led up to the bare andesite
rocks of the ridge connecting Yukikuradake on the west
with Ō Renge on the east.   At 10 A.M. we were on
the highest point (9,800 feet), which commands a grand
and extensive view.   On the south, beyond the Kōshū
mountains, Fuji raises her blunt cone a hundred miles away.
Nearer at hand come Tateyama and the great snow-streaked
peaks of the main chain to the south.   To the north-west
flashes the swift Kurobe-gawa to the Sea of Japan, and the
waters of the western arm of the bay of Toyama are seen
washing the shores of the long peninsula of Noto.   Straight
below us, on the east, wild ravines fall steeply, filled with
snow, and a snow *arête* connects us with Asahi-dake, a
shapely rock peak on the south-west.

On the descent a novel method of glissading down the
snow slopes was adopted by some of my companions, who

H. J. Hamilton, phot.

YUKIKURADAKE, FROM ABOVE THE RENGE ONSEN.

[P. 282.

cut off branches of the creeping pine and used them as toboggans with great effect.

A couple of coolies having been engaged as porters from amongst the visitors at the bathhouse, we set off the next morning *en route* for Ōmachi. Recent rain had made the narrow rugged path in the worst condition, and going was slow. Beyond the Hatchōzaka we passed through a thicket abounding in magnificent wild raspberries, and infested with swarms of *abu,* a very aggressive species of horse-fly. The spot is notorious amongst the peasants who visit the *Onsen.* At the *sonchō's* house we met the owner himself—Nagakura—a fine-looking man, unusually tall, and with a face pleasing to a degree uncommon amongst male Japanese. He apologized for being away when we first arrived, for the "disgustingly filthy accommodation" we had had to put up with, and so on. In the afternoon we took a cordial farewell of our host and of the obliging little policeman Yamazaki. On paying off our coolies, who transferred the baggage to a little *niguruma,* we found, to our disgust, that one of them was a woman! I had not taken particular notice when the caravan started, and saw nothing of the couple for the greater part of the descent. Moreover, the women in these parts work almost as hard as the men, and frequently dress in the same style, wearing a tunic and trousers of a "pegtop" pattern, which make it difficult at times to

distinguish sex. Half a mile or so from the start we
crossed a fine wooden bridge over the Himekawa, which
marks the boundary between the provinces of Echigo and
Shinshū, and of Niigata and Nagano Ken. Evening saw
us coming to a halt at Kudarise, a village whose name
points to the rapids of the Himekawa close at hand. At
our unpretentious inn, the "Zeniya," we had every attention.
A delicious dinner of potatoes and *sakana tempura* was
provided. The latter dish, fish-fritters (of a sort of trout),
is one at cooking which the Japanese excel. In Tōkyō
and others of the large cities some of the most popular
restaurants are those at which this is the only dish provided. Our bills for the night's entertainment only
amounted to 6*d*. each. Peach and apple trees filled the
little garden outside our verandah. The next day, about
2½ miles beyond Kudarise, we found that a path leaves the
main road at a spot called Chikuni for the Renge Onsen.
The whole distance thither is some ten miles, but the route
is unpopular, owing to the belief that on a moor half-way
(known as Tengū-hara) a monster *tengū*, half dragon and
half man, lurks in secret places, waiting for unwary
travellers.* At Mori (also called Shiojima) the valley of
the Himekawa opens out in spreading rice fields. Planted

---

* This particular sort of hobgoblin is usually located in mountainous
places, and is represented in popular art as possessing a very long nose,
wings, and two or three claws on each foot.

in all directions fluttered little paper flags, bearing mysterious inscriptions, that are supposed to protect the young rice from the attacks of noxious insects. These charms, known as *mushi-yoke* ("insect dispellers"), are bought at Togakushi-San, a famous temple near Nagano (Zenkōji). The place is locally celebrated as the spot from which the god Tajikara is said to have hurled the rock door of the cave in which Amaterasu, the Sun-goddess, hid herself when insulted by her brother Susa-no-ō. As I have had pointed out to me in Central Kyūshū the spot where the actual cave is said to have been, the idea of distance seems to be most ingenuously ignored in the legend. Charms of a similar import, affixed to the lintels or door-posts of the cottages and farmhouses, are common all over Japan. The picture of a horse *rampant* is held to keep away small-pox, by suggesting to the spirit of harm that the usual inmates of the house are on a journey. Terrible-looking demons, dogs, or the imprint of a hand—all done in black, on white paper—pasted above the doorway, are believed to be efficacious against evil spirits of various sorts.

As we crossed the broad stony bed of the Matsukawa, a grand prospect opens out to the north-west of the Ō Renge peaks. By following the course of the stream, and then turning up a valley called Kitamata, the southern shoulder of the mountain can be gained. From Iida

(Kamijō) a gentle incline leads round the shoulders of the hills north of Aoki-ko, and then, passing through a narrow defile, brings us in full view of the lovely blue waters of the little lake itself. It is about three miles in circumference, and lies 2,500 feet above the sea. At short intervals further on are two smaller lakes. The road passes along their flat eastern sides, whilst on the opposite banks richly timbered hills rise darkly. As we drew near Ōmachi the hills insensibly fell away, and the northern head of the long narrow Matsumoto plain began to open out. Wooded hills on either hand stretched their long ramparts as far as the eye could reach, but above these, on the west, towered the tall forms of the now familiar monarchs of the range. Once more the "Yamachō" gave welcome hospitality, and a pleasant stay from Wednesday till Saturday made us loth to leave. Finding an office belonging to the local branch of the Nōshōmushō in the village, I went and had a chat with the gentlemen in charge. They gave me a kindly invitation to join them on an expedition to Kurodake, a mountain north of Yarigatake, celebrated for its rock crystals, but my plans would not allow me to accept it. During the course of necessary shopping we paid a visit to the local chemist to purchase a supply of methylated spirits for our "Etna." The article is usually known as *arukōoru* (alcohol), but the chemist told us he could only sell it to customers armed with the doctor's certificate. On repairing to that worthy, he not only provided us with the necessary document, but also sold us a supply of the thing itself! At the shop next door we —or rather Hamilton, the chief baker of our party— instructed the village *panya* (lit. "bread-man," *i.e.* baker, for the Japanese name for bread is merely their rendering of the Portuguese word for the same) in the art of making the real thing. The itinerant pipe-mender, a dear old patriarch with snow-white hair, gave us a kindly salutation as we stopped to watch him at his work.

On Saturday (July 28th), as the sun rose over the Shinshū mountains and began to warm the narrow plain, we were well on our way towards Matsumoto, a walk of 25 miles due south. As we crossed the broken bridge over the wide bed of the Takasegawa, we had another reminder of the force of summer and autumn floods, caused largely here by the melting of the lower slopes of the snow that streaks the dark wall of peaks westwards. Thin veils of white clouds tempered the sun's rays as we traversed the mulberry orchards, or passed through long avenues of sweet-scented pines. The spontaneous respectful bows of the children trudging cheerfully in little knots of three and four to the village school, showed we were still in "uncivilized" (*i.e.* un-Europeanized) Japan. The sun was gaining power as we reached the busy village of Kita Hodaka, where we rested for an early tiffin at the

"Tōshiya," an inn kept by a chemist. Biscuits of native manufacture, but a wonderfully clever imitation of Huntley and Palmer's best, were added as dessert to our meal. Shortly after midday we found ourselves in the long street that constitutes the little town of Toyoshina. Till six months before it had been one of the most prosperous places in the plain, but in March it was almost wiped out by fire. Of its 600 houses no less than 500 were destroyed in an incredibly short space of time, and it was only now rising, phœnix-like, from its ashes. At one end of the desolated street stands a curious erection called *suzume-dai*, or "cooling table." This consists of an elevated platform, shaded by a roof of pine-branches, raised high enough both to catch the refreshing breezes of eventide, and to afford an uninterrupted view of the neighbouring mountains and plain over the tops of the now resurrecting houses.

In another quarter an odd arrangement drew attention to the fact that a house was being rebuilt after the conflagration. At the spot where we should lay a corner-stone, a post was fastened in the ground between a pair of pine poles, bearing a huge arrow with a trident head, a number of small ones of the usual shape, a bow, a fan, and a *gohei*. I have seen similar decorations used in Kōbe without the bow and arrows, and a Japanese friend there once presented me with those he had used on his own house, consisting of three fans (each representing the rising sun), strips of hemp, a sprig of *sakaki* (*Cleyera Japonica,* the sacred tree of Shintō), and streamers of red, white, and green cotton cloth, all fastened to a large *gohei.* The decorations were fixed at the north-east corner of the house, as that is the quarter of the compass from which the most dreaded evils are supposed to come.*

Three miles from Toyoshina we crossed the Adzusagawa, whose stony bed, half a mile wide, was now nearly dry of water, excepting a narrow, shallow stream not two feet deep. On the opposite side the track mounted up close under the shadow of a tree-topped bluff, and then passed through rice fields and mulberry orchards into the town of Matsumoto. On the day after our arrival at Sasai Motoji's (for the worthy innkeeper gave us a welcome, unmindful of the washing bill of twelve months back) I had a visit from the local photographer. He came to bring back some negatives Hamilton had taken to him for developing. As an expression of gratitude he presented us with a box of delicious preserved fruits and biscuits. "Gratitude" on this occasion proved to be chiefly "a lively sense of favours to come," for he followed up his gift

---

* It has been suggested that the origin of the *north-east* quarter being regarded as the likeliest for the onset of evil, may be traced to the early struggles between the Ainu and their Japanese conquerors. As they drove the Ainu aborigines before them, the *north-east* would naturally become the dangerous region to the Japanese, from being the direction of the nocturnal attacks of the enemy.

with a request that we would take him with us to photograph the mountains we were about to climb.

Merchants who had come to trade in silkworm cocoons, helped to fill the inn during our stay, for Matsumoto is one of the chief centres of this important silk district. Several parties of pilgrims also passed the night under the same roof, besides the fleas innumerable they had brought with them. The latter accounted for another sleepless night, and when day dawned many corpses strewed the battle-field.

CHAPTER XII.

" IF at first you don't succeed, try, try again ! "

In obedience to this old adage, Monday, July 30th, saw
me for the third year in succession on my way to Gamada
for the ascent of Kasadake, the "Umbrella Peak," from
which I had on each previous attempt been repulsed through
the inexplicable objection of the villagers to lend me their
aid. Much persuasion in bygone days had induced the
local *panya* at Matsumoto to turn his hand to making
"foreign" bread, and with a couple of dozen tiny loaves
bulging out our rücksacks into knobbly corners we felt
ourselves secure for the ensuing week.

Our route to Gamada was the familiar one, already
described, by way of Hashiba and Hirayu. As we crossed
the dozen miles of gradually contracting plain to Hashiba

we found constant proofs of the increasing popularity of the
silk industry.   At Hadamura (locally known as Endō), in
the pine forest, we found a new filature employing twenty
bright-faced girls.   The motive force for the spindles was
supplied by a machine of one small boy power.   After a
rest for tiffin at Hashiba, we went on with our two coolies,
by a track I had not previously followed, high up above the
right bank of the Azusagawa to Inekoki.   There we
noticed another filature of the same size worked by a water
wheel.   The last few miles of road before reaching
Ōnogawa were so wrecked in many places by avalanches,
landslips, and floods, that we had to cross over to the left
bank and scramble along an old path ordinarily only used
as an approach to the shelters of woodcutters and charcoal
burners.   Here and there we passed across the face of
a cliff over a couple of shaky pine trees insecurely supported
by struts of timber from below.   A slip on the part of a
Japanese companion behind me nearly sent him head foremost on a journey into the boiling torrent some hundreds of
feet beneath.   Fortunately, with cat-like agility he recovered
himself in a twinkling, but the greenness of his blanched
cheeks told of the start it had given him.   In spite of the
mosquitoes and fleas, the old-fashioned inn of Okuta Kiichi
proved a pleasant resting-place, and the old man's charge
was only 4*d*. per head for *hatago* (supper, bed, and breakfast).   The cool air of the mountains was infinitely

refreshing after a broiling at 20° or 30° higher temperature in the sun-smitten Matsumoto plain.

As we topped the ridge above the village shortly after sunrise the next morning, a grand view greeted us of the twin tops of Norikura, streaked with snow, rising in front due west. Delightful memories waked unbidden as for the third time I traversed the dark ravines and great tree-clad ridges. Now, alas, their solitude is echoing the ring of the woodman's axe and the crash of the falling monarchs of the forests. At Hirayu we found Yomosaburō and his household busy with preparations for a feast to be given that night at the *Kōzan* (mine) on Norikura, where Miller and I had fared so well two years ago. The *matsuri*, or festival, was in honour of Kanayama no Kami, " the god of the metal mountain," and supplies of fish, *daikon*, and rice were being cooked to satisfy 400 workpeople besides the massive fat-clothed wrestlers who were to perform for their amusement. A pressing invitation to join their feast we had to decline, and early morning saw us striding gaily down the ravine of the Takahara-gawa with the grey serrated ridges of our beautiful peak glistening in the light of the rising sun and beckoning us onwards. A halt to seize a view of the valley of Gamada from the top of the Kamisaka-tōge was our only rest before the quaint châlets of the little hamlet were reached. Without delay we repaired to the house of

R 2

Jimbei's adopted son and successor, and stated the object
of our visit. But for the third time we met with a refusal
to further our plans. In the first place, he said, he
couldn't take us in for the night, as a Takayama gentleman
had engaged his guest room, and even in his absence it
might not be used by others. Moreover, the woodcutters
and hunters of the valley were that very night to hold
their annual festivities, and no one could therefore be
induced to guide us to Kasadake.

A second fruitless discussion took place later on as we
sat disconsolate on the rugged steps leading up to the
village shrine. We were just turning away in despair
when a bystander offered to give us shelter for the night.
He proved a friend in need, and under his kind attentions
our spirits revived. As I was picking my way over the
rough stones to the village *Onsen*, I fell in with a fine-
looking fellow whose get-up betokened him to be *a ryōshi*
(a hunter of big game). To him I told my tale, and to
my intense satisfaction he proffered to bear us company.
In the afternoon he paid us a visit to discuss plans for
the ascent, bringing with him Nakashima, the chieftain of
the band of hunters to which he belonged. This man
was a strongly-built picturesque person, with a type of
countenance uncommon in my experience. The former
himself, too, was unusually good-looking for a man of
his class, and might almost have come from somewhere on

H J. Hamilton, phot

THE HUNTER CHIEFTAIN OF NAKAO.

[P 244.

the shores of the Levant. A lengthy *sōdan* (consultation) explained the difficulties that these three years past had been raised against my designs.

"The Gamada folk," said Nakashima, "are incurably superstitious. In the lonely cliffs and ravines of Kasadake they maintain that a mighty spirit roams. Should any of the dwellers in the valley venture to conduct a stranger within the precincts of the mountain during the ripening of the grain, &c., a destructive storm would be bound to follow. This they would at once lay at the door of those who had assisted in the sacrilege, and condign punishment would follow without delay." I wondered no longer at my former lack of success, and promising to keep the visit of Nakashima and his follower a secret, we set ourselves about preparations for the climb. Delicious trout from the stream hard by enhanced our evening meal, and we turned in betimes for a start at dawn. At midnight, however, a rattling at the outer *shōji* of our room disturbed our slumbers. The dull glow of a *chōchin* dimly revealed the bronzed faces of our hunters. Nakashima had come to tell us that Jimbei and the rest had got wind of our plans, and threats of vengeance were freely made if we should persist in the attempt. He begged us to postpone the climb until a later date, but as this was impossible we were obliged to refuse. It was a case of "now or never," and to our delight the younger hunter, who laughed at the fears and threats of the villagers, backed us up with reassuring boldness.   So the pair departed, Nakashima first exhorting us to leave Gamada before the inhabitants were astir, and to join him at the châlet where, higher up the valley, he lived surrounded by the huts of his followers.   In the dull grey light of dawning day (August 2), the younger man and a comrade he had brought with him, shared with us our packs, and led us silently and stealthily out of the village.   At Nakao we found our chieftain waiting in the great room that formed his home to welcome us and give us a parting greeting. As soon as we had re-arranged our sacks, amid a chorus of " Take honourable care—come quickly back again," we set off jubilant at having, at the third time of asking, succeeded in our quest.   From the clearing in the forest, where the hunter's settlement shelters by the side of a rustic shrine, we cautiously descended a precipitous bank to the bed of the stream.

Our peak, cloud-veiled, lay almost due north, and in that direction, with little variation, we steadily pursued our way.   The tangled undergrowth of the dense forest, and the steepness of the banks of the torrent, forced us to take to the boulders of its bed.   Then, as the stream forked, and each arm contracted narrowly, with rushing waters filling their channels, we were driven, willy-nilly, into the forest at the angle formed by their meeting.   The prospect here was anything but inviting. The impenetrable nature of the jungle made progress slow and trying to the last degree. The trees were so close together that but little light was cast upon our way. This lay through thick dank grass and ferns soaked with moisture, varied with frequent scrambles over slippery moss-grown boulders and the rounded rotting trunks of prostrate trees. So thickly was the carpet of moss spread that it was sometimes impossible to tell which was solid ground. And frequently the foot plunged through, and left one with one leg dangling in a hole of unknown depth, like the unwary traveller crossing an unsuspected glacier-crevasse. The time that this jungle struggle took, though only an hour, seemed more like ages, and I shall long remember it as the most trying time I have ever passed in mountain wanderings in or out of Japan.

At last we burst out of our damp dark prison, and welcomed the light of day once more, as we rejoined tho *Hidari-mata,* the " left branch " of the torrent, nearer its source. After a substantial breakfast, we laid some pine trees across the turbulent waters to form a bridge. Balancing on these, swept as they were by the swift current, with the aid of a long thin pole we gingerly picked our way over. We breathed more freely as we took to the broken rocks on the opposite bank, and scrambled up a ravine that opened before us, which the hunters called

the *Anage-tani.* This gradually steepened, and at 5,000
feet we reached the lowest level of the snow. Higher up
a lovely little waterfall dashes over a beetling precipice on
the left. On the right a swift-winged swallow flashed in
and out of its nest in the grey cliff. Under the lee of
a huge fragment of rock half buried in the snow we hid
some of our superfluous baggage, to lighten our load,
and proceeded to face the steep slopes afresh. Up the
great gully we mounted on the rough surface of the snow
for 1,500 or 2,000 feet. Then we varied the climb by
ascending curious terraces of broken water-worn rocks on
the right, probably the course of a now dried-up cascade.
Next we tried a steep acclivity of slippery grass on the left,
but this was distinctly uncongenial " going," and we went
back to the gully till it eased off, and gradually lost itself
below a sharp ridge. Turning a little to the left, we came
across traces of bears and wild boar below some slopes
of snow which we mounted to the main *arête* of the
mountain, from which the highest points rise up. As we
topped the *arête* we found ourselves overlooking the valley
of the Sugo-roku-gawa. This stream I had previously
crossed near its confluence with the Takaharagawa just
below the hamlet of Sugo, so probably the ascent could be
made from that place. At this point our hunters halted,
took off their packs, and proceeded to stick some *rōsoku*
(native candles) in a niche in the rocks. These they

lighted, and then bowed their heads, and, with hands reverently folded, offered their supplications to the Spirit of the Mountain.

Turning to the right, we pushed on along the sharp *arête* north-east to the summit. The phonolitic andesite of which it is composed lies, in many places, in curiously evenly piled slabs, one on the other, like layers of tiles for a house roof. They ring to the blow of an ice-axe as if they were meant by Nature for so many bells.

The slopes on the left that fall to the valley of the Sugo-roku-gawa are mainly clothed with *haimatsu*, but on the right wild and broken rocks merge into the western precipices of Yarigatake. The magnificent rock ridge that connects the "spear-peak" with Hodakayama exhibits a vast line of castellated cliffs, thousands of feet in height, that has no parallel in the Land of the Rising Sun. As the wreathing curtain of grey vapour rolls here and there aside, a view of Tateyama to the north, or of Fuji to the south, breaks through. On the summit, reached at 2·45, we found a tiny cairn, erected by the hunters on some former visit. Excepting themselves—or some of their comrades—they told us we were the first climbers, European or Japanese, to set foot on the top. I scarcely wondered that my friend the botanist of two years ago had returned from the lower flanks of the peak unsuccessful. The ascent had occupied so much longer than we had expected that we gave up hopes of reaching Nakao again that day. As we loitered about the top we startled a ptarmigan, but failed to bring it down. Leaving the summit about 3·30, we found the descent unexpectedly easy, and made speedy progress towards the great gully. As we drew near its top, the prospects of a bivouac almost without food or shelter began to strike us as unenviably romantic. Our leading guide, the handsome Ichijirō, told us he knew of a bear's cave some distance away, but, owing to the fact that it was in an exposed spot, where water and firewood could with difficulty be procured, we declined to pay it a visit. At last a suggestion was made to descend and bivouac by the Hidari-mata, and down we went. The descent of the cascade terraces, smooth, almost, as rounded ice, proved trying beyond description to me in hob-nailed boots. My companions all wore *waraji*, and managed to jump from rock to rock with comparative ease.

Finally, I borrowed a pair and fastened them underneath the soles of my boots. The expedient proved a complete success, and what had hitherto been misery was transformed into a pleasure. Quickly we dropped from ledge to ledge, and then glissaded the snowy floor of the gully to its foot. As the sunlight began to die away we found ourselves crossing the Hidari-mata by our primitive bridge. The prospect of spending the night in the forest grew more and more distasteful, so, with all possible speed, we hurried on in the hope of clearing it before nightfall. The way Ichijirō led the party filled me with admiration. In the deepening gloom he scarcely once faltered, and, to our intense relief, the Migi-mata was reached by 8 P.M. Our race against night was ended, and we knew we were safe.

By the side of the noisy torrent we kindled a fire of brushwood, and consumed the scraps of food we had been saving for our prospective bivouac. We then lighted improvised torches, and pursued our homeward way. Instead of retracing our steps entirely down the river bed, Ichijirō took us by a woodcutter's track through the forest on its left bank, which, though longer, was easier going. In Indian file we plodded on through the pitchy darkness, with torches first made of birch twigs and then of shingles torn from the roof of a dilapidated *koya* (a woodcutter's shanty), which we passed on our way. The picturesque dress of the hunters as they held aloft the flaming torches that ever and anon dropped golden cascades of sparks on the damp ground, made a striking scene. By 10 P.M. we were back at the chieftain's house, receiving warm congratulations at the successful issue of the most arduous expedition I had ever undertaken in the whole of my Japanese wanderings.

We were in no hurry, the following day, to leave our kind host betimes, and several hours passed pleasantly in interesting chat before we could tear ourselves away. Hamilton got the worthy hunter to stand for his photograph, clad in full fighting rig, as he goes to hunt big game. The clothing worn on those occasions consists of a short tunic and tight knickerbockers of blue homespun hempen cloth, of a very tough character. The legs are protected against thorns, tree stumps, snow, &c., by leggings of raw hemp or closely-woven straw. Whilst in the summer time the usual straw *waraji* are worn, these are in winter replaced by boots of raw bear-skin, with the hairy side inwards. When chasing game over *soft* snow the hunter fastens circular snow-shoes, made of a creeper called *Kurogane modoshi*, under his boots. If the snow be hard enough to walk on, and smooth, he uses *crampons* called *kanakanjiki*. These are metal crosses, with the ends turned down and sharpened. I have seen other shapes in different parts of the country. For additional warmth in the way of clothing, a chamois skin is thrown over the shoulders. His weapons include an old-fashioned muzzle-loader, a spear, and a heavy knife. Occasionally, in view of hand-to-hand encounters with bears, he carries a double-handed sword. This has a point as sharp as a needle, and an edge as keen as a razor. It is wielded with a skill and strength sometimes sufficient to sever the animal's head almost at a single stroke.

The weather forecasts of some of the peasants are

distinctly interesting. Whilst in some parts of the Empire the Government has established well-equipped meteorological stations, which issue valuable reports periodically, the country folk are mostly without these aids, and have to depend on their own experience. Amongst the signs of clear weather they include the following circumstances :—

When a dog comes out of his usual shelter to sleep in a more exposed place.

When an echo is heard to the pigeon's coo.

When the *tombi* (kite) cries in the evening.

When the charred soot on the wick of the *andon* (a native paper lamp) is red.

When the rainbow spans the east.

Signs of wet weather are seen :—

When the earthworm crawls out of the earth.

When the cocks go to roost earlier than usual.

When the moon looks low.

When the crow (sometimes said to be the Japanese bird of love) washes himself in the water, you may confidently count on rain the very next day.

Wind may be expected :—

When the stars seem to waver in their places.

When ravens croak together in unusually large numbers.

And when the murmur of the river is unusually loud.

The sun was high in the heavens when our gallant
hunters led the way from their hospitable chieftain's home.
Partly to avoid exciting the curiosity and fears of the
Gamada people, and partly in pursuance of our own plans,
we decided to return to Matsumoto by an entirely different
route, and so it came to pass that the superstitious peasants
down the valley saw our faces no more. Our intention
was to cross the mountains south of Yarigatake to some
point whence we could reach the foot of Hodaka-yama, and
so reach the Matsumoto Plain by the Tokugō Pass.
The name of our *col* was the Yakeyama-tōge, the track
—used chiefly by woodcutters—passing to the south of
Yakeyama down to the Azusagawa, close to Hodakayama. The general direction is due east. The heat of the
sun, which smote the little clearing about the hunters' dwellings unmercifully, made us glad to reach the shade of the
forest trees through which the track wound its upward way.
Clear streams of water, deliciously fresh, coursed down the
slopes to find a common union in the torrent at the
bottom of the valley. Near the top of the pass, 7,000 feet,
the vegetation thinned out, and grass and creeping pine
covered the highest point of Yakeyama, the peak that gives
the pass its name. On climbing to the summit of this,
a few hundred feet above the *col*, we found traces of
volcanic activity in the steam and sulphur fumes issuing
from holes in rocks on the eastern side. A grand view

BEAR-HUNTERS OF NAKAO.

[P. 255.

of Kasadake to the N.W., and of Hodakayama due N., and
quite close at hand, rewarded our toil. At the foot of the
pass we came across coolies constructing a hut for herdsmen
near the spot where a spring of hot water gushes out of the
river bank, and bubbles up through the cold current of the
Azusagawa that flows above.* Hurrying up the vale
through which the stream passes, we found ourselves under
the shadow of Hodaka's granite peaks, and, as we drew near
the Tokugō hut, I perceived in the dim twilight the form
of one of my guides of last year on his way across the
ford to Kamonji's 'shooting box.' He soon recognized
me, and came ashore to have a chat, afterwards bringing
half a score of splendid trout, for which he asked the
modest sum of 6½d.

After a pleasant evening at the hut, we pursued our way
to Matsumoto the following day. The feasts of raspberries
delayed us somewhat, and before we bade our hunters
a regretful farewell we photographed them in the forest on
the way from Hashiba. Long bars of golden light shot
athwart the tall pine stems, and the scent of the branches
in the cool of the afternoon was unusually refreshing.

On Sunday morning we had an interesting little church
service at the house of the native deacon, the Rev. Masazao
Kakuzen, who had recently established a branch of the

* The fact that the outlet of this hot spring was some years ago above the
level of the stream, shows how rapidly the river has been filling up its
channel.

S.P.G. work in Matsumoto.   In the afternoon he paid us
a call, bringing with him a present of a tin of native
preserved apricots, put up in Nagano, bearing the inscription : "This apricots is very sweetest."   Another tin—I
think it was a sort of Japanese "Liebig"—was still more
remarkably inscribed : " All the medicines of our company
used to sell are not only manufactured of the pure and
good materials, but also, unless the article are inspected by
the superintendent they not sealed.   It is true that thieir
quality is best.   If there was suspection about it trust
on the official examination.   If, even in the slightest
neglect the result is not good our company should be
responsible for it.   Beware the trade-mark sealing wax
and wrapper of our company."

In this connection I may remark on the curious shop
signs in English (?), composed in cheerful independence of
outside help.   I have seen the equivalent of the English
" Mangling   done   here"   rendered   "The   machine   for
smoothing the wrinkles oe the trowsers."

" Washman, ladies only."

" Clothing of woman tailor.   Ladies furnished in the
upper storey."

"Imstracted by the French horse-leech."   (This adorned
the door of a veterinary surgeon, and referred to the tuition
under which the gentleman had been trained.)

Of   all   the   peaks   seen   from   the   neighbourhood   of

H. W. Belcher, phot.

IRRIGATING-WHEELS IN THE RICE-FIELDS.

[P. 257.

Matsumoto none more impresses the spectator than the graceful triangular form of Jōnendake.

Bad weather in 1893, and other hindrances, had stood in the way of my visiting it as I had intended, but now our party was bound for it in earnest. Leaving Matsumoto on Monday (August 6), by its northern end, we passed by the old castle, whose pagoda-like walls, now cracking and peeling in decay, look down mournfully on the wide expanse of paddy fields that stretch, like some vast chess-board, between it and the westward hills towards which we were journeying. As we pass by some wayside cottage a solitary coolie may be seen engaged in pounding rice at a sort of treadmill. By the pressure of his foot he lifts a huge wooden hammer, which the next moment he lets drop, with dull, monotonous thud, into a mortar hollowed out of the section of a tree-trunk. A hot, dusty journey of seven or eight miles took us through Toyoshina to the hamlet of Iwahara, which nestles at the base of the foot-hills formed by the eastern spurs of Jōnendake. Our first business on reaching the village was to seek out the *sonchō*. As there was no inn in the neighbourhood, I knew we must throw ourselves on him for hospitality and help. Nor were we disappointed. The *sonchō's* house stands hard by a fine grove of cryptomeria, and a large wooden *torii*-like gateway gives access to a courtyard in front of the porch. Passing through a door in

s

the wall on our right, we found ourselves in a lovely little
garden—one of those Lilliputian landscapes in which the
artistic soul of the Japanese so delights.   In response to a
polite greeting, we stepped up on to the broad verandah, to
receive the kindest of welcomes.   First appeared the eldest
son, then the *sonchō* Yamaguchi Yoshihito himself, a stately
old gentleman of three-score.   By-and-by an attendant
brought in tea and cakes.   Then, over the tiny pipes
next produced, we told our business.   Nothing could
have been more delightful than the attentive interest
with which our plans were listened to and talked
over.   With many humbly-worded apologies for what
the Japanese conventional phrase calls the "disgustingly
filthy accommodation," the good *sonchō* placed a lovely
pair of guest-rooms at our disposal ; and that night, as
we lay on our *futon* listening to the sighing of the breeze
in the tall trees and to the weird call of the night hawk
echoing in the hills beyond, we felt we were "in clover"
indeed.

As day dawned we were up and away.   Not only had
the hospitable head-man provided us with a trio of bear-
hunters, to act as guides and porters, but with them joined
us Yamaguchi junior.   He was arrayed, by way of lending
"tone" to the appearance of the party, in a curious black
felt hat and dirty white cotton gloves far too large.   The
combination of these with his Japanese costume   was

H. J. Hamilton, phot.

HOUSE OF THE 'HEAD-MAN' OF IWAHARA.

[*P.* 258.

undeniably odd, and reminded one of the days when, through imperfect acquaintance with Western fashions, some of the officials of a Japanese city I once lived in occasionally appeared in most startling garb. At one time it was thought to be "the thing" to encircle the neck with a bath-towel by way of comforter. I have been told of a gentleman—invited to a morning function—arriving in *evening* dress, without socks, his manly bosom bare of shirt, and with a collar tied round his neck by a piece of string. This, however, was years ago. I have met Japanese of the better classes who looked as well in evening dress as any European. Leaving the *sonchō's* house behind, we passed quickly through the gloomy grove and descended to the bank of the Karasu-gawa (the "crow river"), which flows down from the eastern flanks of Jōnendake. As we slowly forded the torrent we were nearly carried off our feet by the swift rushing of waters whose icy coldness spoke eloquently of their birthplace in the snows far up the mountain.

Then came a glorious tramp, due west, of five miles or more over the wide *hara* (a sort of prairie), which so often covers the lower slopes of the loftier mountains. It is these prairie regions, and the mountain woodlands often connected with them, that form the home of that wonderful variety of plants in which Japan is so rich. No one, as Dr. Rein has remarked, who has viewed this variegated

s 2

floor of living mosaic will wonder at the name by which it sometimes goes—*ō hana batake,* " the great flower-field." Besides familiar English wild flowers, the beautiful *Lychnis grandiflora,* varieties of magnificent lilies, such as the *auratum* and *tigrinum,* the purple iris, and the deep blue bell-shaped kikyo (*Platycodon grandiflorum*), give a gorgeous colouring to the face of the field.

Above the *hara* our track began to wind round the slopes of intervening hills, but the densely-wooded valley then contracted, and we were compelled to take to the bed of the wild torrent below, with the occasional variation of plunging through the dense jungle on the left bank. For the next five hours the work was extremely rough. The route lay up what one might compare to a sort of moraine of smooth boulders, sometimes of enormous size, partly submerged in water and inclined at a gradually steepening angle. Over these water-rounded rocks we made our way as well as we could, leaping from boulder to boulder, wading through the icy water of the swirling rapids, or, by way of a pleasant change, scrambling up or round some intervening buttress of rock and descending to the torrent higher up. At 3 P.M. we reached the first snow, at a height of 7,200 feet, at a spot where, in a gloomy ravine, dark cliffs rose steep and forbidding on either hand. No sooner was the word to halt here given, than at once our hunters threw down their packs and fell to prodding about with their sticks in the holes and crannies of the broken rocks in a state of wild excitement. They told us they were searching for a particular sort of lizard called *san-shō-no-uwo*, which this stream produced to perfection. When caught, skewered on long sticks, and dried, it is highly esteemed as a cure for various diseases of children. In China it is also much valued in the native pharmacopœia, and goes by the name of the " stony son of a dragon." In an advertisement drawing attention to its uses in a native Shanghai newspaper some time ago, it was stated that the medicine made from it was " not only unusually effective against the plague, but it is also infallible against different kinds of cholera, typhus and typhoid fevers, ague, diphtheria, liver and stomach aches, vomiting, diarrhœa, colic, apoplexy, sunstroke, asphyxia, tetanus in children, surfeiting, small-pox, malaria, all sorts of tumours, and inflammatory poisons, &c."

Chief of all reptiles of this class, however, is the Giant Salamander* (*Cryptobronchus Japonicus*), found chiefly on the west or south-west spurs of this range (as well as in some other parts between 34° and 36° N. lat.). It appears to chiefly prefer the clear mountain streams of granite and schist ranges at a height of 2,000 to 4,000 feet above the sea. It feeds chiefly upon trout (in which those streams abound) and upon the larvæ of insects and the smaller

* Cp. Rein's " Japan," p. 188.

batrachians. Its flesh is valued chiefly for its medicinal uses and for keeping the water clean in wells.* The largest specimens, five feet long or so, are brought to the principal cities, where they are found as curiosities in the naturalists' shops. Whilst near relatives are found in China and in North America, its closest kinsman of all is the one whose remains were found by Scheuchzer at Œningen. Owing, however, to its weak reproduction and limited distribution, it will soon follow its departed cousin, that *homo diluvii testis*, and at no distant date will cease to form part of the living fauna of Japan.

From the home of the lizard we had a further two hours' scramble in the torrent-bed, but were not sorry to leave it for a clamber up the precipitous hill-side, thinly overgrown with pines, on its right bank. Then came a stiff pull up disintegrated granite rocks, which finally landed us on a sort of col on the north side of our peak. Here, at a height of about 8,600 feet, on a nearly level ridge, partly covered with *go-yo no-matsu* (" five-needle pine "), we decided to bivouac. It was now 7.15 P.M., and the day dies young and suddenly in these low latitudes even at high altitudes. Some of us set to work to clear out a space for our camp and to make a fire. The rest went off in search of water. This was to have been procured from

* Wells are said to be under the special protection of Suijin Sama, who keeps the water pure and good chiefly by the aid of small fish called *funa*, a kind of carp.

a neighbouring torrent, but as the thirsty summer heat had long since absorbed it, we were compelled to have recourse to a distant slope of snow. My waterproof ground-sheet was therefore requisitioned for a bag. It served its purpose well enough, but left too much flavour of indiarubber about the water to be agreeable.

What a delightful bivouac that was! The shadows of the dark, low pine trees lay all the deeper behind the blazing firelight, and as the logs crackled, the only other sounds that broke on the still night air were the liquid notes of the nightingale, or the ceaseless murmur of the mountain torrent a thousand feet below. When dinner was done, one was loth to leave the warm blaze, with the quaint stories and cheerful chatter of our hunters. The spirits of the men expanded with the genial warmth, and old Fujiwara, the oldest of the trio, a tall, lithe fellow, with curiously curly hair for a Japanese, regaled us with a yarn to explain the strange title by which the mountain is known. Usually, Japanese peaks are named either with reference to their personal appearance, or after some Buddhist divinity to whose care they are supposed to have been committed—the name of Jōnendake is quite an exception to this custom.

"*Mukashi, mukashi,*" a party of poachers—not of game, but of a certain kind of much-prized timber, found only in a neighbouring valley—had frequent occasion to camp near this very spot. One night, however, they were startled to hear, wafted down on the night breezes from the summit, the weird sounds of mingled voice and bell of a Buddhist priest at his evening devotions. Hour after hour it continued, until at length, in conscience-smitten terror, they fled from the spot never to return. When the story leaked out, the awe-struck peasants in the Matsumoto plain gave the mountain the name it still retains—" Jonembō," or " Jōnendake " ("the peak of the ever-praying priest "). An incredulous listener to the hunter's story, however, remarked that the explanation of the title, like the stolen timber, was rather far-fetched.

A grand panorama was unveiled the next morning as the grey mists of dawn slowly melted before the rising sun. Due west of our camp, over intervening valleys, rose the pointed monolith of Yarigatake, with its broken south *arête* running on to the precipitous ridges and towers of Hodakayama ; eastwards the eye sweeps over the Matsumoto-taira (plain) to the hills beyond. Chief amongst them, the volcano of Asamayama rolls up in silvery spirals its grey column of mingled smoke and steam. Towards the south-east the graceful cloud-capped cone of Fuji reminds us that the long breakers of the Pacific are rolling in almost at her feet. While revelling in these delights, the crack of a rifle startled me from my reverie. Presently from the forest came Fujiwara into the camp with the carcase of a curious black and white speckled crow he had just brought down. This was quickly popped into the pot hanging over the fire, and with the addition of some *miso* (bean-curds) and *warabi* (a sort of mountain fern), proved a welcome addition to our hunters' breakfast.

A rough clamber over the broken blocks of andesite on the north *arête* took us in an hour from our bivouac to the top of Jōnendake. For the first time the iron heel of a foreigner was now planted on his rugged head. On the summit (10,000 feet) we found a small cairn erected by Fujiwara and his friends on a previous occasion. It had once been adorned by a tiny shrine dedicated to the *tengū*, but only a few scattered chips now remained. One of the hunters remarked that he and his companions were quite as handsome as the *tengū*, so, in the midst of the clouds now surging round the summit, the trio, with Fujiwara and his gun in the centre, sat for their photograph. On our way down, the old hunter secured a fine ptarmigan, which he shot in the creeping pines near our camp. These creatures, like the hares that are found in the higher thickets, turn white in winter.

Just before reaching the *soncho's* house on our return that evening, Yamaguchi junior very abruptly detached himself from the rest, and, without a word, hurried into

the family quarters. For a while I felt uncommonly uncomfortable, thinking I had unwittingly offended him.
By-and-by, however, a domestic approached, and humbly
begged me to " honourably condescend to enter into the
honourable hot bath." I then realized that my friend's
haste simply sprang from his desire to show hospitality by
having my bath ready on my arrival. It was a little bit
of spontaneous kindness which showed me that getting
into hot water does not necessarily prove one has " put
one's foot in it" with one's friends. The next morning
we said an unwilling *sayōnara* and regretfully departed,
with the reiterated "please honourably deign to come back
again" still ringing in our ears, and mingling with juvenile
farewells. One could not but feel how well deserved is
the title in " uncivilised " Japan, by which in bygone days
this kindly people delighted to call their home, *Kunshi no
koku*—" the land of gentlemen."

During the course of that evening at Matsumoto we
were informed that a visitor was waiting below to see us.
On asking him up he proved to be reporter of the
" Shinano Shimbun," one of the leading newspapers in the
province. He wanted to hear about our travels and to
learn our " impressions " of the people we had met and the
places we had visited.

It was not the first time I had been thus attacked, for
last year, after my journey over the Harinoki-tōge and the

ascent of Hodakayama, &c., he had approached me with a similar request. As his notes, however, were written in Japanese, the reproduction of them here would be of no service.

CHAPTER XIII.

THE culminating point of our tour, we had agreed from
the outset, was to be an ascent of the sacred mountain
Ontake ("the August Peak"), to which I have already
referred in a previous chapter. Accordingly, after a two
days' journey in pouring rain, the evening of Saturday,
August 11, saw us snugly sheltered under the roof of the
Tawaraya at Fukushima, our starting point for the expedition. My boots had sadly suffered during the last few
days, and when I got to Fukushima I forthwith repaired
to the home of the peripatetic cobbler who had done me
good service three years before. He usually spends his
time at this place or at Agematsu, but now he was neither
here nor there, but on his rounds elsewhere. This drove
me to resort to the village mender of fencing gear, who,

after much instruction and many cautions, did what was needful.

On Sunday night the advent of numerous pilgrims—for crowds are constantly coming and going just now—created considerable disturbance, for Japanese pilgrimages very generally partake of the nature of a pious picnic. These Oriental Alpine clubs differ in constitution from anything we are accustomed to in Europe, excepting that each member pays an entrance-fee and a subscription. The former is usually about 5 sen (say 1¼*d*.), and the latter from 1 to 3 sen per month. Shortly before the climbing season begins, the club meets and draws lots to settle who shall represent it on the pilgrimage to the chosen peak. The expenses of those thus chosen are paid out of the common fund. The trip from Kobe to Ontake and back costs about 13*s*. or so. Other members are allowed to join the party, but only at their own expense. An experienced member, familiar with the route and its objects of interest, is chosen as *sendachi*, a sort of guide and manager, and in this respect resembles the "conductor" of a party of Cook's tourists. As has been already mentioned, at each inn patronised on the way, a *hŏ no tenugui* (a sort of Japanese towel), adorned with the club crest, name, &c., is given to the landlord, to signify approval of the accommodation to other members who may follow after. These pilgrim mountaineers are usually distinguished by

their white garments and enormously wide hats, as well as
by the hexagonal alpenstock of plain deal they carry in
their hands. At the chief shrines on the mountain the staff
and clothes are stamped with Chinese and Sanskrit
characters, to denote that the owner has been so far, and
thus remind one of the practice in vogue among certain
classes of tourists in Alpine Switzerland that keeps alive
the familiar legend, " *Ici on marque les bâtons.*"

As Professor Chamberlain has remarked,[*] " Pilgrimages
have been a recognized institution among Japanese
Buddhists from the very earliest times of Japanese Buddhism, the practice having been already in full force among
the Buddhists of China, and before that, again, in India."
Chinese residents near Foochow have told me of pilgrimages they have seen made by white-robed mountaineers
to hill-shrines in that neighbourhood, but I have been
unable to gain much detailed information. In Japan, the
favourite peaks ascended by the pilgrim climbers are Fuji
and Ontake, though Ōmine San in Yamato, of lesser
height, has also a considerable vogue.

But it is with the " August Peak " that we are now
concerned. This remarkable summit is an ancient volcano.
It would fairly be called " extinct " were it not that the
sulphurous fumes that burst from crevices in the rocks in
places, solfataras, and other proofs of dormant activity still

* " Journal of the Anthropological Institute,' May, 1893, p. 359.

H. W. Belcher, phot.

FUKUSHIMA, ON THE NAKASENDŌ.

[P. 271.

show it to be instinct with the breath of volcanic life. It is not, strictly speaking, " dead," but only sleeping, though no eruption has been recorded in historic times. Geographically, it is cut off by a deep and wide depression from the main range of the Japanese Alps. Figuratively speaking, it is still more differentiated from those peaks by reason of the extraordinary hypnotic practices pursued by various of the pilgrim bands whose special goal it is during the months of July and August.

Fukushima, the chief starting point for the pilgrims who approach Ontake from the east (*i.e.* from Tōkyō and the upper Nakasendō), is a picturesque spot some 23 miles from the summit of the peak. The brown cottages with their unusually wide overhanging stone-weighted roofs, remind one vividly of Alpine châlets. From the village, a walk of seven miles or so brought us through cool ravines and shady forest groves to Kurosawa, where the shrine of Iwo-haiden marks the *fumoto* or actual base of the sacred mountain. Here the pilgrims purchase their alpenstocks and get them, as well as their white garments, stamped by the priests to certificate their climb. The *Kannushi*, or " god guardian " in charge of the shrine, proved most kind and hospitable. He even offered to stamp my garments and my Alpine stick (one of Hill's abbreviated ice-axes), and to give me a certificate of the ascent without my troubling to make it ! The characters usually printed on the tunic read :—" Ontake San, Ontake tōzan, Gyōhō Shinriki," and signify " Mount (lit. Mr.) Ontake, the ascent of Ontake, (certificating) the divine power of the practice."

From Iwo-haiden our path wound in and out of the eastern spurs of the great mountain whose blunt summit, scarred with dark red lava streams, and seamed with white slopes of snow, rose far above the forests that clothe its shoulders and lower flanks. As one passed from cool shade to dazzling sunlight under a cloudless sky, the repeated transition nearly took away one's breath. Mounting to a higher grassy ridge, we arrived at the Matsuwo rest-house, the first of the little huts that mark the successive stages of the mountain path. These are the Japanese representatives of the Swiss Club huts, and are supposed to be ten in number—the first at the foot and the tenth at the top. The whole mountain is compared to a quantity of rice, enough to fill a *shō* (a little over three pints) measure, spilt on the ground in a conical heap. This *shō* is divided into ten parts, each called a *gō* or rather more than a gill, so that the huts at the several stages are known as *ichigōme*, *nigōme*, &c., or, as we should put it in sporting language, " first lap," " second lap," and so on. Whilst we were breakfasting at the Matsuwo hut, a band of pilgrims, descending from the summit, clad in ceremonial white, and headed by their *sendachi*, or president, arrived upon the scene. Our curiosity was aroused as one by one they

H. J. Hamilton, phot.

A PILGRIM BAND ON ONTAKE.

[P. 272.

laid aside their dusty garments and passed out of the hut
to where, behind a tall memorial stone, a little cascade fell
with a musical splash into its rocky basin. Soon above the
sound of the waterfall the voice of prayer arose. Each of
the travellers took his stand in turn under the chilly fall,
and with chattering teeth and quivering limbs, repeated
his litany of penitence for past transgression, with prayers
for future freedom from sinning. It is this sought-for
purity of soul of which the white garments are the outward
symbol. To it the ascent of Ontake is believed to conduce.
The *sendachi*, as the leader of the band, however, is
distinguished by additional insignia. A *kesa*, a sort of
Buddhist stole, adorned with tufts of silk, encircles his
shoulders. Up his sleeve, or sometimes stuck inside the
collar of his tunic at the back of his neck, he carries the
sacred *gohei* — the wand with notched white papers
pendent from the top, always seen in Shintō temples, &c.
In his hand he bears a *shakujō*, a staff adorned with loose
metal rings, which is intended to serve the purposes of
alpenstock, siren-whistle, and field-marshal's bâton all in
one. The *shakujō* belonging to this particular *sendachi*
was an especially remarkable instrument. He informed us
confidentially that it was called *Kumo-Kiri*, the "cloud-
cutter." He had obtained it, he said, by means of direct
intervention on the part of the god of Ontake himself in
answer to mystic incantations. Even when the densest

T

mists obscured the way it never failed to point out the proper path. Sometimes a member of the band will carry a huge conch-shell, which is blown from time to time when passing along the road or through the mountain-forests. Its original use was probably to scare the wild beasts that infested the lonely thickets on the higher peaks.

A charming old gentleman, with snow-white hair, consented to join the group we photographed from the door of the hut. He had come, he said, from a long distance, in the hope that the supernatural influences pervading the peak would avail to cure him of disease, for it is at Matsuwo-no-taki (the Matsuwo cascade) that one of the great mountain spirits is believed to dwell. Near the hut a cluster of memorial stones stand like a collection of grave-yard monuments to commemorate the achievements of famous *sendachi* of bygone days. One tells of the hero of 100 ascents, another of 37, of 35 and so on. A huge flat slab is engraved with a portrait of Kakumei-gyōja, the first ascetic-mountaineer to climb Ontake from this direction. His eyes, and the bell he holds in his hand (for he was a Buddhist by persuasion) are brilliantly painted in gold ; whilst on the rock below, a pair of hands, carved in bas-relief and coloured bright crimson, remind one of the times when in Japan at least the red print of a man's hand affixed to a document stood for his seal. (In connection with Mr. Galton's "finger prints" this fact may not be without point.) Higher up a solitary post is adorned with an inscription telling of the first winter ascent of Ontake on January 23, some years ago.

After a farewell greeting to the pilgrim band we mounted quickly to the crest of the grassy ridge above. On overtopping it we were greeted with a sight of the massive form of our familiar twin-topped Norikura, the "saddle peak," nearly due north. The treeless slope we were now on is decorated with a picturesque hut, known as "The Place of the Thousand Pines." The apparent contradictoriness of the title may be explained by the fact that whilst the forest above this limit is Imperial property, all else belongs to the villages below, and so is mostly disafforested. Spaces in the forest, however, are let to the priests attached to the Ontake shrine, and by them again sublet to the keepers of the *koya* or pilgrim huts. On entering the forest belt, at a height of 6,000 feet, we found a profusion of chestnut, birch, *Chamæcyparis obtusa* and several sorts of fir. Passing clear of this some 2,000 feet higher up, we came out on a steep spur covered with dwarf pine, alder, and mountain ash. The rest-house at this point is known as *Nio-nin-dō*, and corresponds to those already spoken of on Fuji, &c., as marking the former limit of woman's freedom in bygone days. There now, however, seems to be little distinction made between the sexes in matters mountaineering, unless it be that while men pilgrims usually wear white stockings as part of their climbing costume, it is more usual for ladies to don leggings of lavender silk.

From the *Nio-nin-dō*, the eastern wall of the crater lip now rose immediately above, and our gradually steepening route lay over rough ridges of lava, streaks of snow, and broken rocks. From its shelter in the low spreading branches of the *haimatsu*, a startled hare shot forth and nearly ran between my legs in its alarm. It was here that we caught up the oddest specimen of a pilgrim I ever beheld. A veritable 'Excelsior' was he : his garments once were white, but were now toned down by exposure to a grimy grey. In this connection I may remark that the greatest proof of sanctity is seen where the dirtiest clothes proclaim the number of ascents the wearer has made on the sacred peak. Round a shaggy unkempt mass of coal-black hair he wore a white towel. On his back he bore a motley load of offerings for the Spirit of the Summit. Amongst others were a wooden tablet decorated with spear-heads, a pine branch, and a thick tress of hair. This last, he said, had been sent as a votive offering by a woman whose proxy he was. To complete his curious outfit, in his hand he bore "a banner with a strange device "—*Ontake jinsha*—" for the Ontake shrine."

Later in the afternoon, as our party reached the top (10,000 feet), and were examining the little shrine with its attendant array of images, guardian gods, and deified heroes of the past, the old man arrived with his load. He presented the offerings with prayers of touching earnestness and gestures of the strangest kinds. Below the summit in various spots, the rock is literally cushioned with the cast-off *waraji* of the pilgrims, for it is regarded as almost a breach of good manners, if not of piety, to omit to change the foot-gear at certain orthodox resting-places. Here and there I noticed pairs of ⊤-shaped *geta* (wooden pattens) lying on the ground. These are worn only by *gyōja* (ascetics) of the strictest sort. The presence of only one piece of wood underneath the sole affords greater immunity to stray beetles, snakes, &c., that are in danger of being crushed, for the earliest pilgrim-mountaineers were strictly Buddhist in their desire to avoid the taking of animal life.* Moreover the obviously greater difficulty of progression from place to place on a one-toothed patten is held to be more meritorious. The idea involved is probably akin to that which in old-time European pilgrimages prompted the traveller to put peas into his shoes.

* This once universal tenet of Buddhism is now gradually dying out, and flesh-meat is being consumed in increasing quantities throughout Japan. Kobe beef is noted throughout the Treaty Ports of the East for its excellence. Nevertheless, a Japanese friend of mine, an engineer, not long ago told me that the hold on the old ideas was still tenacious here and there. The land-lady of a country inn at which he intended to stay one night, turned him away almost in a fury when she discovered that amongst his baggage he had a tin of Kobe beef! "How did he know that the spirit of an honoured relative of his or hers might not be imprisoned in the contents of the case?" To her it was a matter of the most serious importance.

Descending the flight of steps that lead from the enclosure we passed into the hut—the highest on the mountain—and spent the night with Tochiyama, the *Kannushi* who guards the sacred summit.   He was an interesting person, and in spirit he reminded one of the fighting prelates of the Middle Ages.   Talking of the war in Korea then progressing, he waxed eloquent as he told how fond he was of fencing and shooting, at which warlike accomplishments he said he was keeping his hand in. Like old Fujiwara, our hunter-guide on Jōnendake, and thousands of other superannuated aspirants after military fame, he was longing to be called to fight for the honour of his Emperor and his beloved land.   Wherever one went among the people that summer, the same unanimous spirit was manifested.   At Matsumoto I had been warned of the danger of travelling in the interior.   I was told the suspected leanings of England towards China were likely to embitter the minds of the country folk against the English, and matters might go hard with me should my nationality be discovered !   Truly the whole 41,000,000 of this patriotic people were as one in heart and hope touching the progress of the campaign.

On the morrow we repaired, in the small hours, to the little rocky platform on which the topmost shrine is built. Through the grey mists northward the long line of the distant peaks of the Japanese Alps seem literally to uplift

H. J. Hamilton, phot.

THE SHRINE ON THE SUMMIT OF ONTAKE.

[P. 279.

themselves, like rocky islets emerging from a sea of white clouds. Below us lay the highest of the six great craters that stretch in a line along the highest ridge. The waters of the lake that fills it are held to possess miraculous powers to heal and to harm. The day before we had seen pilgrims carrying large bundles of paper on their shoulders down the mountain. These, they informed us, they had previously soaked in the lake, and were taking them to their far-off homes. They are then bestowed on suffering friends, who make them up into pills, which when swallowed are said to cure an astonishing catalogue of maladies. But due reverence must be shown to the water, for, we were told with awe, on one occasion an impious climber who had ventured, travel-stained as he was, to bathe in the lake, was punished with a sudden and shocking death for his act of desecration.

As we stood on our vantage point, 10,000 feet above the sea, the arrival of a number of pilgrims from a hut below told us the sun was about to rise. Reverently the white-robed party approached the shrine, and made their offerings with earnest prayers. They then turned eastwards, as the shrine itself faces, and proceeded, as the first bars of golden light began to steal up into the sky, to pay their supplications to the Goddess of the Sun. First of all, they clapped their hands to call the divinity's attention to their requests, and then broke out into a series of *harai*, or chants of "prayers of purification." Intermingled with the chants were repetitions of the invocation which is also continually heard as a band of pilgrims mounts upwards on the ascent, "*Rokkon Shōjō O Yama Kaisei,*" *i.e.,* "May our six senses be pure, and may the weather on the honourable peak be fine ! " *

Then followed a series of extraordinary pantomimic gestures called *in-musubi,* " seal-knots." The weirdness of these it is almost impossible to describe. With intense energy and earnestness the fingers of both hands are tied and twisted into the strangest combinations of knots, like the "cat's cradles" made by children at play. Each twist, each knot, has its own meaning, and resembles a sort of dumb alphabet, spoken with all the expression that physical action can put into it. For language it is really meant to be, addressed to those invisible powers of evil against whose malevolence the pilgrim is appealing for protection. As each sign is made, a violent grunt accompanies it by way of emphasis. These pantomimic prayers are concluded with a curious digital device called *Kuji-go-shimpō,* " the exorcism of the nine strokes." In this, the pilgrim holds the fingers of his

* This invocation is of Buddhist origin, and the six senses referred to are the eyes, ears, nose, tongue, heart, and body. Few of the pilgrims who repeat it understand its meaning, as the words are mostly Chinese. Those travellers, however, who have heard the chant on the lonely mountain side, only broken by the ringing of the *Sendachi's* bell, will not readily forget its weird effect.

right hand, sheathed, as it were, in his left, to represent a
sword. He then suddenly draws them forth and cuts the
air with nine swift strokes, five horizontal and four

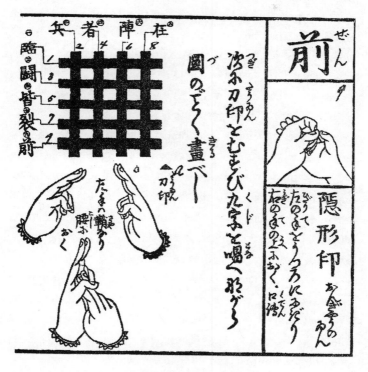

DIAGRAMS OF KUJI-GO-SHIMPO AND IN-MUSUBI, FROM AN
ILLUSTRATED MANUAL.

vertical, alternately. With each movement he utters a
Sanskrit syllable, of the actual meaning of which, however,
he is entirely ignorant. This device is apparently meant

to be both offensive and defensive, typifying as it does both the exorcism of the powers of evil, and at the same time imposing a barrier against their attacks on the soul.

During all this time the *Kannushi* Tochiyama sat stolid in his sentinel box by the shrine. He looked on at the proceedings with a sceptical contempt born of excessive familiarity. To me the whole scene, though now I was by no means witnessing it for the first time, was weird to a degree. But a stranger sight still was in store. As I crossed the platform, I suddenly noticed another knot of pilgrims, who, to escape observation, had hidden themselves behind the shrine. When I came upon them I found them engaged in the uncanniest pursuit of all.

Holding before him, between the palms of his outstretched hands, a *gohei*, one member of the party was squatting on a rock in front of the rest, who sat facing him —as nearly as their confined quarters would allow—in Indian file. It is worthy of notice that the man's legs were not tucked under him in Japanese sitting fashion, but folded in front, like the Hindu, &c. He was acting as a sort of medium (the Japanese word *nakaza* = " seat between ") of communication betwixt his friends and the mountain divinities they had come to consult. Closing his eyes, the *nakaza* sat silent and still. His companions broke out into a subdued chorus of prayer. Soon the face of the medium began to turn a livid hue. Unearthly

From a Kakemono.

FUKAN REIJIN, A PIONEER OF THE JAPANESE ALPS. [P. 283.

gaspings issued from his throat, and the *gohei* trembled
and shook violently in his hands. His eyes turned upwards in their sockets until only about half the iris was
visible. A series of convulsive jerks at length brought the
gohei to a standstill above his forehead. This was a sign
that a god had come. Thereupon the *maeza* (literally,
" the seat in front "), a pilgrim who had been all the time
acting as a sort of precentor to the rest, bent reverently
towards the medium. With his forehead lowly bowed on
the rock between them, he inquired the "honourable
name" of the august visitor who had now replaced the
personality of the medium by his own presence. In a
hoarse whisper came the reply, " I am Fukan Reijin."
This was the posthumous name of the canonized
mountaineer who, exactly a century before, had made
the first ascent of Ontake from the Ōdaki side (sometimes
called the "back-way," in contradistinction to the Kuro-
zawa or "front entrance").

As the *maeza* heard the name, he went on to put the
requests of the several pilgrims. All were simple enough.
Some referred to the weather they were likely to have on
their travels ; the health of those at home, or their business
prospects during the coming year. In a low voice the
nakaza pronounced the god's replies. All were conveniently vague in their oracular orthodoxy, though I
remember he predicted cloudy weather for that afternoon.

Indeed, I had good cause to recollect it when, a few hours later, we were plunging down the slippery slopes in the forest through a thunderstorm of pitiless violence. When all the questions put had been dealt with categorically, the *gohei* in the medium's hands was lowered in token that the spirit had departed, and that the man was now himself again. The *maeza* then arose, and with necessary, well-meant violence, set to rubbing the body and pounding the limbs of the *nakaza*, so stiff and rigid had they turned during the cataleptic trance. Soon the man came to, and the party went away. They had taken no more notice of my presence than of the stocks and stones that surrounded us.

As my party were this year making a sort of *col* of Ontake, we did not retrace our steps of the previous day. By way of variation we descended by a steeper and, in some respects, more interesting route—that reaching Agematsu by way of Ōdaki. Leaving the summit at 8·30 A.M., a rather trying descent of rough lava, loose cinders, and then steep rocks, took us down to the Kongō-dōji hut, or, rather, its shattered remains. The sky soon became overcast, and a tropical thunderstorm, with sheets of rain, drove us for over an hour to shelter in the Ta-no-hara hut. At the Nakagoya lower down we saw diagrams representing the old religious dance descriptive of the legend of Suzume-no-mikoto. During the time Ontake is

open, a troupe of performers give this play at Kurosawa.
The hut-keeper told us that a branch of the Tomoye Kō
(one of the principal pilgrim clubs), on their way up the
mountain, had recently paid $30 for a performance on
their own account. After making the descent, they
gave $15 for an exhibition by way of a service of interces-
sion for the Emperor and for his success in the war with
China.

As we cleared the forest we fell in with a couple of
Shintō priests, with whom we had a chat under the *tōrii*
below the Nakagoya hut. As they stood for their photographs, their dingy garments and shaggy hair contrasted
strangely with the smooth-shaven crowns and brighter,
richer robes always worn by their Buddhist brethren in the
plains. About 2 P.M. a slight detour from the downward
track took us to the foot of the Ōtaki, a lovely cascade
falling over the face of a cliff into a secluded basin shaded
by tall, dark cryptomeria. As we stood watching the play
of light and shadow on the glancing waters, a solitary
pilgrim entered the glen. Stripping entirely naked, he
took his stand under the icy fall, and crossing his hands on
his breast, broke out into an almost agonizing series of
prayers for cleansing from sin and for purity of soul.
Without this purity, I was told, it was useless to ascend
to the mountain top and bend in supplication at the sacred
shrine. And as one listened to the pleadings of what

certainly seemed to be a soul in real earnest, the words
of David vividly came back—

" Who shall ascend into the hill of the Lord ? or who shall stand in His
holy place ?
He that hath clean hands, and a pure heart ; who hath not lifted up his
soul unto vanity, nor sworn deceitfully."

May it not be of such as he that the great Apostle once
wrote, " In every nation he that feareth Him and worketh
righteousness is accepted with Him ? "

Near the base of the mountain a neat new shrine,
sheltering under the lee of perpendicular creeper-grown
cliffs, bears the warning inscription *raku-gaki muyo*
(" Needless scribbling is prohibited"). At Ōdaki, a
finely-situated hamlet perched on a hill-side above the
rushing waters of the Ōdaki-gawa, we spent the night.
Everything was *en fête* in commemoration of the one
hundredth anniversary of the first ascent of Ontake by
Fūkan Reijin, already referred to. When the good man
first made the attempt, he is said to have hopelessly lost
his way. On the second, however, he was aided by a
ptarmigan, which guided him safely to the top.

The *matsuri* (festival) in the climber's honour lasted
through the earlier half of August. A cluster of tall
bamboos, with long streamers fluttering in the breeze, stood
sentinel over a magnificent monolith bearing the great
man's name and titles. This was an oval slab 14 feet by

8 feet, erected on a mound at the entrance to the village. Its presence reminded one of the Chamonix commemoration of Balmat's world-famed feat on Mont Blanc.

After a night at the *Kannushi's* house at Ōdaki, we walked in the cool freshness of the early morning nearly to Agematsu, on the Nakasendō, by one of the loveliest routes in this part of the country. Of all the picturesque characteristics of the scenery on the east side of the Japanese Alps, perhaps the bridges are the most remarkable. Of none is this more true than of Ambabashi, some 2½ miles from Ōdaki. Dark timbers are cleverly fixed against the smooth straight sides of parallel cliffs at a height of 100 feet or more above a deep green pool. The water is so clear that the bases of the cliffs are visible many feet below the surface.

At the bridge of Hashidō further on, the landlord of the little rest-house—where Belcher and I had halted three years ago on our way from the sacred mountain—recognized me at once and gave us a kindly welcome. On reaching the Nakasendō I had to bid a regretful farewell to my trusty comrade, for Hamilton's work compelled him to return to Nagoya before I had completed my tour. Uraguchi and I returned to Fukushima later in the day. As we threw ourselves on the chairless floor of our inn that evening after dinner, we fell to studying the words of wisdom from a Chinese classic, with which a thoughtful landlord had adorned the *fusuma* (sliding screens) of our apartment. One of the inscriptions, quite incidentally, threw a little light on the dilatory way in which that worthy used to call me in the morning.* It declared, " There is here no fixed time for retiring or rising, but each one does as he feels inclined." Another, in a metaphoric vein that displayed a remarkable knowledge of anatomy, warned us sententiously that, " Though life, like the entrails of a sheep, be many thousands of miles long, yet fame is ever as short as the horns of a snail."

The squalling of infants, less than a mile away, not seldom disturbed our rest. The experience, trivial as it may seem to the ordinary observer, is one more worthy of note in a land where it is the fond delusion of the passing globe-trotter to believe that babies never cry. That it is a stern reality, any one who is not deaf and has travelled with his ears open in the country must freely own. An English teacher in one of the higher Japanese schools once received from his pupils a collection of epigrams upon this very topic. One scholar described a crying baby as " a case of *chian bogai* ('disturbing the public tranquillity ')." Another as " a broken wind instru-

* On this subject I may remark that some of the country folk have a great objection to waking persons by force. They believe that the soul, in the form of a small black ball, deserts the body of a person going to sleep. If the owner be waked suddenly the soul is said not to have time to return, hence fatal consequences are likely to follow. This belief is held by other races also.

IN THE 'PARADISE OF BABIES —WHERE "CHILDREN NEVER CRY."

[P. 288.

ment that has to be beaten in order to bring it into proper shape again."

'TRUE TILL DEATH'—THE BUGLER SHIRAKAMI GENJIRŌ, AT THE BATTLE OF SŎNG-HWAN.

It was so long since we had received any news regarding the war, that we were naturally anxious to get the papers

U

promised by our friend Kakuzen from Matsumoto. When they arrived, we read the most curious stories telling of the wave of patriotism sweeping over the country from end to end. No sacrifice seemed too great, if so be even the humblest might thereby advance "the glory of the Emperor." A barber of Nagoya wanted to show his patriotic zeal by shaving all the soldiers of the garrison free of charge. When this was good-naturedly forbidden by the commanding officer, the worthy fellow, it is true, continued to make the usual charge of $\frac{1}{4}d$. per beard, but insisted on giving each man a bottle of lemonade to make up ! The strangest instance of all, however, was this : a party of young men formed themselves into a guild, under a vow to abstain from venereal practices, in order to save money to contribute to the Patriotic Fund ! During the progress of the war, strange stories were told that showed that the same patriotic fire was burning in every breast in this extraordinary nation.

On one occasion an old gentleman received a letter from one of his two sons who had gone to the war. " When my brother and I joined our regiment," he said, " we each exacted a promise from the other that if either met his death before reaching the gates of Peking, the survivor should carry his corpse within the walls of China's capital. But my brother is already slain, and we are yet far away from the great city. I have therefore, in order to fulfil my promise, cut off a portion of my brother's body, which I have placed inside my cap, so that, when we enter victorious

WOUNDED CHINESE PRISONERS BROUGHT INTO A JAPANESE FIELD-HOSPITAL DURING THE WAR—FROM A NATIVE CARTOON.

into the conquered capital, my brother's spirit will behold and know his heart's desire has been accomplished." And as the old man read the letter, he quietly laughed, and said, "Well done, my son!"

An old widow lady, mother of an only son, one day received the news of her darling's death. Her friends at once, *more Japonico*, gathered round to offer sympathy. But, with indignant scorn, she turned away. "Widow though I am," she cried, "I count it but a privilege to give my only son to die for the honour of his Emperor and his country."

How it all recalls the Spartan mother of the old anthology :—

> " Eight sons Demœneta at Sparta's call
> Sent forth—one tomb received them all.
> No tear she shed, but shouted "Victory!
> Sparta, I bore them but to die for thee!""

We made our way back to Kōbe by the Gombei Tōge, the Kōshū Kaidō, and Minobu, and the rapids of the Fuji-kawa. The magnificent Buddhist temple, dedicated to Nichiren, on the quiet, forest-clad hill-side at Minobu, formed a picture whose beauty will long remain fresh in our recollections. At Iwabuchi we took the Tōkaidō train to Kōbe, having as companions a detachment of soldiers bound for Korea. Great enthusiasm, albeit of a quiet sort, was manifested along their route. At several stations the train drew up to find a platform adorned with lanterns and flags decorated with the Red Cross Society's badge, whilst attendants dispensed cold water and tea to the warriors thirsty with a hot and dusty journey from the capital.

And so we bade our farewell to the Alps of Japan. They do not, it is true, display the glories of glacier-shrouded peaks, and the scale on which they are built is only two-thirds that of the famous Alps of Switzerland. But the picturesqueness of their valleys, and the magnificence of the dark and silent forests that clothe their massive flanks, surpass anything I have met with in European Alpine wanderings. And of them with equal truth it may be said, " How many deep sources of delight are gathered into the compass of their glens and vales, and how, down to the most secret cluster of their far-away flowers, and the idlest leap of their straying streamlets, the whole heart of Nature seems thirsting to give, and still to give, shedding forth her everlasting beneficence with a profusion so patient, so passionate, that our utmost observance and thankfulness are but, at last, neglects of her nobleness, and apathy to her love." (Ruskin, " Modern Painters," Book IV.)

CHAPTER XIV.

A FEW remarks may not be out of place with reference to the origin of the curious practices described in the preceding chapter. After several times witnessing performances of them on the mountain side—as well as in a more detailed and elaborate manner at a meeting of one of the pilgrim clubs in private—I can only come to the conclusion that they are simply survivals of old forms of Hindu mysticism, which have reached Japan by way of China and Korea. In the paper by Professor Chamberlain, already referred to on p. 270, he has pointed out that when Buddhism was introduced into Japan, it brought with it a whole museum of Chinese superstitions on the top of original Indian beliefs and practices, themselves the slowly accumulated legacy of a hoary antiquity. Allowing for natural modifications, the present customs in vogue amongst these Ontake pilgrims (and others closely resembling them) are just such as we might expect when we realize how much of the religious beliefs and practices of the Japanese have been derived from China* through Korea. Friends of my own, who have lived and travelled and observed in the less known parts of those countries, tell me of customs almost identical with those I have been endeavouring to describe, although, of course, the practices in their principal features are such as are known to be common to various races at different times.

The famous Buddhist teacher, Kūkai, better known in Japan by his posthumous name of Kōbō Daishi, visited China in 804 A.D., for the purpose of studying Buddhism more closely under the guidance of the great abbot Hui-Kwo. On his return he founded the sect of Shingon, "the true teaching." It is especially in the mystic practices of this and similar sects,—widely spread, though secretly indulged in, throughout Japan, chiefly amongst the lower orders—that we find such a striking resemblance in all essential features to such systems as the Yoga of the Hindus, from which Chinese Buddhism and Taoism largely borrowed.

---

* Cp. "The China Review," vol. iv., p. 78, &c. : "If there be any family in trouble a somnambule is sent for. Incense sticks are lighted and put into that niche dedicated to the spirit of the hearth. As soon as the particulars as to the nature of the difficulty are learned, the medium seats himself on a low stool and crouches down so that his head rests on his knees. He utters incantations; a sudden change comes over his body, which is convulsed with spasms. He apparently falls fast asleep. Questions are put which the somnambule answers in the name of the spirit in an unnatural voice. When all is over he is waked up by loud shouts, etc., from those around." Cp. also Appendix B. on ' Notes on the exorcism of spirits in Korea.'

Interesting notes on the Yoga practices will be found in Sir Monier Williams' " Buddhism," Lecture X., and again in a remarkable book by Surgeon-Major Waddell, on " Lamaism in Thibet." On p. 141 of the latter book we read, " The Yoga doctrine of ecstatic union with the universal spirit had been introduced into Hinduism about 150 B.C. by Patanjali, and is not unknown to Western systems. It taught spiritual advancement by means of a self-hypnotising to be learned by rules . . . . Asanga, importing Patanjali's doctrine into Buddhism and abusing it, taught that by means of mystic formulas,—as spells, the reciting of which should be accompanied by music and certain distortion of the fingers (*mudrâ*)—a state of mental fixity might be reached, characterized by neither thought nor annihilation of thoughts, and consisting of sixfold bodily and mental happiness (*yogi*), whence would result endowment with special miracle-working powers. These miraculous powers may be used for exorcism and sorcery, and for purely secular and selfish objects. Those who mastered these practices were called Yogācārya."

Some of my readers may possibly hold that an inquiry into such things as these is only a waste of time. Others will say that the Christian should have nothing to do with the investigation of phenomena or practices which *by those who carry them on* are avowed to have connection with beings of another world—and that not of the upper order of the supernatural. But, for myself, I cannot believe this. For I hold, with Bishop Westcott,* that "even the rudest 'demon worship' contains the germ of this feeling by which the worshipper seeks to be at one with some power which is adverse to him. It is a witness to something in man by which he is naturally constituted to feel after a harmonious fellowship with all that of which he is conscious—with the unseen and with the finite no less than with the seen and the material."

During the course of my investigations into the origin, &c., of the foregoing practices, I was on several occasions invited by officials connected with various pilgrim clubs to attend the *séances* in private. Although the ceremony of *Kangakari*, or *Kami-oroshi*† as it is called, is thought to be most readily and efficaciously performed on the sacred peak, where the spirits approached are considered to be most accessible, it also takes place, during such time as the mountain is not " open," in private. This is generally in the house of one of the club members, where the regular meetings of the club are held. The following account will show that the details of the service are then, as might be expected, much more elaborate, though the essential features are still the same. The meeting on this occasion took place at the house of a rice merchant in Ōsaka, where

* Cp. "The Gospel of Life," p. 97.
† *Kangakari* = " causing the god to rest," *i.e.* on the medium ; *Kami-oroshi* = " bringing the god down."

the only down-stairs room had been arranged to serve as a temporary chapel.

The *toko-no-ma*—the recess which forms the place of honour in a Japanese apartment—was hung with *kakemono* (hanging scroll-pictures), representing several of the gods who are supposed to hold Ontake under their special patronage. In front of the *kakemono* were placed a *kōrō* (incense-burner), a *gohei*, and offerings of oranges, cakes, &c. The officiating minister was a well-known Shintō priest of Ōsaka. Dressed in white garments, stamped with the characters that denote an ascent of Ontake, and wearing the tall black hat familiar as a part of Shintō priestly costume, he reverently took his seat before the extemporised shrine. Clapping his hands together in the ordinary way, he bent his head in prayer. In the meantime the rice-merchant, who was to act as *nakaza* (medium), entered the bath-room at one end of the verandah close by, and went through a series of lustral ablutions, for much fasting and ceremonial purification are indispensable to a proper performance of the rites. After him, another member of the company arose, stripped himself naked, and followed his example. The *nakaza* now returned adorned in his pilgrim clothes, and wearing over his shoulders a *kesa* or stole, and at his girdle a bell. Taking the *gohei* from before the shrine, he placed it in a little bamboo receptacle at hand. With lighted *senkō* (incense sticks) he wrote

mystic figures in the air, and then returned them to the
kōrō. In quick succession he next told his rosary and
waved the *gohei* violently in each quarter of the room, by
way of purifying the place from evil influences. Each of
these performances he interrupted from time to time with
finger twistings, writing mysterious characters in the air,
ringing his bell, and scattering a purificatory shower of
sparks with flint and steel. Then he sprinkled salt towards
the four cardinal points in order to ward off further evil
and for a similar purpose swept the air again with the
gohei before returning to tell his beads afresh. Then came
another *harai*, or Shintō litany, said as a duet by the
priest who acted as *maeza*, and the *nakaza* himself,
interspersed with frequent repetitions of "*rokkon-shōjō.*"
After more incense-sticks had been lighted, oil was poured
on the head of the *nakaza*, who proceeded to hang up his
kesa before the shrine and to purify the *tenugui*—with
which his head had been bound round—in the smoke of
the rising incense. Now the *maeza* took the lead for a
while, muttering incantations over papers inscribed with
Sanskrit characters, to the accompaniment of finger-
twistings punctuated with energetic grunts. Amongst
other prayers recited by the *maeza* was the *Ō harai*, or
"greater litany." The principal Shintō divinities were
invoked and petitions offered for the protection of the
worshippers and their families, and for the prosperity of

their businesses. After the names of the *San-jū-rokudōji* ("the thirty-six divine children"—certain other Shintō celebrities) had been repeated, a passage of Buddhist scripture in Sanskrit was intoned, beginning "*Hannya haramitsu.*" Finally came the petition for a god to descend, on the ground that the place had been got ready by purificatory rites. "*Koko mo takama no hara nareba,*" "Since *this* also is now (equivalent to) the plain of high heaven."

This concluded the first part of the service, and all was now ready for the medium to become possessed. That person thereupon, seating himself with his back to the shrine, tied his *kimono* (outer ordinary garment) round his legs very tightly, and after crossing them in Hindu fashion in front of him, moved on to a piece of paper on which were inscribed the two characters *kongō himitsu*—*i.e.*, "profound mystery." They were written, he afterwards remarked, by a very famous *sendachi*, now deceased.

The most curious part of the *séance* then began.

The *maeza*—still acting as a sort of master of ceremonies—tied the *nakaza's* towel round its owner's head, in return receiving a purifying sprinkling of salt over his own body. The *gohei* was now placed in the closed palms of the medium, who forthwith sat up erect with fast-closed eyes, whilst the *maeza* waved a *nusa* (a sort of small *gohei*) and twisted his fingers with great rapidity.

In the meantime the medium's face turned a ghastly livid hue, and heavy breathing was succeeded by retching, as if the man were suffering from *mal de mer*. Suddenly the *gohei* was jerked up as a sign that the god had come, and, as the medium trembled violently and gasped for breath, the *maeza* reverently bent his forehead to the floor and inquired the august name of the divine visitant, the whispered reply being, " I am Mikasa."   This is the name, it may be remarked, of one of the lower peaks of Ontake. After thanks for the speedy visit of the divinity had been given, the various members of the club present then put various questions through the *maeza*.

One, a woman who stated her age to be 25, said she had long been suffering from ophthalmia, and asked for the reason and a remedy.

She was told it was a complaint common to females, and advised to consult the doctor ! To her further query as to where the doctor lived, the reply given was inaudible, as was the answer to a request for the medium himself to suggest a remedy.

Another woman asked what was amiss with her child of eight, who was very ill.

The reply was " *Kan* " (a hysterical complaint common to children.)   " The only possible remedy," he added, " lies in burning the child's back with *moxa* " * (a sort of

* Cp. Chamberlain, "Things Japanese," p. 312.

grass used as a cautery, and held to be a panacea for nearly every ill imaginable).

The last petitioner was a man 54 years old. His abnormally bare face and skull shone like a great billiard ball, and his eyebrows were destitute of hair, proclaiming him to be suffering from a sort of leprosy. He looked much in need of active exercise. The advice given to him was to become an earnest believer in the doctrines of the Ontake Kyōkwai (sect), and to make frequent ascents of the "august peak."

No other members of the congregation having further questions to ask, this portion of the service was therefore at an end. The *maeza* then sprinkled more salt about the room, and betook himself to finger-twisting again. At this point the *gohei* in the hands of the medium began to descend, signifying that the god was taking his leave. To yet another accompaniment of *in-musubi* the *maeza* addressed the departing divinity with the respectful farewell " *Kumoi haruka-ni kaerimase* ("Please to return to your distant home in the sky"). He then turned his attention to the medium. First he removed the towel from his brow, but only with great difficulty succeeded in wrenching the *gohei* from the grasp of his stiffened fingers. Indeed the man had become so rigid during the cataleptic trance into which he had thrown himself, that it was not until after soundly belabouring his shoulders and back, and kneading, so to speak, his arms and hands that the *maeza* and his assistant (officially known as *wakiza*, lit. "side-seat") managed to restore him to his normal condition.

The *séance* concluded with more *in-musubi* and incantations in a jumble of Sanskrit, &c., in which the words frequently recurred, "*on saraba Tathâgata.*" * Roughly speaking, the whole service seems to divide itself naturally into four sections :—

1. Prayers for sanctification—that the congregation, and especially the medium, may be rendered fit to receive the divine visitant.
2. Prayers for the descent of the god upon the medium thus sanctified.
3. The god's descent—the *kangakari*—or possession proper.
4. Prayers for his return.

How much of the trance-like condition of the *nakaza* is real, and how much is simulated, it is perhaps difficult to say, and I think it would be beyond the scope of the present volume to enter into any detailed discussion on the subject. But a little light is thrown upon the opinions of the better educated and more enlightened Japanese touching the matter by certain police regulations issued

* The Sanskrit term 'Tathâgata' (Japanese 'Nyōrai') is an honorific title applied to all Buddhas, signifying that a Buddha is one whose coming and going are in accordance with the action of his predecessors. Cp. Murray's "Handbook to Japan," p. 46.

some time ago to the sects who practise *Kami-oroshi* and similar rites.

In July, 1882, the Minister of the Home Department published an order to the heads of these bodies, stating that "only those who are already under medical treatment in the ordinary way are to be allowed to get prescriptions at the *Kami-oroshi* gatherings. In each case such applicants must testify beforehand that they are taking doctor's medicine!"

While the ceremonies which I have described are perhaps the best-known of their kind, though not performed in public, there are others, more uncommon, yet of a similar nature to which it may be of interest to refer.

At the time of the *bon-matsuri*, or "feast of the dead" on the 14th of July, according to the old calendar, a rite known as *go-ō* takes place on a mountain called Futagani San, in the province of Mimasaka. This is to prevent the crows from doing harm to the crops. A person known as the *go-ō-zane* is chosen to become possessed by the god of the mountain, the choice being influenced by the knowledge of his honesty and devoutness of life. For several days before the ceremony he undergoes a rigorous course of ascetic training. Living in the depths of a silent gloomy forest, he spends most of his time in bathing in a pond sacred to the *genius loci*. About midnight on the eventful day the god is supposed to come to the *gohei*, which the *go-ō-zane* carries from the shrine on the summit to a large temple at the mountain foot, where the rites are to be performed. In the central hall of this building all lights are extinguished, and a preliminary service is held. This consists chiefly of *harai*, and repetitions of *rokkon shōjō*, &c., to the accompaniment of the blowing of conch-shells and the rattling of *shakujō*. The effect is said to be weird and awe-inspiring to a degree, as the silent forest echoes and re-echoes to the increasing din. The body of the medium is bound thickly with straw ropes, so that in his subsequent proceedings he may do himself no injury. Outside the temple, hundreds of men, stark naked, are waiting with torches several feet long to follow his movements. After the prayers are finished, the medium becomes " possessed." Leaping up from his seat on the floor, he dashes out of the temple and rushes wildly about the enclosure. At times he rests on stone slabs placed at three of the corners of the sacred garden. To prevent him from falling to the ground two priests hold him by the arms, as he is believed to be unconscious of his actions as well as weakened by his fasting. The rounds he makes of the enclosure are said to be due to the good spirits of the god possessing him. Returning at last to the temple he is dispossessed, so to speak, in the way I have already described, and the spirit returns on the *gohei* to the mountain-top shrine. During his wanderings in the

x

enclosure, the possessed medium strikes with a torch he holds in his hands various persons—thus shown to be guilty of wrong-doing—by way of warning. The fire of the torch on this particular night, however, is held to be quite innocuous. When the torch is finally thrown down, before the medium re-enters the temple, the fragments are eagerly sought after by the spectators, who put them up in their rice fields as scare-crows of exceptional efficacy. Crowds of the peasantry from the neighbouring country-side visit the mountain and watch these proceedings with mingled amusement and awe. The possessed *go-ō-zane* is said to hop about in a very curious manner, instead of running or walking. This is owing to the fact that the god who takes possession of him is the ruler of the crows !

Mr. Frazer (author of the 'Golden Bough') has kindly pointed out to me interesting classical parallels to the above practice in the worship of Apollo Smintheus ("Mouse Apollo") and of Dionysus Brassareus ("Fox Dionysus"). This worship was probably addressed originally to the Lord of the Mice (himself a mouse) and to the Lord of the Foxes (himself a fox), to induce them to use their authority with their subjects (mice and foxes respectively) and forbid them to ravage the fields and vineyards. The worship of Baal-zebub ("Lord of the Flies ") was probably similarly directed to the Lord of Flies as a means of getting rid of the plague of flies.

The Greeks offered special sacrifices to gods who were supposed to have the power of driving away the flies.*

Before leaving the subject of these curious practices, I may add one other instance of methods of divination, though it is quite different from the foregoing. Amongst the ordinary, now dying-out class of persons known as *miko* or "diviners," is one called *kitsune-tsukai, i.e.,* "a fox-possessor." The divination is carried on by means of a small image of a fox made in a very odd way. A fox is buried alive in a hole with its head left free. Food of the sort of which foxes are known to be most fond is placed just beyond the animal's reach. As days pass by the poor beast in its dying agony of hunger makes frantic efforts to reach the food, but in vain. At the moment of death the spirit of the fox is believed to pass into the food, which is then mixed with a quantity of clay, and shaped into the form of the animal. Armed with this extraordinary object the *miko* is supposed to become an infallible guide to foretelling future events of every kind.

* See Pausanias, v. 14, 1 ; viii. 26, 7; Pliny, Nat. Hist., x. 75.

CHAPTER XV.

" POSSESSION " AND " EXORCISM."

THE belief of the mass of the Japanese people in the power of certain animals to "possess" human beings is so widely spread, that references to the general subject of possession itself would scarcely be complete without special mention of the familiar superstitions known as *tanuki-tsuki* ("badger possession"), and *kitsune-tsuki* ("fox possession"). Mr. Chamberlain has remarked that Chinese notions on the subject entered Japan during the early Middle Ages. Certainly the folk-lore of both countries, *mutatis mutandis*, seems to point to such a conclusion. A curious fact connected with such possession is that the person bewitched is commonly in the habit of behaving as much like the animal itself—be it badger, fox, or what not—as it is possible for a human being to do. An instance that came to my notice in Japan some time ago will serve as an illustration.

Mr. Chamberlain* remarks that badgers are generally players of practical jokes rather than seriously wicked

* " Things Japanese."

deceivers. A common trick of theirs is to beat a tattoo on their stomach. In art they are generally represented thus diverting themselves, with an enormously protuberant abdomen, for all the world like a drum. It is not, however, always so. For some time I had in my service a Japanese as house-boy, who ultimately was re-engaged by a friend of mine, his former master. One day news was brought to my friend that the man was ill. Enquiries elicited the information that "the fact is, a badger has taken possession of him;" and forthwith a visit had to be paid to the unfortunate person's room. Grovelling and leaping on all fours about the place, the bewitched one dashed from end to end of the matted floor. "There, there!" cried the man's wife, excitedly; "don't you see the badger has got hold of him? Listen to the way he grunts and growls, see the food we have had to bring him; watch him jumping to and fro—only a badger could make him do that." In truth, the unhappy individual's behaviour was remarkably like that of the *tanuki* itself. He ultimately, in a moment of comparative calmness, called for a sword with which to slay his tormentor, apparently forgetful of the fact that immediate disaster or death is held to inevitably result from such an act of madness. The man eventually died in hospital, the doctor's verdict being, I believe, one of brain-disease.

It is, however, chiefly with the fox that such disorders

are connected. Their power of "possessing" is so generally
feared that shrines and temples in their honour exist in
nearly all parts of the country. So popular is the chief of
these (on the outskirts of the former capital, Kyōtō), that it
gives its name to the railway station built years ago for the
accommodation of the throngs of visitors who flock to the
various festivals held in the temple precincts. Practically,
all foxes were once supposed to be subject to Inari Sama,
the Goddess of Rice, though now in popular belief Inari
Sama *is* the Fox-Goddess. Opposite the holes inhabited
by these creatures stand small *torii* and shrines with images
of foxes in clay or stone, with propitiatory offerings of the
food they are known to delight in. Doubtless this attention is owing to the fear which the wily animal inspires.
At the season when the rice is ripening the fox is supposed
to act as a sort of torch-bearer to the Rice-Goddess when
she goes on a tour of inspection of the crops. A sort of
will-o'-the-wisp, caused by the gaseous exhalations then
prevalent, forms the ground of belief in what is known
as *kitsune-bi, i.e.* "fox-fire." The peasants affirm that
the mysterious fire-brands are composed of torches made
from human bones. The lights never set the crops ablaze,
but merely make them visible. They are oftenest seen
after light rains, and seem to run along the ground, unit-
ing and separating, disappearing and reappearing, from
time to time.

To return, however, to the actual question of the alleged possession by foxes—the phenomena by which it is accompanied are various. Sometimes the victim loses entire possession of himself quite suddenly; or, again, the lack of self-control may be only partial. At other times he is quite unaware of the coming of the fox, the only manifestation being strange and apparently unaccountable swellings in different parts of the body, or various forms of nervous disease. Sooner or later the possession shows itself unmistakeably by an uncontrollable trembling of the hands and feet, contraction of the muscles, violent facial contortions, unmeaning noises, together with actions resembling those of the actual animal itself. Occasionally the sufferer takes to the woods and hills, and lives on berries, etc., all the while running or crawling about on all fours. This state lasts sometimes only a few hours, more usually a few days, though cases have been known to last for many months. On obtaining deliverance, the patient is almost invariably quite prostrated, and frequently knows absolutely nothing of what took place during the period of possession. There are said to be different grades of possession. When the victim only grovels and grunts he is said to be under the control of a fox of low degree. Intelligent speech reveals a higher rank; while, where the power of divination is held to exist, the most exalted order has been reached.

The possession is usually attributed to the malevolence of some fox or other, which has failed to receive from the victim something in the way of food, etc., it particularly desired. At times it is declared to be the result of the desire for vengeance on the part of a human enemy through the agency of *kitsune-tsukai,* *i.e.,* "fox possessor," or witch. The fox is said to enter its victim either through the breast or through the space between the finger-nails and the flesh. Where once he has so entered the creature lives a life of his own, entirely distinct from the real *ego* of the possessed person. When first I became aware of this fact, I turned my attention to the phenomena of hypnotism, to which this curious state appeared to be so closely allied. Eventually I found Dr. Baelz, a well-known professor at the Imperial University of Tōkōy, and physician to H. B. M.'s Legation, had studied the question from a medical stand-point. Dr. Baelz kindly communicated to me some of his conclusions, and as these practically coincide with my own, I cannot do better than quote them as also given in Mr. Chamberlain's already mentioned work on "Things Japanese."

After the entrance of the fox into its victim "there thus results a sort of double entity or double consciousness. The person possessed hears and understands everything that the fox within him thinks or says. The two often engage in a loud and violent dispute, the fox speaking in a voice altogether different from that which is natural to the individual. . . , It is almost exclusively women that are attacked—mostly women of the lower classes. Among the predisposing conditions may be mentioned a weak intellect, a superstitious turn of mind, and such debilitating diseases as, for instance, typhoid fever. The explanation of the disorder is not so far to seek as might be supposed. ' Possession ' is evidently related to hysteria and to the hypnotic phenomena which physiologists have recently studied with so much care. The cause of all alike is the fact that, whereas in healthy persons one half of the brain alone is actively engaged . . . . . leaving the other half to contribute only in a general manner to the function of thought, nervous excitement arouses this other half, and the two— one the organ of the usual self, the other the organ of the new pathologically affected self—are set over against each other. The rationale of possession is an ' auto-suggestion,' an idea arising either with apparent spontaneity, or else from the subject-matter of it being talked about by others in the patient's presence, and then overmastering her weak mind exactly as happens in hypnosis. In the same manner, the idea of the possibility of cure will often actually effect the cure. The cure-worker must be a person of strong mind and power of will, and must enjoy the patient's full confidence. For this reason, the priests of the Nichiren sect (which is the most superstitious and bigoted of

Japanese Buddhist sects) are the most successful expellers of foxes. Occasionally fits and screams accompany the exit of the fox. In all cases—even when the fox leaves quietly—great prostration remains for a day or two, and sometimes the patient is unconscious of what has happened.

"To mention but one among several cases : I was once called in to a girl with typhoid fever. She recovered ; but during her convalescence she heard the women around her talking of another woman who had a fox, and would doubtless do her best to pass it on to some one else, in order to be rid of it. At that moment the girl experienced an extraordinary sensation—the fox had taken possession of her ! All her efforts to get rid of him were vain. 'He is coming ! he is coming !' she would cry, as a fit of the fox drew near. ' Oh, what shall I do ? Here he is !' And then, in a strange dry cracked voice, the fox would speak, and mock his unfortunate hostess. Thus matters continued for three weeks, till a priest of the Nichiren sect was sent for. The priest upbraided the fox sternly. The fox (always, of course, speaking through the girl's mouth) argued on the other side. At last he said : 'I am tired of her. I ask no better than to leave her. What will you give me for doing so ?' The priest asked what he would take. The fox replied, naming certain cakes and other things, which, he said, must be placed before the altar of such and such a temple, at 4 P.M. on such and such a day.

The girl was conscious of the words her lips were made to frame, but was powerless to say anything in her own person. When the day and hour arrived, the offerings bargained for were taken by her relations to the place indicated, and the fox quitted the girl at that very hour."

Exorcism of the fox-spirit is not only largely practised at celebrated shrines connected with the Nichiren sect—such as those of Minobu and Kato Kiyomasa (near Kumamoto in Kyūshū), but in some more out-of-the-way spots there are actually hospitals which exist solely for this purpose.

One of these, accommodating some 30 patients, is situated some 4 or 5 miles from Hachiōji, on a picturesque hillside in connection with a shrine of Inari Sama. The female patients live on the ground floor, the males above. On one occasion some friends of mine happened to be walking in the neighbourhood, when their attention was attracted by the screams of a childish voice close by. On turning the corner of a rocky cliff they found a man holding under the icy waters of a cascade a struggling child, a girl of fourteen. Enquiries elicited the information that she was possessed by a fox, and that she was undergoing treatment for its exorcism. Three times a day for several weeks her father brought her to the waterfall, holding her under it for some minutes at every visit. Her ankles were chained together in order to prevent the fox-spirit from hurrying her away to destruction. On leaving the spot she was compelled to struggle across the stones over which the torrent dashes on its way after leaving its rocky basin beneath the fall.

Although (particularly amongst the lower orders) circumstantial stories of the curious hallucinations above referred to are almost without number, the belief of the people in the fox's supernatural powers to work them harm is gradually, even if very slowly, dying away before the spread of education and general enlightenment. But whilst many foreign residents in Japan are more or less familiar with the superstitions connected with it, the subject is one of which comparatively little is known to the outside world. And it is for this reason, chiefly, that I have ventured to dwell on it at rather greater length than I should otherwise have done.

CHAPTER XVI.

As it has been intimated that some hints on travel in the higher mountain districts of Japan might be profitably added, a few suggestions are accordingly offered in the hope that they may be of use to those whose experience has not yet reached to the districts remote enough from the beaten tracks to need a little special care and preparation for travel of a rougher kind than that to which the ordinary visitor is accustomed.

With regard to dress, a Norfolk jacket with plenty of pockets, and loose knickerbockers of a strong grey flannel will be found serviceable, whilst for underwear the lightest and thinnest woollen, or silk-and-woollen, vests and shirts are best, since there is less risk of getting a chill after being over-heated. The best material for this is that made by Dr. Jaeger's Company. A light travelling maud is also useful during halts at high altitudes, or bivouacs in the open.

If *waraji* are worn, care should be taken to have the

soles of the *tabi* much thicker than those used by the
natives, otherwise the feet are likely to suffer.   The *waraji*
give a better foothold on smooth rocks than hob-nailed
boots, but the latter are best for ordinary walking.   The
blue cotton gaiters called *kiya-han* afford much more protection to the legs than woollen stockings when a way has
to be made through the rough undergrowth so often found
on the lower slopes of the mountains.

For ordinary boots a supply of Pound's waterproof
grease is invaluable.

A sheet, made into a bag and capable of being tied at
the top; a ring air-cushion to put under the hip when
sleeping on the ground; and a water-proof ground sheet
will be found useful when nights are spent away from inns.
In such cases a good substitute for a tent can be made by
means of three large pieces of strong oiled paper.   One
piece is ∧ shaped by folding it over a line stretched
between two uprights, and the other two are tied to it by
strings fastened on the edges.

For carrying purposes, the native *kori* is most convenient
for provisions, books, instruments, &c., and if two or more
are taken, they should fit into each other in such a way
that when one is emptied the other may be put into it and
so lessen the bulk.

For clothes and soft things, however, the Swiss *rück-sack*
is far better than anything else in the way of knapsacks

and similar contrivances. It is sometimes made of Willesden canvas, but I have found a sort of water-proof cloth better. It consists of an oblong bag, say 24 inches by 20, fastened at the top by a cord which can be attached to a brass ring about two inches in diameter. On this ring are sewn two straps which go over the shoulders, and passing under the armpits, are fastened to the lower corners of the bag so as to allow the weight to rest in the strongest part of the back, just above the loins, the position being regulated by ordinary buckles. This "sack" is much the most comfortable and convenient device of the kind, and has only to be used to be appreciated. By fixing straps and buckles under the lower end of the bag a mackintosh, shawl, or coat may be carried with little extra trouble.

For carrying drink a vulcanite bottle covered with thick felt may be strongly recommended. If the liquid is wanted hot, the felt covering will keep it warm for a long time; while if it be desired to have it cool, the bottle should be dipped in cold water, the evaporation of which from the soaked felt will keep the contents cold.

Maps, note-books, etc., should be wrapped in some thin water-proof material to preserve them in case of one's clothing getting wet on the march.

A railway reading-lamp is a great boon when in country places, where the native lamps are usually of a poor kind;

and it is far more satisfactory also than the native *chōchin* when walking has to be done at night on strange roads or rocky hillsides.

The question of food is, to most persons, of considerable importance. The man who is able to subsist entirely on the scanty resources of an out-of-the-way hamlet is a rarity, and even if he is able to, it is a question whether it is wise to do so.

Sometimes, however, one may be cut off from all sources of supply for several days, and it is well to have as much as possible in concentrated forms. "Bovril" makes a capital soup, and where hot water for this cannot be got, Valentine's meat juice, with a little cold water, is a valuable stimulant.

Halford's curried fowl is very appetising at the end of a day's work, and De Jongh's cocoa is the most conveniently made, and perhaps the most easily digested by those who care for that kind of drink. Some travellers carry cold tea on the march, and consider it both stimulating and refreshing. This is best made with cold water, and not with hot water afterwards allowed to cool. Few people would believe the difference there is between the two until they have tried both. The ordinary quantity of tea should be used, but instead of standing five minutes or so it should stand for as many hours. Where it can be taken, however, cold coffee is perhaps still more refreshing, and can be strongly recommended.

A handful of good prunes, raisins, or dates may be put into the pocket at the beginning of a climb, the last being especially sustaining as well as tasty during the walk. Rice can generally be got where the dwellings of men are met with, sometimes fish, and often eggs.

A few simple medicines for ordinary ailments will generally be carried, and it is possible to get most of such things put up in the form of tabloids. Of these perhaps the most handy and suitable for the ordinary traveller are the compressed drugs prepared by Burroughs, Wellcome, & Co., of Snow-Hill Buildings, London, E.C., and made up into a small pocket case under the name of "The Alpine Case." This is recommended by Mr. Clinton Dent, formerly President of the Alpine Club, a well-known physiologist and surgeon, as well as a celebrated mountaineer. It only weighs 8 ozs., and costs 21*s.*; a somewhat larger and more complete thing of the same kind being the "Mountaineer's Case," weighing 1¾lbs., and costing 25*s.* Where the use of simple remedies is properly understood, much gratitude is the sure result of a little kindly employment of them in cases here and there met with amongst rustic folks, who never see a doctor once in a lifetime perhaps, and know little of proper treatment for their common ailments.

A few little trifles taken as presents often help to secure the goodwill of those on whose aid one is often quite dependent. A pocket-knife or a small compass given to the hunter who acts as guide, a pair of scissors to an inn-keeper, or a doll to his little daughter, cost but little, and may bring in what is, under the circumstances, a consider-able return. Above all things, be always as polite in your way, as the natives are in theirs, and you will often find things work much more smoothly. One generally finds that on many of the highways of foreign travel in Japan, the manners of the innkeepers, &c., are extremely objectionable. There may be other explanations, but one certainly is this :—the lack of politeness and courtesy too often shown by the foreign traveller himself, the repetition of which in succeeding instances comes at last to be reflected in the unmannerly behaviour of the native himself.

Whilst ice-axe and rope can practically be dispensed with in the Alps of Japan, a piece of stout line often comes in useful, and so will a good Alpine walking-stick, such as is sold for about 25s. by Hill & Co., 4, Haymarket.

As it is often necessary to do one's own cooking, whether at the country inns or when bivouacking on the mountain side, some sort of canteen is essential. It should be as compact and as light as possible. After trying various kinds, the present writer has at last found one which answers the above requirements almost completely. It is made of strong block tin, and consists of a sort of saucepan, 6 inches square at the top and $5\frac{1}{4}$ at the bottom, the depth being $4\frac{1}{2}$ inches. A double handle of strong iron wire, about $\frac{1}{8}$th of an inch in thickness, is fixed at one of the corners, being made so as to fold flat with the sides when not in use. Inside this pan is another which fits closely, but can be taken out and replaced with readiness. Inside this again are four oblong boxes, the lids of which overlap the bodies an inch or so, fitting as tightly as possible. These can be used for tea, coffee, jam, condensed milk, or whatever may be needed for constant use. The cover of the whole forms a frying-pan, having a folding handle at one corner, whilst at the bottom and closely fitting on to it are a couple of plates, though of course the number may be easily increased if wanted. The weight of this canteen is about $3\frac{1}{2}$ pounds, and with the addition of a couple each of enamelled iron* cups, knives, forks, &c., it meets the needs of two persons. Of course, a spirit lamp must also be taken with it, though it can be used, if necessary, over a fire or *hibachi*. Supplies of spirits of wine are to be obtained at chemists' shops in such towns as Takayama, Matsumoto, Takatō, and elsewhere. At all these places milk also is obtainable, but must be ordered overnight. One of the greatest annoyances, from which there is rarely any escape in native houses, is the ubiquitous domestic flea. Sometimes Keating's "Insect Powder" will

* Aluminium is still better.

keep it off, unless it be unusually hungry and correspondingly reckless. A solution of Jeyes' fluid in water, when used for washing the hands, arms, and neck, is also often efficacious. Another source of trouble is the unpleasant odour common to all Japanese inns, though this may generally be overcome by the constant use of a solution of Jeyes' fluid, a concentrated and more portable form of which, however, is to be had under the name of Creoline. This is also good for washing scratches and cuts, which may be further treated to advantage with the ointment known as Lano-creoline.

The above suggestions, it is hardly necessary to remark, may be added to or modified according to individual preference, though as nearly every item enumerated has been tested by the present writer in practical experience on a number of journeys in the mountain districts off the beaten tracks in Japan, it is believed that they may be of some little help to those travellers who wish to undertake journeys of a similar kind.

None of the writer's country trips have been made in the company of the "guides" usually taken on the most popular routes, with the result that expenses have been correspondingly low. A good companion is most desirable, and if the traveller has not enough knowledge of the Japanese language to make himself understood, a trustworthy native servant who understands him will be found sufficient. This plan is strongly recommended by some of the most successful of the travellers in the interior known to the writer, though he has found that even the country people are, as a rule, so intelligent that a very little Japanese generally goes a long way.

In conclusion, the all important question of expenses claims a word. These are, naturally, much less when one travels *off* instead of *on* the ordinary routes most frequented by foreigners. In the former case innkeepers usually charge from 15 to 40 or 50 sen for *hatago* ("supper, bed, and breakfast"), though a *chadai* is of course expected in addition. In the latter, the almost invariable price is 75 sen, whether the native food is eaten or not.

The heaviest expenses are those of transportation of baggage, and, where a *jinrikisha* is available, of the traveller's person. For these, the remarks in "Murray" should be studied, though, it may be pointed out, the prices actually paid will often depend upon the persuasive powers one can employ in that most trying of all situations —striking a bargain. In any case this should be done overnight, loss of time, patience, and money being thereby avoided.

APPENDIX A.*

" UNDOUBTEDLY the range is of very ancient date ; doubtless it dates from Palæozoic times, and then consisted chiefly of granite and crystalline schists. Since that time the cones of Norikura, Ontake, Tateyama, and several others have been formed. I may ·. say that the oldest peak is, I think, Yarigatake, which consists of very hard ancient porphyry breccia. The youngest peaks lie at the north-east, and consist of three very fine volcanoes of a very much later date than any others.

" For the mineralogist there are many interesting places, especially in the neighbourhood of Tateyama. Near the base of Tateyama there have been very extensive beds of limestone. These, by metamorphic action, have been converted into highly crystalline marble ; and in this there is a remarkable combination of minerals, which, I think, does not exist anywhere else, except in one other part of the range, and at Ishiyama at the south-eastern extremity of Lake Biwa. The minerals embedded are graphite, wollastonite, magnesia, mica, and actinolite. There are several other parts of the range where we find garnets and many other minerals I need not name. Its chief value is on account of the ores found in it. I have made a special exploration of the ore-bearing districts, and from Mr. Weston's paper I find there is a mine which must have been very much developed since I visited it. When I was there, there were only four men working at the place. On the west side of the range, near a place called Funatsu, we have very extensive and valuable ore deposits of argentiferous galena

* From remarks offered by Mr. W. Gowland, F.C.S., F.S.A. &c., on the paper read by the author before the Royal Geographical Society, December 9, 1895.

and copper pyrites, and several mines, in one of which, fifteen years ago, I found no less than 750 men working, and the annual product amounted to 140 tons of copper, 170 tons of lead, £18,500 worth of silver from all the mines in the district during 1890. Further we find extensive deposits of plumbago, of which, in 1890, 4,500 tons were extracted. Passing northwards, we have manganese. Then, going round to the eastern side, we have deposits of silicious shale, very rich in petroleum, but they do not yield so much as they ought to do if worked by more modern processes; then, still further down the range, at Kurodake, there are extensive deposits of iron ore, but, unfortunately, in such an inaccessible position that I am afraid it will be many, many years before the Japanese can utilize it for the manufacture of iron. In order to get to them from the east side, you have to cross over the front range, varying from 7,000 to 8,000 feet high. Then we have, of course, sulphur on all the volcanic peaks. And in the river which flows down the eastern side of the plain of Shinano, I found asbestos derived from the tributary ranges, and it is curious that in very early days this asbestos was worked and fire-proof paper was made from it. Two famous springs, Shirahoneyu and Norikurayu, contain calcium sulphides, the temperature of the former being 128°.

" The sulphur springs of Tateyama have extremely strong mineral water, very much stronger than any other, which consists of a solution of lime, and contains free sulphuric acid. The temperature of the water is boiling-point.

" Now with regard to the flora. This is rich, varying from sub-arctic to temperate, making it one of the finest fields for the study of Japanese botany. The plants represented are arranged in different altitudes. With regard to economic botany, my researches bear out what Mr. Weston has said with regard to climatic conditions. On the west the vegetation is not nearly so luxuriant as on the east. On the east, I found rice growing up to 4,000 feet, ordinary potatoes to the same height, barley about 4,200 feet, buckwheat about 5,000 feet.

" Besides these interesting minerals and so forth, on the plains and the low hills on the eastern side there are some very interesting archæological remains. Towards the north-east end of the Shinano plain there are dug up from time to time stone arrow-heads and stone axes of such a form that we must conclude that at a very early period indeed that part of the country was inhabited by the aboriginal Ainus. If we come further south in the plain, we find a most interesting series of dolmens and chamber tumuli. Near the town of Namabo there are a great many in a ruined state; but Matsushiro has eight in fairly good preservation, of four of which I took measurements. They consist of rude rectangular chambers in stone, the length of which varies from 14 to 18 feet, the breadth about 7 feet, and the height about 8 feet. Two of them are neolithic; two are constructed of very large stones, entered by a narrow gallery 4 feet in width, the door facing south within a few degrees. The remains found in them consisted of iron swords of the dolmen period, and bronze rings plated with gold, besides a considerable quantity of sepulchral pottery. Remains, absolutely the same as these, have been found in the great dolmen districts in the centre of Japan, and they show distinctly that the dolmens of that part are of approximate age with those of Central Japan; therefore not later than the fifth century, and probably much earlier, that part of the plain of Shinano was occupied by the Japanese, and not by the aborigines."

APPENDIX B.

NOTES ON THE EXORCISM OF SPIRITS IN KOREA.

[Kindly communicated to the author by E. B. LANDIS, Esq., M.D., of Bishop Corfe's Medical Mission, Chemulpo, Korea.]

A VISITOR cannot be long in Korea without hearing somewhere in the neighbourhood a loud ding-dong sound of clattering cymbals, with the beating of drums, and if he proceeds in the direction of the sound he will see a woman (usually an old, ugly-looking hag who reminds him of pictures of witches seen in his youth) dancing and posturing or going round and round, keeping time to the drums and cymbals, which are kept going by two or three younger exorcists, or may be only pupils, who are sitting on a mat spread out in front of her. The sorceress herself uses a fan and dresses up in most fantastic attire, usually that of a man, and further sticks into her hair pieces of paper of the exact pattern that one sees before Shinto shrines in Japan. The twisted Shinto rope is also used, and a number of the ceremonies are so similar that one begins to ask whether Shintoism is not after all Shamanism, which was obtained from Korea together with Pottery, Literature, Buddhism and almost everything else a Japanese possesses, excepting probably his conceit, which is so marked that it could not possibly flourish anywhere excepting on Japanese soil. The ceremony which Mr. Percival Lowell describes, in a paper read before the Asiatic Society of Japan, as a purely Shinto rite, and which is supposed to be met with nowhere else, can be seen almost daily in any large Korean town, the entire ceremony only differing in the size of the wand used and in the fact that, whereas in Japan the exorcist is a Shinto priest, in Korea a woman is the chief actor in the scene. Below will be found a few notes on exorcisms as practised by the sorceress in Korea.

PRELIMINARIES TO EXORCISM.

The exorcist (in Korea always a female) must not occupy the same apartments as her husband for a period varying from a month in the case of the higher spirits to three days in the case of those of a lower grade. During this time the exorcist must abstain from fish and flesh, and must generally fast (not severely). Ashes are first steeped in water and the exorcist takes this liquor and, walking round the house to be exorcised, sprinkles it as she goes. She then takes pure water and goes through the same performance. The spirit of the Ridge Pole (No. 7) is then supposed to come out and invite her to enter.

There are 12 varieties of exorcism.

I. THE SPIRITS OF GOODS AND FURNITURE (No. 8).

This is the chief of all exorcisms. By having this performed, virtues descend to the household, and goods are accumulated in plenty.

Tai Am Chyei Syek, Syo Am Chyei Syek and Po Ki Chyei Syek are invoked to give to the sons long life and to the daughters many virtues. The origin of these three spirits was not in the mountains of silver nor was it in the mountains of pure gold. Their paternal ancestor was a philosopher of Hwa Ju. Their maternal ancestor was a lady from the Dragon's (Emperor's) Palace. At the age of 7 they first met, and again at the age of 17 they met. At this time their maternal ancestor became pregnant, and in due time their father was born. The hour, day, month and year were taken and the horoscope was cast. When the child was three years old, the mother died, and in his 7th year the father died. The child had nowhere to go, so he went to his uncle's house and said, " You are my uncle by blood, but my aunt is not my blood relative. I will therefore become your servant." His aunt treated him very cruelly, feeding him with cold food and with refuse vegetables,

which were all put into a basin. His tears dropped into the basin
and mixed with the food. After many days and months of this, on
New Year's Day he was compelled to go and gather faggots. He
tied a rope around his waist and took a scythe under his arm and a
sickle in his hand and ascended the mountains of pure gold. Here
he gathered a bundle of dolichos faggots. He then descended the
mountain, and as he was gathering a bundle of oak faggots, a monk
came down the mountain chanting, and seeing him he asked,
"Where do you live? There are many days and months in the
year: therefore why do you gather faggots on New Year's Day?"
He answered, "I am not of low birth, I am Chyei Syek's son; my
parents died early and I went to my uncle's house to live. They
sent me out to gather faggots to-day, and I was compelled to obey."
The monk said, "You are the noble son of a noble house, but your
horoscope is bad. It makes me sad to think of your sufferings.
Would you like to go and live with me at the temple?" The boy
was pleased and followed the monk. They walked alone over a
high mountain pass and then ascended the highest peak, on the top
of which was a temple. Here was the place where the monk dwelt.
There were several temples attached to this one monastery. The
highest was three stories in height, and the lowest was two. They
proceeded to the largest of the temples, where there were images
of the three Buddhas. Before these were the Buddhas of the five
quarters and the four guardians, as if chanting. In front of the
table on which the images were sitting was an old monk, who,
grasping the rosary, was chanting with frequent prostrations. The
boy walked all round the temple, and after he had seen and examined
all, he had his hair cut off and became a disciple. The monk then
asked him whether he would first learn his letters or whether he
would study Buddhist rites and ceremonies. He said he would first
study his letters. He then began with the "Thousand Character
Classic," and then studied in succession all the text books. He
was wonderfully clever. It was only necessary to teach him one
character and he knew the meaning of the whole line. After he
had studied all the classics, he studied the rites and ceremonies of
Buddhism. After he had studied all the Buddhist Sutras, the monk

said to him, " If any of the nobles' sons were as learned as you, they would obtain a doctor's degree. For you the study of Buddhist literature is useless. Take your bundle, your rosary and your staff and go down the hill, and the first house you come to, you must beg for rice." The disciple then did so. He went to the house, where he saw a young woman weaving cloth. He begged for rice, which was given him. He looked into her eyes and she became pregnant. In due time she brought forth three sons. These three sons were you, oh spirits ! You have given blessings to the world, so that now in all houses offerings are made to you.

When offerings are made to these spirits, no meats are used, which points to a Buddhistic origin. All houses, when the ridge poles are erected, have offerings set out. If you ask the ordinary man the meaning of this, he will say he does not know. But the following gives the origin of it.

II. THE SPIRIT OF THE RIDGE POLE.

This spirit is the chief of all the spirits of the house. If a death occurs or any calamity which causes weeping, this spirit becomes angry and leaves the house. If he does, one calamity follows another, and the house goes from bad to worse. The exorcist is then called in, who induces the spirit to return. As this spirit is the chief, after he returns the other spirits also return and bring good luck with them.

III. SPIRIT DEMON OF THE YI FAMILY.

This is the spirit of a former Crown Prince of Korea. He wished to attack China, being so puffed up with pride, but as he was only Crown Prince, he was compelled to remain quiet. He was very impatient and angry with his father, the King, for not allowing him to carry out his mad scheme. Once, during his fortieth year, when his father the King went in procession to the tombs of his ancestors, he forged an order in the King's name declaring war on China. This was an act of rebellion and of course he had to be killed, which was done by one of the King's faithful ministers. His spirit now roams about, injuring all that come in contact with it. Should a man in good health suddenly drop dead or disease infect several members of one family, or some one have a frightful dream, it is due to this spirit. If the spirit comes to a house, he will not be appeased until a man dies, or an ox or a pig. Therefore if the spirit visits a neighbourhood or a house, a pig must immediately be killed to appease him and induce him to leave. The pig must not be cut up but boiled entire, and offered up entire. The exorcist will then take two knives and go through the sword dance. Sometimes the exorcist dances and works herself into such a frenzy that she falls down as in a fit, frothing at the mouth. Cases have occurred in which she actually died. She invokes the powers in the following words : " Oh Master and Mistress of our Kingdom, May you ever exist in peace. Once in every three years we invoke you with music and dance. Oh make this house to be peaceful ! "

Wood is then brought out and a box is made. The native official hat and robes are then placed in it, as well as clothes suitable for a lady of the palace. This box is then placed on top of the family clothes horse, and sacrifices frequently offered.

Regularly every three years, as is implied in the invocation, a special service is held in each district to appease this spirit.

IV. Spirits of Mountains and Hills.

In exorcising these spirits, the exorcist puts on a man's hat and a minister's official robes. In one hand she takes a three-pronged lance. She then dances and whirls around, working herself into a frenzy. While doing this, she puts the leg of a pig on the middle prong of the lance (which is longer than the others). She places this upright on the end of the handle in front of the sacrifices which are offered, and, strange to say, it remains in an upright position. Before doing this, her whole body trembles, involuntarily when the demon is supposed to take possession of her. She then scolds and abuses the spirit, until it asks for pardon. Then a sheet of paper is rolled into a hollow roll and set on fire. This is done for each member of the family. If the burning paper ascends, that particular member of the family is supposed to be quite innocent. If the paper does not ascend, but tumbles over, that special member of the family is supposed to be guilty of some fault.

V. Spirit Attendants of III.

In exorcising this spirit, a red hat and red official robes are worn, and the insignia of a minister are tied to the belt. The exorcist then dances and invokes the spirit as well as the spirit of the Hong clan and the ambassador spirits of the twelve feudal States. She scolds the master of the house for not setting out more offerings, even though many have been set out. Paper is then rolled up and burnt as in IV.

VI. Spirits of the Ancestors.

This exorcism is for male or female ancestors to the fifth generation. The exorcist will take in her hand a picture of the three Buddhas and, dancing, the spirits will come and sit on her shoulders. The exorcist weeps, and says that the ancestors told her that their graves were disturbed for some reason or other, or that the house site is bad, or some like reason, which causes sickness or other calamities to befall the family. Female ancestors have nine souls, and male ancestors have twelve souls. For all the relatives of the family a sheet of paper is burned. This for relatives to cousins five times removed.

VII. The Spirit of Small-Pox.

In exorcising this spirit, the exorcist wears a soldier's hat and takes bells in her hands. White cakes (made of rice flour and water and baked) and water only are offered. She dances until the spirit takes possession of her, and through her says that there are 53 spirits of small-pox, but, as Korea is a small country, only one-third have taken up their residence here. The spirit furthermore announces himself as chief of the small-pox spirits, and promises, if

properly reverenced, to see that no calamity befalls the household
through small-pox.

I may add that small-pox is a common and very much dreaded
disease in Korea. The number of persons who are blinded or
crippled in other ways through this disease alone is frightful. The
natives have a way of vaccinating by introducing virus from a
small-pox patient into the nostril, but the evil effects of this is only
exceeded by those of small-pox itself.

VIII. Spirit of One's Own Self.

This spirit always accompanies a person. The exorcist will take
a sheet of paper in her hand, and having exorcised the spirit, she
will be told by it that the spirit having accompanied a man to a
certain place could not enjoy the food, and for this reason he has
afflicted the family with illness or interfered with the trading done
by the master, as the case may be. The paper which the exorcist
holds in her hand is then fastened to the eaves of the house, and
another sheet is taken and burned.

IX. Spirits which take the Forms of Animals.

There are certain animals which come to a house and bring
blessings with them, such as a species of snake which belongs to
the python family, or weasels. If these animals are seen in one's
dreams, blessings are sure to follow. They take up their residence
beneath the pile of brush-wood. If the spirits of these appear, silk
or satin clothing should be made, and these, with some money, put
into an unoccupied room. If this is done the family may become
quite wealthy. To obtain these blessings, the exorcist should be
called to invoke these spirits. Sacrifices should be offered on the
first and fifteenth day of each month, when many offerings in the
way of food should be made and paper burnt.

X. The Spirits of Jugglers.

These spirits only resort to houses which have in the family one
person who has passed the literary examinations. These spirits

are only exorcised when there are a large number of spectators. A young virgin exorcist dances and sings, while the spectators throw her money, which she hangs in her belt and fastens on to her clothing. This is one of the most profitable from a financial point of view to the exorcist.

XI. Spirits which reside in Trees on the Hill Tops.

If anyone dies before reaching a cycle (*i.e.*, 60 years of age) the spirit will reside in a tree, usually on the top or the side of a hill. This tree is known by its gnarled appearance. Should persons die of the pestilence, or by the roadside, or women die in childbirth, the spirits are sure to take up their residence in a tree. Offerings are made to these spirits of cake, wine, and pork, but should the tree be the residence of the spirit of a man who has been killed by a tiger, the flesh of a dog is offered instead of pork. The exorcist puts on red clothing, and dances invoking the spirit, saying that a large number of wicked spirits have come to this house, and have troubled the master; will the spirit in the tree deign to drive these malevolent spirits away? The sorceress then calls the master of the house, and scolds him, telling him that he has done wrong. After this a number of small tables are set out with offerings for the spirits.

After any of the above exorcisms the sorceress comes to the yard in front of the house and offers cakes of grain, rice, soup, vegetables, fish and coarse wine, and raw flesh. She takes portions of these and scatters them to the four winds for the spirits to eat, and then invokes them as follows : " Do not trouble this house more, or visit it for three years, and after this period of time we will again appease you by offerings."

Women do not become exorcists by birth. Whether a woman is rich or poor, high or low in the social scale, virgin or widow, a spirit may take possession of her. If a spirit takes possession of her she first becomes ill. She may be only slightly ill, or she may be very ill indeed, and the period of her illness may last one month or it may last three years. In her sleep she will dream of peach

z

trees in blossom (peaches are said to be the fruit of the gods), or a rainbow in the heavens, or a dragon. She may also dream of a man in armour, who suddenly changes himself into an animal. These dreams will impress themselves on her mind until she becomes as one who is insane. After this when she is awake she will see acrobats, and all sorts of curious things, and from this time it will not be long until she speaks as the oracle of the spirits. She will then announce to the family that a great messenger from heaven, and a great messenger from earth, and a great messenger from the lightning, have told her that if she is not allowed to exorcise spirits the members of the family, or the domestic animals belonging to the family, will die. Should her relatives lock her up and refuse to allow her to have communication with the outside world she will become more and more ill, and finally die. If she be'ongs to a noble family, as sometimes happens, they may probably, and very often do, kill her, as the disgrace would be felt so keenly that the family would feel that nothing could ever wipe it out. But we will suppose that the family bow to the inevitable, and allow her to have her own way. The first thing she does is to go into an empty room and fill it with flowers, either artificial or natural, as an offering to the spirits. The next step will be to get the clothing and instruments and various paraphernalia of a deceased sorceress. She will therefore go to the house of a descendant of a sorceress, and ask for the clothes, &c. The descendant will always be glad to get rid of them as, until he does so, there is a great danger of one of the members of his family becoming possessed. The sorceress will carefully inquire at what age the former owner of the apparel became possessed, at what age she died, and what her family name was. She will then demand the clothing, and an amount in money to procure her a full outfit, as a number of suits of new clothing are needed, the clothes of the deceased sorceress probably not being in a condition fit to be worn. It is not necessary that it be worn; only that the newly-possessed sorceress gets possession of it, and after the spirit has taken full possession of her it can be destroyed. But when a sorceress has died the drums, &c., cannot be destroyed, and they must be kept until a new sorceress comes and asks for them. After the clothes, &c., are given, the newly-possessed sorceress will at once exorcise all the spirits of the donor's house that the members may live in peace, and after this she goes to the neighbouring house, where she obtains rice and money. She will then write the names of donors on tablets, and placing them in a little house she will invoke blessings down upon them for three years. After this she can go to other houses to exorcise spirits. Should the sorceress belong to a noble family she will not be allowed to exorcise spirits anywhere excepting in her own house, and when she dies, she will be buried in a hole in the mountain side, with all her clothing and instruments of exorcism, and if a person in the neighbourhood is newly-possessed she will be sent to the place of burial for the clothing and instruments. A sorceress belonging to a noble family is called a messenger of the spirits. Often a sorceress will build a small house near her own, and will not go abroad at all for the exorcism of spirits. Those of the neighbourhood who wish to have spirits exorcised will send to her the necessary money and offerings, and she will exorcise them in her own house. Of late years it is the custom for the daughter of a sorceress to be taken out with her mother, and taught from an early age, so that she almost invariably becomes a sorceress as she grows older.

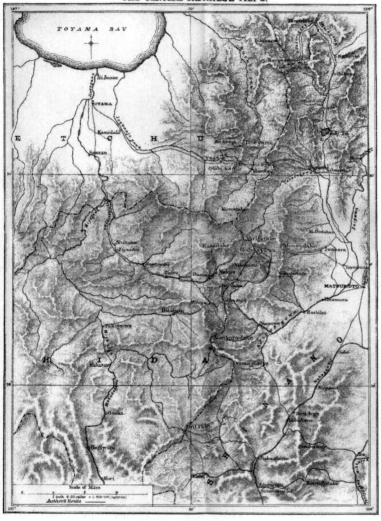

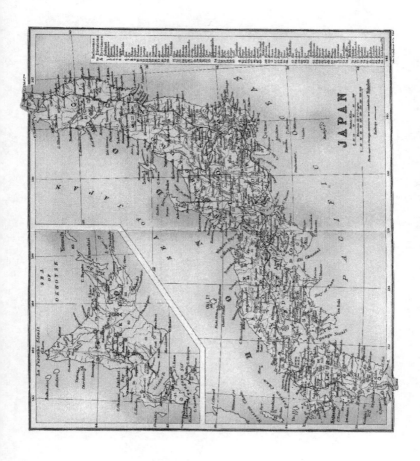

INDEX.

Miller, Dr. R. S., 61, 68.
Milton, 214.
Mineral springs (cp. Solfataras), 89, 96.
Mines, 73, 156, 165, 231, 243.
Minobu, 292.
Misaka-tōge, 206.
Mistleto, 85.
Miya-tōge, 64.
Mosquitoes, 170.
Motoyama-tōge, 99.
Mulberry, 19, 237.
Murayama, 194, 210.
Murray's Handbook to Japan, 131, 146.
Myōgi-san, 5.
Mythology, 42.

NAGANO (Zenkōji), 119, 221.
Nakao, 246.
Nakasendō, 40, 199.
Nakatsugawa, 202.
Naoetsu, 221.
Newspapers, 218, 267.
'New Woman,' 102.
Nezame-no-toko, 44.
Nionindō, 144, 210, 275.
Noguchi, 131.
Norikura, 16.
,, ascent of, 75 et seqq.

Oaks, 70, 124.
Oba-ishi, 144.
Observatories, 121, 253.
Ūdaki, 286.
Ō-jigoku, 147.
Ōkawara, 104, 112.

Ōmachi, 125, 236.
Ōmiya, 209.
Onna-taka, 102.
Ūnogawa, 85, 168, 242.
Ontake, 41.
,, ascents of, 41, 271 et seqq.
,, summit of, 277.
Ō Renge-san, ascent of, 231.
O'Rorke, H. W. L., 197 et seqq.
Osaka, 63.
Ōta, 199.
Outfit, hints on, 317.
Oyashirazu Koshirazu, 224.

PAIN, Japanese disregard of, 69.
Passports, 61, 217.
Patriotism, 278, 290 et seqq.
Photographers, 239.
Pilgrims, 43, 215, 269 et seqq., 285.
Pines, 204.
Policemen, 61, 105, 111, 197, 217, 226 et seqq.
Politeness, 19, 21, 39, 66, 106, 129, 266.
'Possession,' 282, 294 et seqq., 304, 310 et seqq.
Proverbs, 184.
Provisions, 18, 318.
Ptarmigan, 32, 78, 265.

RAILWAYS, 13, 118.
Rain, praying for (amagoi), 160 et seqq.
Rhododendrons, 47.
River terraces, 55.
Ruskin, 93, 293.
Ryūzan-jita, 139.

THE END.

Made in the USA
Middletown, DE
28 April 2017